PRAISE FOR THE MUSIC FILMS OF ROBERT MUGGE

"Filmmaker Robert Mugge has . . . established himself as the cinema's foremost music documentarian, with a career that includes . . . chronicling individual performers (Al Green, Sun Ra, Rubén Blades) and various music styles (blues, reggae, bluegrass, etc.)."
—Frank Scheck, *The Hollywood Reporter*

"To describe the recent films of the documentarian Robert Mugge as cultural reference books doesn't mean to imply that these explorations of the musical byways of Southern rural America are lacking in pungent musical sap. Documents of a flourishing below-the-radar culture, they are archival records as well as entertainments."
—Stephen Holden, *The New York Times*

"The prevalence of documentaries about musicians is a curse, because most of these films do a terrible job of showcasing music. One rare exception is the work of the director Robert Mugge, whose film *Sun Ra: A Joyful Noise* . . . is one of the most satisfying portraits I've ever seen."
—Richard Brody, *The New Yorker*

"Years from now, when . . . filmmaker Robert Mugge leaves behind his remarkable legacy of priceless documentation . . . musicologists, cultural historians and just plain folks are going to hail Mugge as a national treasure. Retrospectives of his work will stretch into the future, providing a timeless record of artistic expression and pure entertainment."
—Jeff Shannon, *The Seattle Times*

MORE BOOKS FROM THE SAGER GROUP

Students Write the Darnedest Things: Gaffes, Goofs, Blunders and Unintended Wisdom from Actual College Papers
by Pamela Hill Nettleton, PhD

Big Noise from LaPorte: A Diary of the Disillusioned
by Holly Schroeder Link

Meeting Mozart: A Novel Drawn from the Secret Diaries of Lorenzo Da Ponte
by Howard Jay Smith

Lavender in Your Lemonade: A Funny and Touching COVID Diary
by Chris Erskine

Sarabeth and the Five Spirits:
A Novel about Channeling, Consciousness, Healing, and Murder
by Mike Sager

The Deadliest Man Alive:
Count Dante, The Mob and the War for American Martial Arts
by Benji Feldheim

Lifeboat No. 8: Surviving the Titanic
by Elizabeth Kaye

The Pope of Pot:
And Other True Stories of Marijuana and Related High Jinks
by Mike Sager

See our entire library at TheSagerGroup.net

ROBERT MUGGE

Foreword by William Reynolds Ferris

A Filmmaker's Journey
through American Music

ROBERT MUGGE

Foreword by William Reynolds Ferris

A Filmmaker's Journey through American Music

THE SAGER GROUP

Artifex Te Adiuva

CONTENTS

Foreword by William Reynolds Ferris

Filmmaking is clearly not for the faint of heart, as Robert Mugge viscerally details in his fascinating book *Notes From the Road: A Filmmaker's Journey through American Music*. A self-described "American nonfiction filmmaker," with his unswerving, focused eye, Mugge has produced thirty-six documentary films over four decades. Mugge both thrills and exhausts us as he describes the process of making his films. Constantly on the move with his film crew, he captures performers and their music in graphic detail.

Mugge views life through the lens of music, and he likens his four-person film crew to a jazz or rock quartet. He shifts his camera lens deftly from classical music to bluegrass to jazz to Tex-Mex to gospel to reggae to Hawaiian slack-key guitar. Thankfully, Mugge is both a gifted filmmaker and a fine writer, and with eloquent prose he introduces us to musicians, record producers, and his trusted film crew, who at times include his wife Diana. He pulls back the curtain to reveal his struggles with fundraising, temperamental musicians, and difficult producers. For the aspiring documentary filmmaker, this book is a perfect primer for the road that lies ahead.

The book opens when Mugge is in film school at Temple University and discovers that Sun Ra and members of his Arkestra live in the Germantown section of Philadelphia. After shooting Sun Ra on stage, at his home, and elsewhere, but not yet able to pay him, Mugge asks him to sign a letter of agreement that he can share with potential investors. Sun Ra lectures Mugge for two hours explaining that he is "immortal" and "could never sign an agreement with someone who would 'end up in the graveyard.' "

Once their agreement is in place, Mugge gives Sun Ra a large check and drives him to his bank. The white bank manager refuses to cash a check payable to "Sun Ra." Only after Mugge explains that the real name of his friend is Herman "Sonny" Blount, and he does business under his stage name, does the manager cash the check. Thus Mugge began *Sun Ra: A Joyful Noise*, a film on one of the most colorful, beloved jazz artists of the twentieth century. As Mugge recalls, Sun Ra mastered "jazz composition, arrangement, instrumentation, vocalizing, band leading, and overall presentation, and then stretched the boundaries of all of them."

From jazz, Mugge turns his lens to Memphis and the music of Al Green. After releasing an endless stream of popular soul songs produced by Willie Mitchell—including "Let's Stay Together," "Love and Happiness," and "Tired of Being Alone"—Green's life is shaken when a girlfriend scalds him in the shower with a pot of hot grits and then shoots and kills herself, leaving a suicide note in her purse. Shortly thereafter Green founds his own church in Memphis, where he sings only gospel music.

Mugge ultimately spent thirteen months pursuing Green to Memphis, New York City, and elsewhere before finally gaining permission to make *Gospel According to Al Green*. Shooting began on the seventh anniversary of Green's Full Gospel Tabernacle, with Rev. Green "screaming at the top of his lungs, racing around the room, and sweating profusely. One after another, approving female church members rose to their feet as well, filling the aisles with their own sense of abandon."

Mugge views these early films on Sun Ra and Al Green as a platform that allows the musicians "to speak and perform for themselves." It is an approach that he applies to all of his films.

Mugge's *Cool Runnings: The Reggae Movie* led him to the Bob Marley Performing Arts Center in Montego Bay, Jamaica. As he exits the airport, someone offers to sell him ganja. Then his host John Wakely takes him "on one of the most harrowing, two-hour rides of my life. As we raced around mountain roads at night, featuring only one lane in each direction and zero visibility beyond the next curve, John would simply lean on his horn and race towards whatever awaited us."

One evening Mugge awakens to "a loud pounding" on his door. Wearing no clothes, he opens the door "a crack, and looked out at a pair of uniformed guards, each of whom was armed and holding the leash of a German shepherd." The guards demand that he pay for his room, and "realizing how vulnerable I was, standing naked behind the door with a small supply of ganja in my closet," he decides "what was happening here was a shakedown," yells that he will pay for his room the next morning, and slams the door. He reflects, "All just another day of doing business in the so-called Third World."

Inspired by his passionate love for music and his incredible recall of details about each film, Mugge relentlessly immerses us in his films and their performers. After completing films with subjects ranging from Hawaiian music and dance to Mississippi Delta blues performers, he turns to Creole musicians in Southwest Louisiana. There he discovered "a scene in which older generations of musicians were . . . passing the torch to younger ones; in which musical styles were evolving rapidly." He films in "live music clubs—usually dark, smoky, and somewhat cramped . . . packed to capacity with dancers."

At the Hook'd Up Bar and Grill in Youngsville, Louisiana, Vasti Jackson performs his "Zydeco Crossroads" (title song for Mugge's 2015 film of the same name) in which he describes the connection between blues and zydeco.

> Down at the zydeco crossroads,
> Where the Delta meet the bayou,
> Got the gris-gris and the mojo,
> Down at the zydeco crossroads.
> We put the rhythm in the blues,
> Yeah, we make your body move,
> A little waltz and a two-step;
> We slow drag and shuffle fast.

Wishing to celebrate those who support regional American music, including in Mississippi and Louisiana, Mugge profiles Bruce Iglauer, founder of blues label Alligator Records, and Marian Leighton Levy, Bill Nowlin, and Ken Irwin, founders of eclectic Rounder

Records. In Shreveport, Louisiana, he films *Louisiana Hayride* veterans, after which a consultant and her husband demand that he pay them for musicians he had not agreed to film. As Mugge "backed up our vehicle, the two of them grabbed hold of my door, yelling like characters from the old *Dukes of Hazzard* TV show that they would get me for this. Finally, I dislodged the two of them, yanked my door closed, and screeched away, happy in the knowledge I would never speak to them again."

While in nearby Monroe, Mugge films "colorful gospel deejay Sister Pearlee Tolliver, 'the jewel of the dial' on radio station KYEA as she reads her indescribable commercials for bail bondsmen, clothing stores, auto parts companies, and arthritis medications, all of which were a key draw for her shows."

After filming Alida and Moise Viator perform Cajun music near Eunice, Mugge and his crew discover an unpleasant part of "living and working in such close communion with nature." Their van is filled with mosquitos, and the "flying, bloodsucking vermin made the return to our Lafayette hotel, almost an hour away, something of a challenge."

Mugge never forgets that "in documentary filmmaking, anything not captured in the moment it happens is literally gone forever." He captures musicians with intimate conversations and performances in each of his films. In *New Orleans Music in Exile*, Mugge, his partner (and future wife) Diana Zelman, and their film crew arrived in the city two months after Katrina struck on August 29, 2005 to profile struggling musicians. He recalls how "at the Parc St. Charles, we found ourselves living side-by-side with Red Cross workers, FEMA staff, and Blackwater mercenaries wearing uniforms of black boots, slacks, T-shirts, and berets, and with automatic weapons hanging at their sides. . . . Wi-fi . . . was virtually nonexistent . . . gas was in short supply . . . finding eating establishments open and stocked with food was an ongoing struggle . . . what proved literally lifesaving for us was the fact that an old favorite, Mother's Restaurant, was less than three blocks up Poydras, and they were open for breakfast . . . whether it was po' boys, étouffée, or eggs and toast, we were always grateful."

Like many other musicians, Irma Thomas's home was severely damaged. She shows Mugge "her ruined furnishings heaped into piles out front, taped-up refrigerators lining the sidewalk . . . Inside, Irma pointed to a three-dimensional image of herself, now appearing to have a tear falling from her eye."

New Orleans musician and songwriter Eddie Bo gives Mugge a tour of his Check Your Bucket Café at 2107 Banks Street. Wearing surgical masks because of the fumes, Bo and Mugge enter the club where "tables and chairs had floated around the room, cases of soft drinks had exploded, refrigerators had fallen on their sides, and keys on Eddie's electric piano had frozen in place."

Throughout their complex shooting schedule in New Orleans, Diana is constantly on the phone as she buys Mugge a new laptop, arranges to have their laundry done, and books vans, flights, and hotel rooms for the group. When they leave New Orleans and drive toward Mugge's home in Jackson, Mississippi, Diana drives one of their two minivans and finds a Popeye's restaurant that serves both shrimp and oyster po' boys. She constantly delivers comfort and security to her collaborators.

Mugge and Zelman arrive in Jackson, wash and dry their clothes again, and collapse, only to find that the backers of their New Orleans film have asked for "updated budgets, copies of all collected releases, a list of every person we had interviewed on camera, a list of every person who had performed on camera, and a *separate* list of those who had both performed and been interviewed on camera. Naturally, they wanted these reports immediately, or else we could forget about coming payments that would be needed just to begin viewing and editing all of the footage we had shot. . . . The following day (Friday, November 11) Diana and I drove our two rented minivans the three hours back to Memphis, turned them in at the airport, picked up my own minivan, ate dinner, and drove back to Jackson again. Then, over the weekend, Diana flew home to Philadelphia, at which point I immediately started missing her." Mugge allows us to see all the pieces necessary to produce his films. His candor is refreshingly honest and offers an unvarnished view of the struggles every documentary filmmaker faces.

Mugge concludes *New Orleans Music in Exile* as Dr. John performs his song "Sweet Home New Orleans," which he updated in response to Katrina.

Lootin' and shootin', poor people ain't got a dime.
And poor people been livin' like this for too long a time.
I pray to the spirit world for help from dreams,
In Katrina's wake, to heal my New Orleans.

On February 4, 2006, Mugge films a final project interview with Dr. John at the Keswick Theatre in Glenside, Pennsylvania, a suburb of Philadelphia. That same day in Philadelphia, Diana's granddaughter Anabella Grace Hoback is born. Mugge blends personal and professional worlds as he reflects how "once again, this project combined the joyful, the tragic, and the simply bittersweet."

Robert Mugge describes himself as a "music filmmaker" and suggests that we view his documentaries as "spirit catchers." The subjects of his films are iconic American musicians, and in *Notes From the Road* we look over his shoulder as he makes films on their lives. Of his thirty-six films to date, the twenty-five music documentaries discussed at length in this memoir create a unique portrait of American music, and this book offers an intimate view of his struggles as a filmmaker and his unswerving determination to capture our nation's music on film. For that every American should be deeply grateful.

William Reynolds Ferris is the Joel R. Williamson Eminent Professor of History Emeritus and the Senior Associate Director Emeritus of the Center for Study of the American South at the University of North Carolina at Chapel Hill. An author and filmmaker, Ferris served as chairman of the National Endowment for the Humanities and was founding director of the Center for the Study of Southern Culture at the University of Mississippi.

Preface and Acknowledgements

Where to begin? I am an American nonfiction filmmaker. Over a period of more than four decades, I have produced three dozen documentary films, with most but not all of them focusing primarily, or exclusively, on music and musicians. Most also have involved literal adventures in which, with the help of collaborators, I have explored influential artists, enduring traditions, and isolated music scenes (many of them communities of color), and for context, I have examined related historical, cultural, political, spiritual, racial, and geographical issues. Yes, in a few cases, the script has been reversed, with some of the latter subjects becoming primary concerns, and music mostly used to accompany, enhance, or comment upon the rest. Nevertheless, in every instance, music has played a part in my filmmaking process, and generally speaking, has been the heart of the matter, which is why I have long termed myself a *music filmmaker*.

As a producer-director, I have always believed that films should speak for themselves, and I have devoted huge amounts of time to them, not only teaching them to talk, but also carefully crafting what they should say. Of course, what makes it to the screen is only a partial reflection of my own exploits in making these films, and typically ignores the months or years of fundraising, negotiating, building relationships, conducting research, scouting locations, and then shooting, editing, promoting, and distributing them; in other words, process rather than product. From such extensive efforts come thoughts, concerns, and images just as rich as those designed for release, yet there is no simple way to share them. With this book,

I hope to convey what attracted me to these projects, how crew members and I went about capturing my chosen subjects, and what such experiences have meant to us, to those subjects, and to many in our audiences.

Like other so-called *independent* filmmakers (those eschewing a regular salary and consistent corporate backing in hope of controlling and even owning their own work), I practice a unique art and craft, the execution of which is far more expensive than writing, painting, composing, dancing, and so forth, if only because the cost of crews, equipment, film or video stock, travel, and assorted technical work can be greatly prohibitive. For this reason, I have always kept my budgets as low as possible, trying to determine exactly what my esoteric subjects (those that excite me, whether they appeal to others or not) may be worth to domestic and foreign broadcasters, home video companies, small theatrical distributors, grant-giving organizations, and related entities that typically underwrite productions. I begin such efforts knowing that some of my proposals will attract funding, while others will not, and that pressures (both personal and professional) will build in direct proportion to their rejection. This being the case, filmmakers, like professional gamblers, must know when to fold a weak hand (or rather, abandon an unfunded project) and attempt to regroup. After setbacks, the goal becomes broader appeal, yet still in service of a sustained vision. (As others have noted, an artist's initial work stands on its own, while all that follows conforms to precedent, giving birth to a personal style, and possibly decreasing originality.)

This also is why, when examining someone's filmography, one can never assume it reveals the director's full intentions. Instead, it likely records only those projects that were funded and completed, establishing, in retrospect, a more limited career tally than what had been envisioned. Any patterns or connections identified by critics rely solely on work that made it to fruition, at least in some form, and cannot factor in the many films left unproduced. That has been true for me as well, of course, with various feature-length films and nonfiction series failing to be funded, even though I saw them as crucial additions to what auteurists would call my *oeuvre*. And yet, looking back over my career to date, I can hardly complain, if only because of the great number of films I have completed, a majority of which have been widely distributed, and with rights to most residing with me. Overall, I have done well, and that includes never accepting a project I did not feel could be pulled in the direction of my own goals and ideals. As a result, I have a body of work that is diverse in every sense, that is distinctly my own, and that archives a world in which I myself have enjoyed living.

Regardless of unrequited labors of love, in addressing my fully realized films for this book, I have made one all-important choice, which is to focus only on those that are unashamedly *about* music, and not on those that include music but which I would not term "music films," as I myself define the term. A second choice I am making with this book is not to spend time on films that I have completed but which, for one reason or another, have never received proper commercial releases. Although I believe that all the works in this latter group have value and, as of this writing, can be viewed via my website, or else as bonus features with home video releases of other of my films, I do not see them as fully equal, whether in ambition or in accomplishment, to my twenty-five primary music-related films, and therefore I address them only in passing.

Otherwise, in organizing my stories about the making of these films, I have elected to avoid the easy route, by which I mean discussing them in precise chronological order and making this a straightforward autobiography. That route, I feared, would have led to too many step-by-step, matter-of-fact descriptions of what my associates and I have done, as well as how and when. All very prosaic, and probably of interest to very few. Yes, I have engaged in some of that, especially where I sense that fans of certain films may enjoy it. However, overall, I have chosen to organize twenty-five of my films thematically, which allows me to draw connections among groups of them, even if they were produced years or even decades apart. Using that approach, I also can emphasize how particular artists or traditions have influenced others, and how a handful of regions, especially in the American South, have given birth to what we consider our national musical heritage. In other words, to the extent possible,

I have tried to shift the emphasis of this book to what is interesting about my subjects, rather than what some may consider interesting about my filmmaking approaches, although, certainly, both are addressed at length.

I believe it also is important to declare, right from the top, that I have never claimed to be a music historian, a music journalist, or an ethnomusicologist, though I have friends and acquaintances who are, and I have drafted many of them to serve as advisors and onscreen guides for my films, helping me to document significant musical trends that are, themselves, built upon longstanding American traditions. Their major contributions are noted throughout the text. At the same time, in my films, I encourage musicians to speak for themselves.

Another area in which I have needed, and frequently found, major assistance is that of project funding. One of the great truisms of filmmaking is that it requires a group effort, even if a single individual is ostensibly, or even officially, in charge, and that is certainly true of fundraising. In many cases, I have conceived an idea for a film, then sought to secure financial backing, sometimes successfully and sometimes not, but frequently with the help of others. In a handful of cases, one or more individuals have wanted a certain film made, knew that I had produced something similar, and therefore sought me out. On such occasions, if the person or persons had financing in hand, had chosen a subject that appealed to me, and proved willing to grant me a certain degree of creative control, we were able to work together; but when any of those factors was missing, we were not. So, yes, many fine people, in many different circumstances, have helped to underwrite my projects, and except for the few situations where promises were broken or power struggles ensued, my most generous backers, or facilitators, have remained among my closest friends. Indeed, whom should I value more than those who, for whatever reasons, have enabled me to practice my craft and, in earlier days, feed my kids? Many of them are mentioned in the coming pages.

Also among my closest friends are the talented crew members who have returned to my projects again and again, accepted less than their going rates in order to stretch my meager budgets, exhibited as much passion for every project as I have myself (even if, to paraphrase the Ginger Rogers comment about dancing with Fred Astaire, they have contributed as much as I have, "only backwards and in heels"), and who have seemed to derive genuine joy from the places we have traveled, the music we have heard, the food we have eaten, the people we have met, and the fellowship we have shared. They, too, are mentioned throughout the text, and this book is dedicated to *them*, in particular.

Finally, I must acknowledge a few individuals by name: my parents, Dr. Robert H. and A. Elizabeth Mugge, who, along with family friend Marvin R. A. Johnson, FAIA, were the first to support my creative interests; Philadelphia attorney Richard P. Jaffe (assisted for a time by fellow attorney Gary Azorsky), who spent a couple of decades protecting my legal interests and creative rights, most often without payment; film lab owners Roger Robison and Pete Garey, who literally brought my films to life; pioneering agents and distributors Ed Seaman, Jessica Berman-Bogdan, Angus Trowbridge, Bruce Ricker, David Kinder, and Mitchell Block, who have sold my films around the world; historian and folklorist Dr. William Reynolds Ferris, a major role model of mine, who has honored me with his magnificent foreword, as well as his ongoing encouragement; frequent collaborators Chris Li, Craig Smith, and Bob Maier who have shared important recollections of our time together for this book; jazz experts Lee Mergner and Nou Dadoun who read my manuscript and offered helpful advice; acclaimed author and journalist Mike Sager who invited me into the creative family of his Te Adiuva Press; LeRoy "Lee" Morais, the talented painter, film director, and professor who taught me the art and craft of filmmaking; Rich Turansky, also a fine painter, who has built and expanded my website over the past two decades; and my wife and filmmaking partner, Diana Zelman, who, since 2005, has helped to make my life worth living and my projects worth pursuing. My heartfelt thanks to you all.

Introduction
(Nuts and Bolts)

I n May of 1971, British singer Rod Stewart turned an English-language aphorism, "Every Picture Tells A Story," into a hit song and record album. And what he sang, though ambiguous, was inherently true. Whether in the form of a painting, a photograph, or what used to be called a "motion picture" (or "picture show," or simply "picture"), such creatively captured and organized images tell stories, perhaps most ambitiously when a great many are screened in succession, as they are in the twenty-four frames per second of celluloid, or thirty frames per second of video. In fact, in the case of motion pictures, later labeled "movies" or "films," one work can tell a single story, or it can tell multiple stories on as many levels, with viewers either discerning them as the filmmaker intended, or interpreting them through their *own* experiences, perspectives, and preconceptions. In other words, every picture can tell a great many stories, whether ones that were intended by the storyteller, or ones that were not. And of course, over the years, the meanings of stories can change, just as the people viewing or recalling them will change.

Less than a year before the release of Stewart's hit song, I started film school at the University of Maryland, Baltimore County Campus (UMBC), where Screen Arts Department head Professor LeRoy Morais allowed me to create my own academic major titled Film and Associated Art Media. By then, once bulky, heavy, and cumbersome camera and audio recording equipment had become smaller, lighter, and less expensive—that is, more easily utilized by smaller groups of filmmakers in a wider variety of situations—and the earlier, upright film editing systems had largely been replaced by more user-friendly editing *tables* that were easier to operate and to teach. All of these changes—especially the mobility of cameras and recorders—had led to films and television programs being shot and recorded in locations other than on studio lots and in studio sound stages, and a new, more intimate form of documentary storytelling had evolved in the 1960s, called *cinéma-vérité* in France (where its greatest proponent was Jean Rouch) and *direct cinema* in North America (where its best-known early practitioners were Robert Drew, Richard Leacock, D. A. Pennebaker, the Maysles brothers, and Frederick Wiseman). But these changes also made possible a whole range of other so-called *independent* filmmaking—fiction and nonfiction filmmakers working on small budgets and shooting anywhere in the world—including one small subset, which was the making of music documentaries, and that would eventually become my own primary pursuit.

All of us who eventually tried our hands at music-centered non-fiction filmmaking were influenced by such pioneering music docs and directors as the following: *Jazz on a Summer's Day* (1959) by Bert Stern and Aram Avakian; *Dizzy Gillespie* (1964), *The Blues Accordin' to Lightnin' Hopkins* (1968), and many others by Les Blank; *Festival* (1967) by Murray Lerner; *Don't Look Back* (1967), *Monterey Pop* (1968), and more by D. A. Pennebaker; *Woodstock* (1970) by Michael Wadleigh; *Gimme Shelter* (1970) by Albert Maysles, David Maysles, and Charlotte Zwerin; and beginning in 1968, a series of Mississippi Delta folklore films by Professor William Ferris, including unfiltered views of blues musicians, gospel singers, folk artists, and rural tale spinners. The best of these filmmakers would continue turning their lenses and microphones toward popular and traditional musicians, dancers, artists, writers, and more for decades to come, and in relatively short order, they would be joined by younger filmmakers, such as myself, whom they had inspired.

Of course, in all the years since 1927, when Al Jolson and *The Jazz Singer* showed that American movies could sing as well as talk (even if, to our enduring historical shame, doing so in blackface), many filmmakers found ways to bring music to their fiction and nonfiction stories, and not simply by placing it on the soundtrack to emphasize onscreen action. As I grew up in the second half of the twentieth century, impacting me from my own time and from decades before were the wit and wisdom of Ernst Lubitsch, almost singlehandedly inventing screen musicals, beginning with such examples as *The Love Parade* (1929), *One Hour With You* (1932), and *The Merry Widow* (1934); the sexy surrealism of producer Max Fleischer's Betty Boop cartoons, sometimes combining performances of flesh-and-blood jazz musicians like Louis Armstrong and Cab Calloway with kinetic, mischievous, dreamlike, and (once again) occasionally racist imagery in largely animated shorts such as *Minnie the Moocher* and *I'll Be Glad When You're Dead You Rascal You* (both 1932); the cleverly fragmented and kaleidoscopic visuals of film choreographer and director Busby Berkeley in musicals such as *The Gold Diggers of 1933* and *Footlight Parade* (both 1933), *Dames* (1934), and *The Gang's All Here* (1943); the physical grace, lighthearted romance, and fluid naturalism of actors/singers/dancers Fred Astaire and Ginger Rogers in films such as *Flying Down to Rio* (1933), *Top Hat* (1935), and *Swing Time* (1936), the latter stained by blackface still again, this time during Astaire's heartfelt homage to African American dancer Bill "Bojangles" Robinson; the breathtaking visual and musical storytelling of producer Walt Disney's animated masterpieces *Snow White and the Seven Dwarfs* (1937) and *Fantasia* (1940); the mature flowering of the direct-to-screen musical (as opposed to adaptations from the stage) with Gene Kelly and Stanley Donen's *Singin' in the Rain* (1952) and George Cukor's *A Star is Born* (1954); British director Richard Lester's refreshingly upbeat, phrenetic, and satirical rock musical *A Hard Day's Night* (1964), made in collaboration with worldwide pop rock phenomenon The Beatles; British director Ken Russell's dramatized film and television portraits of frequently tormented creative geniuses including Dante Gabriel Rosetti in *Dante's Inferno* (1967), Isadora Duncan in *Isadora Duncan, the Biggest Dancer in the World* (1967), Frederick Delius in *Song of Summer* (1968), Pyotr Ilyich Tchaikovsky in *The Music Lovers* (1971), and Gustav Mahler in *Mahler* (1974), all of which compared and contrasted the artist's life with his or her creative work.

It should go without saying that everyone—perhaps artists in particular—stores up images, ideas, and approaches absorbed from countless works of art and entertainment witnessed over a lifetime.

So, even though I have never knowingly attempted to make a film like any of the ones mentioned, I have no doubt that these, as well as other works long forgotten, have helped to shape the consciousness I bring to everything I do myself. Just as traditional American musicians see themselves as carrying forth (and perhaps expanding upon) inherited musical techniques, approaches, styles, and forms, so do filmmakers see ourselves as part of an evolutionary process, perhaps making contributions, but doing so with a sense of what has come before, and what could yet come after.

Now, just as every picture tells a story, every production depends upon an appropriately selected and utilized crew. In my own case, crews have ranged from a two-person unit (myself and a cinematographer), to a four-person group resembling a basic jazz or rock quartet (director, cinematographer, camera assistant, and sound person, more or less paralleling a lead guitarist or horn player, and a rhythm guitarist or keyboard player, supported by a bass player and a drummer), to ensembles of ever-increasing size and scope. For instance, while a several-person crew might do fine for the conducting of interviews, the documentation of intimate performances, or cases where a larger group could prove disruptive or provoke restrictions on its movements, other situations cannot be adequately documented without greater numbers and resources. On the films I make, the prime example of the latter would be large-scale concert shoots which require multiple camera operators (I prefer no fewer than four in such cases); perhaps an assistant for each camera person; grips or production assistants to haul equipment, run cables, and assist with hanging lights; a gaffer and electrician to create or adapt stage lighting; sometimes Steadicam or dolly operators to liven the coverage; a mobile recording truck equipped with at least twenty-four-track audio equipment and two or three technicians to handle miking, recording, and mixing; my usual audio director to record interviews, as well as to oversee the interface of the sound truck with the rest of us; a production manager or line producer to assist with larger production issues while I focus on the demands of directing; and eventually one or more film or video editors (though I always edit my own films).

Fortunately, I have a core group of camera, audio, and general production people with whom I have worked for decades, and whenever a project moves forward, I simply supplement that group with whatever additional personnel is needed. The process is not unlike that of a closely knit group of musicians that keeps its numbers small enough for each member to be paid sufficiently, while also holding performance fees to what the market will bear, except on occasions when a so-called "big band" is financially feasible. The scale of my productions, and therefore the size of my crews, is determined in each separate case by my ambitions for the project in question, by the inescapable demands of what I intend to document, and perhaps most importantly, by the amount of funding available.

At any rate, as I suggested in the preface, aside from the stories told by finished films, the productions themselves engender stories that rarely are shared at length, even if partially addressed in film-maker interviews or so-called "bonus features" created for home video releases. By contrast, this book exists solely to recount how twenty-five of the key music documentaries I have directed over four decades came to be, with emphasis on the challenges, the controversies, the camaraderie, and the generally gratifying results.

It should go without saying that, since leaving film school, neither I nor any of the highly accomplished friends who studied with me have completed all of the films we would have liked, or perhaps even a single one that exactly matched our initial intentions. But as always in life, it is the journey that matters; not the destination. And with that in mind, what follows are twenty-five stories—concerning twenty-five journeys—that resulted in twenty-five films—each of which I consider among the best of my music docs. I hope you enjoy the ride, as I certainly have myself.

Chapter One
Music Beyond Time

George Crumb: *Voice of the Whale (1976)*

Gather at the River: A Bluegrass Celebration (1994)

I n early 1976, I received a grant from the National Endowment for the Arts that permitted me to produce an hour-long film on Pulitzer Prize-winning composer George Crumb. The resulting portrait, *George Crumb: Voice of the Whale*, was my first professional film after leaving the graduate filmmaking program at Temple University in Philadelphia. At the time, Professor Crumb was teaching at the University of Pennsylvania and living in the Philadelphia suburb of Media, Pennsylvania with his musician wife Elizabeth and their two young sons, David (a future composer himself) and Peter. Their grown daughter, Ann, was already a professional singer and actor in New York City.

Growing up in Charleston, West Virginia, with parents who were, themselves, classical musicians, George displayed an early talent for composition, but also a love of nature and a sense of spirituality derived, at least in part, from the rural gospel music of the region. Now, of course, he was world-renowned for writing hauntingly beautiful music that upended classical conventions by incorporating unlikely instruments (the didgeridoo from Australia, the nipple gong from Thailand, the Indian elephant bell) and unique vocal and instrumental techniques (from singing through a flute to placing a glass rod on strings inside the piano), the cumulative effect of which was a dazzling range of unexpected timbres. He also was employing alternative styles of notation, with his scores often forming visual images (a circle, a spiral, a peace sign) which underlined his intentions.

From left, flutist Carole Morgan, composer George Crumb, music director Dr. Richard Wernick, pianist Lambert Orkis, and cellist Barbara Haffner. (photographed by Marvin R. A. Johnson, FAIA, 1976)

Once NEA funding was in hand, George and I agreed to center my planned portrait around a full-length performance of his 1971 composition, "Vox Balaenae for three masked players," commonly known by its English translation, "Voice of the Whale." We also agreed to entrust that performance to the renowned Penn Contemporary Players (flutist Carole Morgan, cellist Barbara Haffner, and pianist Lambert Orkis) under the leadership of Crumb's fellow composer and University of Pennsylvania teaching colleague Dr. Richard Wernick.

The piece was written for amplified flute, cello, and piano, with the flute evoking the singing of whales, the cello sometimes suggesting the cries of seagulls, and the piano illustrating the slow, but sometimes turbulent passage of time on Earth, as marked by three principal movement titles: "Vocalize (. . . for the beginning of time)," "Variations on Sea-Time," and "Sea-Nocturne (. . . for the end of time)." The middle of the piece is divided into five shorter parts designating the successive geological eras of the Earth, and the arrival of human beings is announced through a quote from Richard Strauss's Nietzsche-inspired composition, "Also sprach Zarathustra," which today is best-known for having been featured in Stanley Kubrick's 1968 film *2001: A Space Odyssey*, as co-written by Arthur C. Clarke. The result conveys a mysterious and seemingly endless sense of cosmic time and space in which human beings play a belated, clearly impressive, yet possibly temporary role, and Crumb reinforces this notion by instructing that the three musicians be masked throughout the performance, explaining that their masks "tend to symbolize the impersonal forces of nature [and] isolate the performers, in a sense, from the audience." The piece would be performed for us, one section at a time, in a theater space on the University of Pennsylvania campus, with Bill Barth, then the longtime audio director for the public television station in Hershey, recording and mixing live, without overdubs. Bill would go on to become the location audio person for nearly all of my films.

Crumb and I also agreed that Dick Wernick would conduct the key, onscreen interview with him, in which he would be asked to discuss his intentions as a composer, the political and spiritual dimensions of his work, the unique calligraphy of his musical scores, his thoughts about teaching, and his time growing up in West Virginia (including making his own fireworks for the Fourth of July). In addition, my small crew and I recorded George advising one of his composition students in a campus studio, interacting with his wife and sons at home, and demonstrating some of the exotic instruments and performance techniques he had utilized in his compositions. As he told us, "I guess that I've always been interested in sounds, and possibilities of new sounds, as expressive devices in the music. I've borrowed instruments from other cultures."

Finally, director of photography Larry McConkey and I visited Philadelphia's Franklin Institute, the Smithsonian in Washington, DC, a New Jersey beach, and a section of rural West Virginia in order to capture images for use in illustrating the complete performance of "Vox Balaenae." These included dinosaur skeletons, a seagull in flight, model airplanes and spacecraft, an overhead model of an enormous blue whale, clouds casting shadows over a West Virginia mountain-side, and waves striking the New Jersey shoreline, one of which washed away my own footprints in the sand.

Crumb has stated that, growing up in the Appalachian River Valley of West Virginia, his "ear was attuned to a peculiar echoing acoustic" which influenced his music, in that he loved "sounds that have long, slow decays to them." Moreover, he revealed that rural revival tunes he heard growing up had made their way into his music: "certainly echoes of them if not exact quotations." So, while Larry and I were in West Virginia, we also walked into a small, country church and were granted permission to film gospel performances at a service that evening. The often solemn and slowly paced songs offered at least a surface connection to the dreamlike pacing of Crumb's own music, and gospel revival lyrics suggested how he may have come to adopt his view of spirituality in nature. That was especially true of one song in particular ("There Is a River," composed by Max and David Sapp, with apparent inspiration from Psalm 46:4, then adapted and performed in the film by The Happy Three), which makes the point especially well: "There came a sound away from heaven. They said it was a rushing and a mighty wind. They tell me that it filled their hearts with singing . . . that it gave them peace within. [chorus] There is a river, that flows from my God above; there is a fountain, and it's filled with His great love."

Compare those lyrics to sample passages from the work of Spanish poet Federíco Garcia Lorca, as incorporated by Crumb into his 1970 piece, "Ancient Voices of Children":

I have lost myself in the sea many times
with my ear full of freshly cut flowers,
with my tongue full of love and agony.
I have lost myself in the sea many times
as I lose myself in the heart of certain children . . .
My heart of silk
is filled with lights,
with lost bells,
with lilies, and with bees,
and I will go very far,
farther than those hills,
farther than the seas,
to ask Christ the Lord
to give me back my ancient soul of a child.

Or consider how George described his own work to us: "The music is meant to be a kind of nature music."

In the film, Crumb also commented on three other issues of note: (1) On his approach to writing music: "I found that I was unable to compose a music that was highly structured in the sense of a pitch ordering, and . . .what I did write had to be more . . . intuitively composed." (2) On his thoughts about time, which he manipulated freely in "Vox Balaenae": "I think music is a beautiful medium to discourse upon time." (3) On the nature of composition, which he appeared to relate to the sense of loneliness and spirituality evident in his work:

Composition is an incredibly lonely business. And as you know, there's something a little bit monastic about writing a piece of music. And the only sense of collaboration you get is in working with performers. But this is after the fact. So, I think that being involved in composition normally imposes a rigor of a kind. And temperamentally, one would have to be willing to accept this rather secluded sort of existence.

Composer George Crumb (right) and music director Dr. Richard Wernick study Crumb's score for "Vox Balaenae for three masked players." (photographed by Marvin R. A. Johnson, FAIA, 1976)

With overall content set, all that remained was to determine the film's structure. In doing that, I was inspired by two film theorists, the great Slavko Vorkapich, with whom a few friends and I had studied at the American Film Institute Theater in Washington, DC (ten Monday nights, from January through April of 1974), and Noël Burch, who wrote an influential book titled *Theory of Film Practice*. Vorkapich's theory of "kinesthetic montage" affected how I edited the performance sections of the film, and Burch's ideas on creating formal structures in films led me to organize my material in such a way that some of the film's themes would be underscored, or even introduced, by the structure itself. At the heart of Burch's philosophy was the notion of dialectic, wherein two separate ideas come together to create a third. And because I knew my film would lean heavily on an alternation between scenes of George Crumb the person and a performance of one of his best-known compositions— a piece, incidentally, that Crumb suggests be performed under blue light—I decided to shoot the film largely in black and white, to tint most of the central performance blue, to tint the interview and related documentary sequences green, to intercut these separate *art* and *life* threads throughout the film, and, finally, to merge the two in full-color footage, proposing what should be obvious, which is that art and life are simply two sides of the same reality.

Among the other more formalistic techniques I employed were the following: (1) shooting a series of seated, close-up, full-color portraits of Crumb and then using them, one at a time, along with actual whale sounds and rhyming onscreen titles, as introductory sequences for each section of the film; (2) shooting Crumb's upper body profile in silhouette, and using that as the opening image of the film, quickly switching it from green to blue, again and again, in order to establish the color-based dialectic that would operate from that point forward; (3) filming George walking through woods near his home, leaning against a large tree, and skipping rocks across a body of water, then, in the editing, manipulating picture and sound in ways that not only called attention to the plastic elements of the medium, but also made further connections among the composer, the natural world, and the fabrications of artistic creation; and (4) gently satirizing the clichéd ways in which interviews typically are handled in documentaries by placing the two composers at opposite ends of a large sofa and shooting their casual conversation with faux formality.

This is the only time in my career that I have utilized so many formalistic approaches for a nonfiction film, and it stuns me to this day that George, his family, and his colleagues trusted such a young filmmaker (twenty-five at the start of the project) to frame and visualize his life and art in such audacious ways. However, the avant-garde nature of Crumb's work, his cosmic concerns, and his international stature—contrasted with his friendly and unassuming personality, his sense of humor, his West Virginia roots, and his idyllic home life in suburban Philadelphia—seemed perfectly suited to a merging of his personal experience and unlimited imagination. In the end, of course, Crumb is shown to be an extraordinary artist, whose work is just as American, and just as important, as that of Aaron Copeland, Charles Ives, and other of our greatest composers.

Although I no longer recall the date, sometime in the Bicentennial fall of 1976, I leased Philadelphia's historic Walnut Street Theatre for a Sunday afternoon screening of the finished film. George and I both invited friends, family, and colleagues, and though George and his wife Elizabeth let me know how much they enjoyed our finished product, George also expressed amusement at how *green* his face had appeared in nonmusical sequences. Happily, soon thereafter, PBS agreed to a national broadcast, and my friends at the Maryland Center for Public Broadcasting who, in January of 1973, had broadcast my hour-long student film about a Western Maryland mining town called *Frostburg*, now agreed to act as the so-called pass-through station for the Crumb film broadcast. It took another year and a half to get it onto the national schedule, but I eventually mailed out a printed invitation reading as follows: "Robert Mugge cordially invites you to join him in viewing the television premiere of his musical portrait film *George Crumb: Voice of the Whale* Tuesday evening, June 6, 1978 at ten o'clock on PBS in the comfort of your own home."

With this film, I developed techniques for the making of music documentaries that would serve me for decades to come. And yet, I would never again impose a formal structure on a production of mine because, working over time as a documentary filmmaker, I learned to value documentation and communication over overt self-expression, and to see myself, increasingly, as assisting other artists by providing them the means for presenting their own work, philosophy, experience, and more, from which we all can learn. Still, I remain proud of what my collaborators and I achieved with the George Crumb portrait, and grateful that it taught me how to inspire talent, motivate crews, devise narratives, impose rhythms, compose visuals, establish moods, capture performances, and construct portraits that are at least as true to their subjects as to my own creative intentions. In short, I had laid out the template for the rest of my career, whether I always chose to follow it or not.

***

Eighteen years after completing *George Crumb: Voice of the Whale*, plus a dozen more films in the interim, I was offered a project with connections to my first. To my surprise, a company called BMG Video, a short-lived division of corporate music giant BMG, asked me to document the 1993 World of Bluegrass events, which would soon be held in Owensboro, Kentucky. At the time, I was seeking funding for a film about independent music label Rounder Records, which I saw as the perfect sequel for my recent film on independent label Alligator Records (my initial collaboration with BMG). Ultimately, though, I convinced David Steffen, founding head of the video company, that if he would support both films—the World of Bluegrass film and the Rounder Records film—I could produce both simultaneously for just a bit more money than he would pay for one alone. In fact, I later pushed to add a third film to the project (one about zydeco music in Southwest Louisiana) which led to my crew and me shooting three films simultaneously during one big swing through the American South. Of course, information about those other two films can wait, because the bluegrass film—shot in the fall of 1993 and released in February of 1994—is the one with obvious connections to my portrait of George Crumb.

How this came about is that, in 1990, the IBMA (International Bluegrass Music Association) established the annual World of Bluegrass events, which included concerts, a trade show, and awards presentations. For the first seven years, these gatherings were staged at RiverPark Center in Owensboro, Kentucky, after which they relocated to Louisville, Kentucky; then Nashville, Tennessee; and then Raleigh, North Carolina. But again, in 1993, David took enough of an interest in the World of Bluegrass that I agreed to produce a feature-length film about it which BMG could release on video, along with a shorter version that his co-funder, TNN (The Nashville Network), could broadcast as a one-hour special.

The priority for the IBMA and TNN was documentation of the awards show. So, once David and I agreed to handle that, we also were given access to the IBMA trade show, day and evening concerts on an outdoor stage, artists and experts we could interview, jam sessions (which could break out anywhere), and presentations elsewhere in the community. I therefore scheduled several days of shooting in Owensboro, immediately preceded by separate shoots in Memphis, Austin, New Orleans, and Southwest Louisiana for the Rounder Records and zydeco films.

From previous experience (most of which I have skipped over for now), I knew that, once we were on location, themes would emerge with little inducement; all we had to do was set up, then respond to what happened. And yet, for the bluegrass film in particular, I felt that some early planning would ensure its special character. For example, noting that Owensboro was perched beside the Ohio River, I decided to call the film *Gather at the River: A Bluegrass Celebration*, which I figured would instill immediate resonance. In addition, I knew an effective way to organize a plethora of information and performance was to employ a charismatic figure who could lead audience members from point to point throughout the production. In this case, we had been warned that "father of bluegrass" Bill Monroe was in bad health and therefore would not be present in Owensboro. So, I reached out to another musician who had received his start in Monroe's band; who was a large man with a winning personality and a powerful yodel; whose talent as a singer, songwriter, and musician was widely respected; and who was then known almost as well in the rock world as he was in the bluegrass community, which perhaps could broaden the film's appeal. That man was Peter Rowan, whom I actually knew best from his late sixties and early seventies countercultural bands such as Earth Opera, Seatrain, Muleskinner, and Old & In the Way, in which he collaborated with the likes of David Grisman, Richard Greene, Bill Keith, and Jerry Garcia of the Grateful Dead.

Peter was already planning to be in Owensboro, of course, if only to network, socialize, serve as a presenter during the awards show, and perform in concert with his hand-picked band called the Panama Red Riders. Now, however, at my request, he would also pose on camera as a kind of troubadour, regaling us with stories about his mentor, Bill Monroe, and the essence of bluegrass, and helping to devise scenes that I could later insert throughout the film and use to guide viewers from one section of narrative to another. Moreover, on our behalf, he would interact with fellow musicians, including West Virginia native and activist singer-songwriter Hazel Dickens, with whom he would sing a few key lines (repeating the only ones they could remember) from our title song, "Shall We Gather at the River":

Shall we gather at the river,
The beautiful, beautiful river;
Gather with the saints at the river
That flows by the throne of God.

Yes, these well-known lyrics, written in 1854 by poet and Baptist preacher Robert Lowry, strongly paralleled the ones previously sung by local West Virginia church members for *George Crumb: Voice of the Whale* (e.g., "There is a river that flows from my God above . . . There is a fountain, and it's filled with his great love"). In fact, what most connects these two films is their shared focus on nature, time, and spirit, as rooted in the rural mountain culture of both George Crumb's West Virginia and Bill Monroe's Kentucky. And even George's evocation of whale songs in "Vox Balaenae" resembled the high-pitched, "high lonesome" vocals of bluegrass singers echoing plaintively out of an Appalachian holler. Both suggest a kind of cosmic loneliness and a recurring sense of loss.

At one point while we were shooting *Gather at the River*, Peter Rowan improvised the following statement about bluegrass traditions: "The music came out of the hills, out of the mountains and out of the woods, the streams and the rivers. And you can hear that in the sound of the banjo and the mandolin; the fiddle, the guitar, and the bass. It sounds like the earth itself: the wind blowing down; the heaven and earth meeting and creating a new music . . . bluegrass style." Then, also for the film, Peter and his band performed "Walls of Time," a well-known song for which Bill Monroe wrote the music and Peter wrote the lyrics (punctuation added):

The wind is blowing 'cross the mountain,
And down on the valley way below.

It sweeps the grave of my darling;
When I die, that's where I want to go.
Lord, send the angels for my darling,
And take her to that home on high.
I'll wait my time out here on earth, love,
And come to you when I die.
Our names are carved upon a tombstone.
I promised you before you died,
Our love would bloom forever, darling,
When we rest side by side.
I hear a voice out in the darkness,
And it moans and whispers through the pines.
I know it's my sweetheart calling;
I hear her through the walls of time.

Robert Mugge (center) interviews Ralph Stanley (right of center) as Bill Burke (left rear) shoots and Bill Barth (behind him) records the interview. (photographed by Craig Smith, 1993)

Not surprisingly, notions of time, loss, loneliness, and changing generations were ever present at that year's World of Bluegrass.

Among the most respected artists performing in Owensboro that year were such first-generation pioneers as Doc Watson ("Ramshackle Shack"), Ralph Stanley ("Mountain Folks"), Mac Wiseman ("'Tis Sweet to Be Remembered"), and the somewhat younger Hazel Dickens ("You'll Get No More of Me") and Del McCoury ("I Feel the Blues Movin' In" and "Queen Anne's Lace"). Also performing were prominent members of the next generation of artists: the Nashville Bluegrass Band ("Father I Stretch My Hand to Thee" and Bill Monroe's "Dark As the Night, Blue As the Day"), the recently revived Johnson Mountain Boys ["Duncan and Brady (He's Been On the Job Too Long)"], Tim O'Brien of former fan favorite Hot Rize ["The Church Steeple (High On a Hillside)" and Bob Dylan's "When I Paint My Masterpiece"], fusion group California featuring master guitarist Dan Crary ("California Traveler"), and dobro wizard Jerry Douglas, demonstrating his instrument with lightning-fast fingers. These younger musicians mostly respected the genre's enduring traditions, yet some also offered new variations almost certain to offend their more nitpicking forebears.

Present as well, and demonstrating the global reach of an initially localized music, were Kukuruza from Russia ("Porushka-Poraniya" and "Wayfaring Stranger") and the Nakashima Family Band from Japan ("Cindy" and "Turkey in the Straw"). But perhaps most suggestive of coming change was Pete "Dr. Banjo" Wernick's awards show presentation of a group of stunning young players who performed Bill Monroe's "Wheel Hoss," and who did so with the youthful zeal one might expect with an average performer age of thirteen. (Incidentally, Wernick had cofounded the popular band Hot Rize with Tim O'Brien, and among these adolescent virtuosos were mandolin player Chris Thile and blind fiddle player Michael Cleveland, each of whom would one day be a world-renowned star of the genre.)

Again, the assortment of styles, techniques, and even generations on display was a cause of concern for the more vocal traditionalists. But so, too, were the IBMA's efforts to strengthen the community through an injection of showbiz glamor and the courting of media, which, that year, included production of our film. In fact, concerns about "growing pains" in the so-called "bluegrass industry" were most poetically expressed by beloved artist John Hartford (increasingly ill, then and later, with non-Hodgkin lymphoma), who told us the following on camera:

> This music, right now, is a wonderful small town where we all live, where we don't have to lock our doors at night. And what we're trying to do here in this organization is, we're trying to get GE [General Electric] to come in on the outskirts of town and build a great big plant. And with it is gonna be all the ills of civilization. And I'm not sure we're ready for that, or I'm not sure *I'm* ready for that. I know that's what everybody's workin' for, [but] progress has a tendency of canceling itself out.

Del McCoury (center, on guitar) performs with his sons Ronnie (left, on mandolin) and Rob (right, on banjo). (photographed by Craig Smith, 1993)

As planned, in Owensboro, the themes of the film were revealed rather than imposed: the notion that time passes, as do we all; that traditions, even when respected, continue to evolve; that nights in the mountains can be dark and lonesome; and that beauty comes from the fragility and impermanence of life. And yet, as Peter Rowan, our intrepid guide, showed with another of his reverberant songs, "High Lonesome Sound" (performed in the film with his friends, the Nashville Bluegrass Band), mountain folks, their descendants, and their worldwide disciples could still light up dark and lonely nights with moments of pure, transcendent joy:

> Y'all come with one another,
> Just to do a little pickin',
> Everybody now gather round.
> The camp fire's burnin'
> An' tonight my heart is yearnin',
> For the sight of that old camp ground.
> And that high lonesome sound,
> When that evenin' sun goes down.
> I'm gonna dance right off the ground,
> When I hear the fiddle play that high lonesome sound.

In such moments, the players, the dancers, and the listeners all transported musically to a place beyond time.

Chapter Two
Jazz Without Limits

Sun Ra: A Joyful Noise (1980)
Saxophone Colossus (1986)

Thrext 1972 Ann Arbor Blues & Jazz Festival changed my life. With old friends James and Harriet Castrataro, and new one Krin Gabbard, I saw performances by, among others, Muddy Waters, Howlin' Wolf, Luther Allison, Junior Walker & The All Stars, Bonnie Raitt with Sippie Wallace, Miles Davis, and Sun Ra & His Solar-Myth Arkestra. All were extraordinary, but the artist who resonated with me most was Sun Ra. The reasons included his electronic keyboards, squealing saxophones, pulsing horns, Afro-Caribbean percussion, soulful vocalists, myth-evoking chants, writhing dancers, sci-fi costumes, gospel-like fervor, sense of spectacle, and jazz constructions stretched to their musical and lyrical limits. Although still an undergraduate film student at UMBC in Baltimore, I resolved that, one day, I would create a film about this most singular of artists.

A little over a year later, I moved to Philadelphia to attend graduate film school at Temple University. When I arrived, I learned that Sun Ra and core members of his Arkestra lived together in a row house in the Germantown section of the city. I also quickly realized that, when not on the road, Sun Ra and his fill-in-the-blank Arkestra (the full name was constantly changing, as did the group's precise musical lineup) would perform somewhere in the area. As often as I could, I took in such concerts, and Sun Ra must have sensed my enthusiasm because, on two separate occasions, while leading his parading musicians through the audience, he suddenly reached over and hugged me.

Anxious to begin my filmmaking career, I left Temple after just two semesters and started writing screenplays. Then, in 1976 and 1977, while waiting in vain for someone to purchase those screenplays or provide the funding I needed to turn them into feature films, I managed to produce long-form portraits of two famous Philadelphians, composer George Crumb and law-and-order mayor Frank L. Rizzo, and saw that perhaps my future was in nonfiction filmmaking, rather than in the more glamorous and potentially lucrative alternative. At any rate, by early 1978, as I started distributing the Rizzo film, I decided it was time to make my long-delayed portrait of Sun Ra. All attempts to secure funding for such a film had thus far fallen short, but I refused to be discouraged. Instead, I made an unannounced visit to Sun Ra's home in Germantown, purchased a few of the privately released LPs that he and Arkestra members sold there, often with individually designed album covers, and broached the idea of making a film about him.

I told him straight out that I did not yet know where to find production funding, but also suggested that, if I could pull together some sample footage, demonstrating that the project was under way, money would surely follow. Although rightly wary, Sun Ra informed me that he would be performing a concert for the Left Bank Jazz Society at Baltimore's Famous Ballroom on July 23, 1978, and that, if I were to be there with a crew, he *might* allow me to film the show. At the time, my only income was a share of money derived from the sale of the Rizzo film to Swedish television, and I used that to buy enough film stock and audio tape to shoot and record a lengthy concert.

I then reached out to assorted filmmaking friends (including Larry McConkey, who had shot my George Crumb and Frank Rizzo

films; Dave Insley, who had shot and co-produced my undergraduate documentary *Frostburg*, then went on to shoot features for John
Waters; and Bruce Litecky, a sound man friend of Larry's who had
assisted in small ways with the Rizzo film) and convinced them to
assist me again on merely the *possibility* of one day being paid, not
only for their labor, but also for use of their cameras, recorders, tripods, lights, and more. Dave also brought along DC-based cameraman Chris Li, who offered an all-important third camera, and who
would go on to work with me for decades to come. And finally, I
huddled with Pete Garey, owner and operator of Baltimore's Quality
Film Labs, who had been my unofficial outside teacher while I attended UMBC, then oversaw postproduction for my George Crumb
and Frank Rizzo films before, most magnanimously of all, agreeing
to defer payment for film processing, film work-printing, and audio
transferring for the unfunded Sun Ra film.

Fortunately, on the Sunday in question, the Left Bank Jazz Society embraced our presence, including offering me reasonably priced
fried chicken dinners for my crew. But even more important, Sun Ra
and his Arkestra proved happy to see us. So, with genuine relief, we
arranged our motley assemblage of lights, cameras, tripods, and recorders around the room, then filmed the two-plus-hour show with
all the competence and enthusiasm we could muster.

Midway through, however, in response to the music's tonal
and rhythmic unpredictability, I encouraged Larry (long known as
"the human dolly") and Dave to shoot handheld and, when suit-
ably inspired, create their own swooping camera movements and
racked focus (switching primary focus from a foreground object to
a background one, or vice versa) in covering nimbly unhinged keyboard and saxophone solos. Our obvious intention was to echo the
Arkestra's digressions from traditional tonality with our own digressions from conventional shooting techniques. Employing such an approach was risky, of course, but I knew that, whenever Larry's and
Dave's more unrestrained coverage became challenging for viewers,
Chris's tripod-steadied camera would provide a visual safe harbor.

Considering our small and minimally equipped crew, the shoot
went surprisingly well, our only unresolved question being, could we

successfully record a large ensemble without multitrack recording equipment, or even the cables we needed to patch into the mixing board of the house PA system (something I would never again be without)? But sound man Bruce Litecky improvised as well, coming up with usable audio by pointing one mike at the house PA speakers and another at whichever musician or vocalist was currently taking the lead.

As the concert wound to a close, and we realized we had made it through without serious mishap, we all breathed a sigh of relief. But then, as we began to pack up our equipment, I was suddenly encircled by Arkestra members who insisted that I remain in place while Sun Ra had a word with me. It turned out that, as Sun Ra went on to announce, "because of four hundred years of slavery," he was now in charge, and I would need to turn over my "tapes." I slowly realized that he meant our *audio* tapes, rather than our exposed film stock, which was at least a partial relief. However, I explained to him that, without those tapes, the film we had shot would be worthless. He countered that, until he was sure we had faithfully recorded his music, he could not endorse the project. Naturally, I objected. So, Sun Ra proposed to leave with the tapes, but to allow Bruce and me to accompany him to Germantown where we could spend the night reviewing them together.

Seeing no alternative, Bruce and I followed him to the house and began playing the tapes for him on Bruce's recorder. Yet, right from the start, I was nervous, because I could hear the many spots where our limited number of microphones made for poor separation among the assorted players. However, as we listened, a funny thing happened. Sun Ra, who claimed to have come from Saturn, to be immortal, and not to need sleep, began slipping unexpectedly into brief naps. On each occasion, he would doze in his seat for perhaps fifteen minutes, then suddenly revive himself and comment on what he was hearing. I had read that people who claim not to sleep at all actually take periodic cat naps, as he was doing here, and that these invigorate them sufficiently that they can carry out their daily activities.

To my enormous relief, Sun Ra must have slept through the most egregious audio issues, because he eventually gave his approval, and sometime after dawn, Bruce and I headed home. Sun Ra did insist that a third party hold the tapes until I secured funding, but after a time, I convinced that person I could not begin editing without audio to synch with picture, and he finally turned them over.

Robert Mugge prepares to shoot a performance by Sun Ra and his Arkestra on the roof of International House of Philadelphia. (photographed by Larry Keffer, 1980)

Not long thereafter, Sun Ra came to realize that, with this project, I was offering him the chance to present as much of his music, his life, and his cosmic philosophy as could be fit into a single film. Therefore, going forward, the project became a true collaboration, with each of us proposing ideas for scenes, and the other trying to be accommodating.

In the weeks that followed, Larry and I, along with whomever else we could convince to assist us without pay, filmed Sun Ra and his key musicians multiple times in or around their Germantown house, which actually was owned by the father of saxophone player Marshall Allen. There, for instance, we captured multiple interviews, a solo keyboard performance, and an Arkestra rehearsal that, to Sun Ra's increasing frustration, was disrupted by repeated phone calls. As he complained at the time, "People don't interrupt Pablo Casals when *he's* rehearsin'. Why do they interrupt *me?*"

We also filmed Sun Ra reciting his poetry beneath the "Playing Angels" sculptures beside the Schuylkill River in Fairmount Park; Arkestra member Danny (Ray) Thompson showing off Pharaoh's Den, his neighborhood convenience store located a short distance from the house ("Pharaoh fed the nations of the world for seven years, so I might be here seven years, maybe."); Sun Ra presenting interstellar soliloquies as he walked among the Egyptian columns, sphinxes, and more at (what was then known as) the University Museum of the University of Pennsylvania, with Larry once again improvising visually as Sun Ra improvised verbally; and the Arkestra performing a requiem for a recently deceased musician at a West Philadelphia nightclub called Danny's Hollywood Palace. Reportedly, the recipient of this requiem was only loosely affiliated with the Arkestra and had died of a drug overdose. Yet, despite Sun Ra's aversion to drug use by Arkestra members, he himself proposed the tribute, and even hoped to squeeze a hundred drummers into the cramped club. Ultimately, though, he settled for just his usual lineup of musicians, and my crew and I settled for filming them from a single vantage point beside the bar.

Of course, working with Sun Ra, even daily routines could prove a revelation. For example, there was a room in the Germantown house called the Room of Chaos, so stuffed with memorabilia that it was simply impassible. There was a culinary staple dubbed "moon stew" that, like the literary "stone soup," consisted of whatever vegetables nightly diners could contribute. There were the aforementioned homemade LPs, the covers of which were personally designed by Arkestra members and sold both at the house and at Philly's Third Street Jazz and Rock record store. Finally, there was the time when, while driving through Sun Ra's neighborhood, I heard a loud thump at my left. Upon reaching the house on Morton Street, I checked the exterior of my driver's side door, discovering, just below the window, a hole from an apparent 22-caliber shot that, had it been an inch or so higher, would have shattered my window and struck me in the side. This, of course, had nothing to do with Sun Ra or his Arkestra except, perhaps, as a reflection on the neighborhood where they currently lived and worked.

There also were the times Sun Ra asked me to film his upcoming appearances in Boston, in Connecticut, in Europe, and at the United Nations because, of course, each would be unique in its own way, and he had yet to understand the cost of extensive filming on the road. Eventually, though, expenses aside, he asked that a small crew and I at least accompany him to Washington, DC so that we could film his philosophical cutting contest with a newly arrived Indian mystic who had declared himself a "representative of the Creator of the Universe," not unlike Sun Ra himself. Although I did agree, and we ultimately spent several hours driving from one DC address to another, we never did find the man. Therefore, just so the trip would not be a total waste, I asked Sun Ra if, before returning to Philadelphia, we could film him in front of the White House. It was then he came up with his notion that, as a matter of racial justice, a "Black House" should be built across the street. We actually talked in that spot well into the night, until the omnipresent Secret Service announced "last call" by shutting off lights on the White House behind him. And of course, for the second time, much to sound man Bruce Litecky's rightful irritation (since he had a paying job set for the following morning), we did not make it back to Philadelphia until dawn.

Throughout this period of off and on production, the person who did nearly all of the talking on camera was Sun Ra himself. The only notable exceptions were four of the seven Arkestra members then living with Sun Ra in the group's Morton Street home—John Gilmore, Danny Thompson, Elo Omoe, and James Jacson—plus a longtime friend named Walter Miller, who occasionally flew up from Birmingham to visit and sit in with the band. Even Marshall Allen, who would one day take over leadership of the Arkestra after the deaths of both Sun Ra and John Gilmore, gently demurred when asked for comment, and so did June Tyson, Sun Ra's incredibly soulful, New York-based lead vocalist, and the only female member of his inner circle. All of them were there in support of Sun Ra's art and ideas, and it therefore followed that, if we filmmakers had any questions, he should be the one to answer them.

After amassing much amazing footage, I spent several months editing it together. Then, when I finally had something to show, I invited Sun Ra over to have a look. Of course, I was then living in an Italian American enclave of South Philadelphia, which had been fine while making my films on composer George Crumb and Mayor Frank L. Rizzo, but was a bit problematic during the making of this one. Local residents were not accustomed to African Americans entering their neighborhood at night, especially ones who were so distinctively dressed. So, when Sun Ra and a few Arkestra members arrived wearing only slightly less than full concert regalia, and my neighbors seated on lawn chairs in front of their row houses showed concern, I did my best to reassure everyone, as I also ushered my guests from the crowded street into my second-and-third-floor corner apartment.

Once inside, we all climbed the stairs to my third-floor editing room and watched everything I had assembled thus far. To my great relief, they loved it all. But what took me aback was how, whenever Sun Ra delivered philosophical concepts onscreen, he and his companions would break out laughing. What I quickly deduced was that, although Sun Ra and his followers believed all of his sci-fi riddles and spiritual parables (to the point where the musicians who were closest to him called him "Master"), they also realized his presentation was a show—an enormous, multileveled artwork—and that it utilized a unique form of cosmic jive. So, they could fully subscribe to his overriding message, while still being amused by his audacity. In effect, I had been invited behind the wizard's curtain and permitted to witness his conjuring first-hand.

At that point, happy with what he had seen and heard, Sun Ra pulled out a 16mm print of the fiction film *Space Is the Place*, a production in which he had starred, but which he had not yet allowed to be released. Like other Sun Ra fans, I had purchased the film's soundtrack record several years before, then waited in vain for the film to follow. What had happened, Sun Ra said, was that he had been involved in the film's creation and truly enjoyed those sections seeking to dramatize his musical mythology. However, he was distressed by the Blaxploitation elements—namely, pimps and prostitutes—which had been added later on, probably to increase the project's commercial appeal. Therefore, Sun Ra now asked that I watch the film with him, then remove everything that he felt cheapened his message, and that I thought could be sacrificed without damaging the narrative.

He then phoned the producer in California and declared that he would be returning the print to him, and that what remained after our cuts could be released. Although I had no further involvement with the production, I feel sure that the sixty-four-minute version available largely on VHS for the next two or three decades was the one Sun Ra had approved that night, only after he and I had abridged it. Eventually, of course—years after Sun Ra's death—the scenes that had so offended him would be restored, and the entire film widely released at last.

Regardless, with Sun Ra's business out of the way, we returned to my second-floor living room where I served my guests chocolate chip cookies and iced tea, and Sun Ra surveyed a poster for *Amateur Night at City Hall*, my seventy-five minute portrait of Philadelphia Mayor Frank L. Rizzo. This bellicose former cop and police commissioner was nationally known as a racist and autocratic bully, yet was loved and admired in the city's white working class neighborhoods, including the one in which I currently resided. As Sun Ra turned away from the poster again, I fully expected him to excoriate Rizzo, at least for the infamous police assaults on hippies, Black Panthers, protesting Black schoolchildren, and others that had happened on his watch. However, hewing to his trademark unpredictability, Sun Ra expressed "no problem" with Rizzo. To the contrary, he said he merely wished "that *Black* people had a Rizzo," by which he meant someone to protect them and watch over their interests, exactly as Rizzo did for those who had elected him.

Next, learning that I owned LP collections of early Fletcher Henderson and Duke Ellington recordings, he asked to hear some, and I proudly complied. As each new song began to play, Sun Ra would explicate the arrangement for us, and since he had been a pianist and arranger for Henderson's band in the late 1940s, there was no reason to doubt his explanations.

In fact, I suddenly realized that this giant of modern music was giving a jazz master class in my living room, just as he no doubt did on a regular basis at the house in Germantown. And what I took away from that night, as he produced his ever-present cassette recorder and taped his favorites of the numbers now playing, was total confirmation that he had mastered basic jazz theory and practice before dragging both into the Space Age. Later, he said, he would transcribe these arrangements and teach them to his musicians.

The year that followed was tough for me. My experiment in "producing a film without money," as I liked to say, had started well, thanks to my cohort of eager enablers. But all the outstanding footage I had assembled was not enough to convince public television stations, keyboard manufacturers, or anyone else to provide the funding I needed for completion. And without the means for paying project bills, I had no way of paying personal ones, either. Indeed, that I survived at all was due to the generosity of my parents, of our family friend Marvin Johnson, of my South Philly landlord Joseph Orlando, of my University City barber Pete Colabelli, of my (then entirely pro bono) attorney friend Richard P. Jaffe, and of Italian Market store owner Claudio the King of Cheese, who so appreciated his inclusion in my recent Frank Rizzo portrait that, whenever I stopped by his shop, he slipped enough free-of-charge Jarlsberg and pepperoni into my bag to last me the week.

Of course, Sun Ra, too, was anxious for me to secure funding, if only because his costs of supporting a large jazz ensemble were never-ending, and I had promised to contribute something as soon as I could. And yet, as our time together proceeded, he came to view our collaboration as never-ending as well. As Sun Ra put it himself: If my crew and I were making a film about him, and he never stopped moving, changing, and creating, why should our filming ever stop? That is, he was a work-in-progress, so the film should remain one as well. Naturally, I loved this vision of our project, and I wished I could indulge it. But with my own situation growing increasingly dire, my primary goal was to find the backing I needed both to complete the film and to remunerate my subject.

Eventually, I showed up at the house in Germantown and asked Sun Ra if he would be willing to sign a letter of agreement that I could show to potential investors. Of course, simply saying "no" was not the Sun Ra way. So, instead, in something between a lecture and a sermon, he spent the next two hours (perhaps less, but it surely felt that long) explaining to me that he was "immortal" and that, as a result, he could never sign an agreement with someone who would "end up in the graveyard." Finally, as my frustration grew, I blurted out that he, too, would wind up in the graveyard, the same as everyone else. And just as quickly, I wished I had not.

Sun Ra was visibly crushed by my words. In fact, slowly, quietly, like a hurt child, he asked me how he could work with someone who did not believe the things he said. Without waiting to be asked again, I quickly apologized for my response and assured him that I did, indeed, believe what he told me, including his claim of immortality. Fortunately, we were then able to part on good terms. But I recognized that, until I had something material to offer, I could make no further appeals.

Finally, in early 1980, a friend of mine named Nainsi Niebuhr convinced a friend of hers named Daniel Kahn to invest $15,000 in the project. Today, I could barely accomplish anything with such an amount. But at the time, it was enough for me to pay Sun Ra, to stage and shoot an additional performance, and to underwrite all aspects of postproduction. Of course, the first thing I did was to take a check to Sun Ra himself, which he received in exactly the manner one might expect: "See that? Mugge's got money! Things must be gettin' better in the universe!"

Still, no sooner did I return home from that visit than Sun Ra called to say that the closest branch of my bank was refusing to cash his thousand-dollar check. Naturally, I drove right back to Germantown again, picked up Sun Ra and another Arkestra member (Elo Omoe, I believe), and headed for the bank. There, I had the unique challenge of convincing an unbelieving white bank manager that Herman "Sonny" Blount did business under the name of "Sun Ra," that I therefore had made out this relatively large check to that name, and that I expected my bank to cash it for him.

In time, we wore the man down, at which point Sun Ra asked me to stop at a nearby grocery store so he could spend some of his newly acquired cash. Frankly, I can imagine few experiences that would compare to my accompanying one of the most original and influential musicians of the twentieth century, dressed as if he truly believed he was born on a science fiction version of Saturn, and watching as he took brightly colored boxes, bags, and cans from the grocery store's shelves. Such a juxtaposition of the celestial and the mundane reminds me of Werner Herzog's 1976 film *Heart of Glass*, in which a character proclaims, "The chaos of the stars makes my head ache." In Sun Ra's case, chaos apparently made him hungry.

During this same period, another friend of mine named Linda Blackaby ran the Neighborhood Film Project at International House of Philadelphia, an institution on the edge of the University of Pennsylvania campus which provided housing for foreign students, while also sponsoring cultural activities for residents, other Penn students, and the general public. With Linda's help, I secured permission to shoot a performance on the roof of the building, which I figured was as close as I would get (short of cheesy special effects) to suggesting Sun Ra's connection to his notion of outer space. I also hired Larry McConkey and Dave Insley to do interpretive camerawork again, and Bill Barth to do the same sort of live, multitrack recording and mixing he had done for my George Crumb film on the nearby Penn campus.

"Human dolly" Larry McConkey shoots Marshall Allen playing alto saxophone as Sun Ra listens to John Gilmore playing tenor saxophone on the roof of International House of Philadelphia. (photographed by Larry Keffer, 1980)

The rooftop performance was as dazzling as I had hoped, marred only by the fact that it was 100 degrees out that day. In fact, because the flat roof was bookended by tall concrete walls on either side of us, the heat was magnified to at least 120 degrees while the musicians played and we filmed. As some of the Arkestra members later remembered, it was so hot that the flip-flops they were wearing literally melted beneath their feet, as did the colorful makeup on Sun Ra's face. Fortunately, though, by the time we did a final standup interview with Mister Ra (as in, "some call me Mister Ra, others call me Mystery") on the edge of the roof, the University of Pennsylvania and Drexel University campuses stretching out behind him, the temperature had cooled somewhat, but Sun Ra himself beamed as brightly as ever.

On Friday, October 24 of the same year (1980), we returned to International House, though this time to their climate-controlled theater for what was dubbed the "Planetary Premiere" of my sixty-minute finished film. Sun Ra and his Arkestra were present, of course, as they would be again on June 26, 1981 when the film premiered at the Carnegie Hall Cinema in New York City. And there, on the big screen—in spite of delays, a recurring lack of funds, and more challenges than on any of my productions to date—was the film I had resolved to make more than eight years before. All it had taken was will power, sacrifice, and an incomparable group of friends who, by the end of that project, included Sun Ra himself, and interviewers such as Terry Gross of WHYY's "Fresh Air" (along with her executive producer Danny Miller and her jazz reviewer Francis Davis) who helped me to promote my launch of the film.

When I first set out to produce *Sun Ra: A Joyful Noise*, I wanted to portray Sun Ra as one of the greatest jazz artists who ever lived, and yet, as so much more than that. He was someone who initially had learned all there was to know about jazz composition, arrangement, instrumentation, vocalizing, band leading, and overall presentation, and then stretched the boundaries of all of them. As John Gilmore, one of the finest tenor sax players of his day, and one of Sun Ra's most loyal collaborators, said in the film:

He was the first one to really introduce me in the higher forms of music, you know, past what you might would say, what Bird,

Monk, and the fellows were doing. I didn't think anybody was ahead of them, until I met Sun Ra, you know . . . And I said, "My gosh, man, this guy is more stretched out than Monk!" It's unbelievable that anybody could write any meaner intervals than Monk or Mingus, you know, but he does. His intervals—knowledge of intervals and harmony—very highly advanced, you know. So, when I saw that, I said, "Well, I think I'll make this the stop," you know?

Yet, beyond even that, like his fellow Philadelphia composer George Crumb, Sun Ra's work is full of dialectics—in his case, freedom versus discipline, electronic instruments versus acoustic ones, ancient Egypt versus outer space, White House versus Black House—and I worked hard to see that all such dualities were represented on screen.

Of course, the one thing I did not anticipate was that, one day, Sun Ra would be considered a pioneer—perhaps even the founder—of Afrofuturism, with a whole new academic field blossoming in his wake. All I knew then was that his art was as exciting, and as involving, as any I had witnessed, and that his wondrous mythology had envisioned an African American identity as deeply rooted in African history as in the vastness of space, each of which suggests a spiritual dimension superseding the indignities of his life. Sun Ra's so-called "omniverse" (the all of everything) took him beyond jazz; beyond his Jim Crow beginnings in Birmingham, Alabama; beyond this mortal coil (he "left the planet" in 1993); and in many respects, beyond the judgement of a particular time and place, whether during his life or after.

As jazz great Max Roach said privately to Sun Ra (who later informed me): "Your music is in code." Exactly. And as Sun Ra himself said in our film's conclusion: "A lot of people have tried to contain me or to limit me. But you see, that is not my type of bein', to be limited. You might call me a catalyst. A catalyst changes everything, but it remains unchanged. Everything that's unknown is part of the myth, and I'm sure that the myth can do more for humanity than anything they ever dreamed possible."

***

To clarify further, I first met Francis Davis, jazz writer extraordinaire, in 1980 when he reviewed my Sun Ra film for Terry Gross's "Fresh Air" program, then a three-hour weekday show on Philadelphia's WUHY-FM (later WHYY-FM) and not yet heard throughout the country via National Public Radio. Among his generous words, the first ever written (and in this case *spoken* on Terry's show) about the film, were the following: "*Sun Ra: A Joyful Noise* marks a decisive use of the art of film to illuminate the often enigmatic art of jazz, and I urge those of you committed to film to see it whether you are interested in jazz or not." There, again, in a somewhat different sense, is that theme of going beyond the limits of jazz.

After that initial meeting in 1980, when we both appeared on *Fresh Air* (as Francis did regularly, and as I did nearly every time I completed a film during those early years of Terry's show), Francis and I became good friends, often having lengthy phone conversations, especially regarding music and film. As was more common in the days before emailing, texting, social media, and even cell phones, we placed no limits on our free-ranging chats between his office-in-the-home and my own. Then, in early 1986, having recently completed my third film in a row for Britain's Channel 4 Television, I was trying to figure out another project that someone, whether at Channel 4 or elsewhere, might be willing to fund. It was then that Francis phoned me about his delightful experience interviewing tenor saxophone great Sonny Rollins.

At the time, Sonny and his wife Lucille owned a house in Upstate New York, but also an apartment on Greenwich Street in New York City, which is where Francis had interviewed Sonny and also gotten to know Lucille. Still reeling from the experience, he wanted me to know that Mr. and Mrs. Rollins were two of the most gracious persons he had met, which was especially surprising where Lucille was concerned. Many top jazz musicians had spouses who served as buffers between the artist and the world and, typically, that spouse might act as manager, booking agent, accountant, or record producer, but most at least served as a gatekeeper, deciding who was allowed to interview the artist, or even to communicate with him or her. As a result, some gatekeeper-spouses developed reputations as being "difficult," because they cared more about protecting the artist from intrusions than they did about advancing the interests of inquiring journalists, songwriters, club owners, label executives, or fans. Lucille, who was involved in all aspects of her husband's business, had developed exactly such a reputation, but Francis said that she could not have been more approachable.

Francis also wanted me to know that Japan's powerful Yomiuri Shimbun newspaper—owner, among other things, of a baseball team, a concert hall, a symphony orchestra, and television and radio stations—had commissioned Sonny to write a long-form composition that he would shortly premiere in the media conglomerate's Tokyo Koseinenkin Hall, in collaboration with its Yomiuri Nippon Symphony Orchestra. The piece Rollins had composed, titled "Concerto for Tenor Saxophone and Orchestra," consisted of structured orchestral movements, against which Sonny would perform improvised saxophone solos. After writing all the major themes, he had convinced his Finnish composer friend, Heikki Sarmanto, to arrange and orchestrate everything, as well as to conduct the initial concerts. But otherwise, both of them still considered it to be Sonny's piece.

Like Francis, I was not the sort of purist who believed jazz should only be played in smoky clubs, with concert halls reserved for classical music, folk music, or international music. And neither did I believe, as did some, that jazz should never have moved beyond swing, or at least beyond bebop, or that its artists should utilize only traditional song structures, instrumentation, vocal stylings, and the rest. To the contrary, as Francis knew, I had long been drawn to experimentation and to all forms of synthesis, as had been evident in my two most recent films—one exploring Al Green's integration of gospel with rhythm and blues, and the other chronicling attempts by Rubén Blades to move Latin music into the American musical mainstream.

For this reason, with Francis's introduction, I phoned Lucille myself and found her to be every bit as charming as he had reported. When I told her how much I loved such ambitious jazz creations as John Coltrane's "A Love Supreme" and Duke Ellington's "Sacred Concerts," and wished that cameras had recorded their premieres, she and I were in total agreement. Moreover, Lucille believed that her husband was playing the best of his career and that, despite his well-known reticence, she wanted this uniquely creative period to be as fully documented as possible. Therefore, when I asked her permission to film the premiere in Tokyo, it was not such a surprise when she once again said yes, plus offered to put me in touch with everyone involved in Japan. Now, all I had to do was figure out how to pay for an international production.

Somehow, in the weeks remaining till the premiere concerts set for May 18—one in the afternoon and one in the evening—I did manage to convince Michael Phillips, the Channel 4 executive newly in charge of jazz programming, to provide significant funding, a small theatrical distributor named David Mazor to provide almost as much, and the Yomiuri Shimbun people to give us general access in return for Japanese home video rights. Phillips, in particular, already a friend, was enthusiastic. Still, the combined support from all three sources was barely sufficient, and therefore, the only crew members I could afford to bring were cameramen Larry McConkey and Erich Roland, along with audio director Bill Barth. Fortunately, though, Kazunori Oki of Yomiuri Shimbun made us feel at home; a couple of still photographers and production assistants were provided to us on the day of the concerts; and Katsunori Fusegi, a student recently returned from living in New York City, served as our driver, guide, translator, and production manager throughout our stay.

When we first arrived in Tokyo, we observed a rehearsal in the concert hall, staked out our positions for filming during the concerts, shot a more intimate rehearsal featuring Sonny and Heikki alone, and recorded outdoor interviews with each of them. For his part, Heikki told us, "I have never heard this type of piece being written for symphony orchestra. So, this whole experience was very new for all of us—for Sonny, myself, and the orchestra." Then, on the big day, we filmed concertgoers arriving at the hall, filmed the cameramen who were shooting the first performance for a live television broadcast, and then filmed the second performance ourselves, while also taking a live feed from the multitrack audio truck which was recording and mixing music for FM radio broadcasts.

In Tokyo, Japan, Sonny Rollins improvises on saxophone as Heikki Sarmanto conducts the world premiere of Sonny's "Concerto for Tenor Saxophone and Orchestra." (photographed by Japanese crew, 1986)

I knew, from the start, that shooting with only two film cameras, each of which would need a change of magazines every ten minutes, would not permit us consistent coverage of the entire concert. Therefore, for our remaining days in the country, we collected colorful images of life around Tokyo, so that I could illustrate each movement of the concerto with a separate visual theme. The piece, which none of us had heard before arriving in Tokyo, was as rich as I could ever have wished—sometimes gentle and other times ferocious—and I hoped to do it justice with my own interpretation. As it turned out, only five of the concerto's seven movements made it into the film, because Sonny decided the other two needed work. But that was fine with me, because the piece was long, and I wanted the film to include American scenes as well.

Truth be told, for our crew, the highlight of every evening was when Katsunori Fusegi would surprise us with a different type of Japanese restaurant, always including ample supplies of Japanese beer and sake. I suppose our two favorites were one where shabu-shabu was prepared for us as we sat on the floor around a large grill, with each new bit of meat or vegetable hurled towards us as it became ready; and another where we were brought a pyramid-shaped display of assorted types of seafood, some of which, to our mild discomfort, was still alive as we ate it—most notably, a lobster, lying on its back, its body cubed and ready for eating, while its flailing legs still fought to get away. The latter led to our private joke, repeated long after we left Japan, which was that Japanese cuisine was nothing if not "fresh."

Over the next couple of months, in addition to screening several of my recent films at festivals in Seattle, Washington; Vancouver, British Columbia; and Sydney and Melbourne, Australia, I began editing together the large amount of footage we had brought back from Japan, while also deciding what still was needed to create a well-rounded portrait of Mr. Rollins. In further conversations with Sonny's wife and manager Lucille, I learned that he was scheduled to perform a more traditional jazz concert aboard a ship sailing around Manhattan at night. This came on top of knowing that, although Sonny had grown up in New York City, his parents had come there from "the islands" of the Caribbean, and that, in the early 1960s, he had taken a two-year sabbatical from public performance and, instead, practiced for hours every day on New York's Williamsburg Bridge. Therefore, I planned to emphasize the fact that Rollins was a singular talent, with an obsessive, lifelong drive to develop his art—disproving, in a sense, the inherited wisdom that "no man is an island." And to do that, I would draw connections between his incredible popularity on the islands of Japan, his heritage in the islands of the Caribbean, and his upbringing on the island of Manhattan, which we would emphasize by shooting his performance as he sailed around the latter at night.

Unfortunately, I soon learned that the ship in question had little light onboard, and its owners refused to provide the power needed to operate lights of our own. So, out went the idea of shooting Sonny as he sailed around the city, and with it, too, went my plan for a fully developed island theme. Truly, though, it was for the best, because Lucille then revealed that, on August 16, Sonny was scheduled to perform an outdoor concert on the late Harvey Fite's sculpted rock quarry, Opus 40, in Saugerties, New York. When I phoned Tad Richards, the manager of the site and stepson of the original sculptor, he could not have been more welcoming.

So, I booked large enough HMI lights to compensate for a setting sun, a generator to run them, a communication system for use in directing my crew, twenty-four-track recording equipment for the music, and a large crew including audio director Bill Barth, director of photography and Steadicam operator Larry McConkey, Larry's brother Jim to serve as his assistant, and cameramen Dave Sperling, Chris Li, and Joe Meccariello.

This time around, Rollins would be fronting a more traditional ensemble, featuring his longtime bass player Bob Cranshaw, Mark Soskin on piano, and Marvin "Smitty" Smith on drums. Yet, this, too, would be an unconventional jazz concert: first, because the musicians would be performing outdoors on a stage made entirely of rock; and second, because, although their set list would include the usual jazz standards and Caribbean tunes for which Sonny was best known he would open with a song no one had yet heard. Indeed, when the big day arrived, Sonny came directly out of the gate in a kind of fury, like Barbara Stanwyck's Jessica Drummond and her forty horsemen riding at full gallop, sometimes right at the camera, in the opening shots of Sam Fuller's 1957 western *Forty Guns*. Titled "G-Man," Sonny's new song stretched the boundaries of jazz every bit as much as Rollins's concerto, but in totally different directions. As critic Robert Christgau wrote in the December 29, 1987 issue of the *Village Voice*, when he gave the film's eventual soundtrack album on Milestone Records an A+:

> ["G-Man"] is 15 minutes of Rollins at a peak—a showman who never shows off, a virtuoso who's never pretentious or (in this situation) even difficult. It's like what some teenager might imagine both "free jazz" and "a honking session" sound like from reading LeRoi Jones or John Sinclair—riffs jumping and jiving long past their breaking points, notes held so long it's a wonder Rollins hasn't passed out . . . Free jazz and honking sessions rarely get this good. I haven't enjoyed a record so much all year.

With the shift to Opus 40 for our second concert, I had decided to call the film *Saxophone Colossus*, borrowing the title of Sonny's most beloved album. In turn, that led me to start our coverage of the concert by having Larry point his camera at the rock obelisk standing high up behind the performance area, then, with Sonny's opening notes, use his Steadicam to glide down a long rock ramp and directly up to Rollins, similarly towering over the stage, and his horn at full intensity. Right off the bat, Sonny had set his terms and established his dominance. From here, the colossus could play whatever he wished, and the crowd seated on lawn chairs, lying on blankets, eating picnic suppers, and tossing Frisbees would have zero complaints.

A second part of the concert would become just as legendary, and prove just as revealing, as the opening song. After a time, Rollins signaled his musicians to drop out, then began an extended period of solo improvisation. As was typical for such portions of his shows, he moved rapidly through dozens of quick musical quotations, from "Somewhere Over the Rainbow" to "The Daring Young Man on the

Flying Trapeze" (both of which were especially appropriate on this day), also employing unexpected honking sounds and sudden changes of mood or rhythm. What was different this time was that, the longer Sonny improvised, the more visibly anxious he became, pacing back and forth across the front of the stage, acting as if he might literally jump the six feet down to the next level of rock, then just as quickly pulling back again. Finally, though, unable to forestall the inevitable, he did jump, hit the ground with both feet, fell backwards, and then simply lay there on his back without moving.

Unsure whether or not he was seriously hurt, I instructed my crew to keep shooting and recording, even as I threw down my headphones, ran around to the back of the rock stage area, and got as close to Sonny as I could without being seen. But before I could ask if he was okay, he suddenly pulled his right leg up over his left (as if to cushion it), brought his saxophone back to his lips, and began playing again from that same position, lying there on the ground. This time, he played the luscious opening notes of "Autumn Nocturne," which caused all concerned onlookers to breathe a sigh of relief. As for his musicians, they were briefly convulsed with nervous laughter, then rushed to accompany him as best they could, especially considering they were still six feet above him.

Later, during an interview I conducted with Sonny and Lucille on a windy day in New York City's Washington Market Park, a short distance from their apartment, Sonny tried to explain what had happened, though the cast on his right foot somewhat beat him to it. Often, he said, during a concert, he liked to leave the stage and play his sax while wandering through the audience. Unfortunately, this time, he had misjudged the distance to the ground below and had broken his right heel. And yet, he said, he was happy he had been able to continue playing for a time, first while lying on his back, and then from a standing position. He had, indeed, performed a few more songs, then allowed Tad Richards and an employee of Tad's to help him to his car, and Lucille to drive him to a nearby hospital.

During an ensemble performance at the Opus 40 sculpted rock quarry in Saugerties, New York, Sonny Rollins jumps off the rock stage and breaks his right heel but begins playing again while lying on his back. (frame from film, 1986)

Certainly, that was the story for public consumption. Later, though, Lucille would tell me what he had said privately, which requires some background. In the performance sequences we shot in Tokyo in May, the finish on Rollins's saxophone had lost its luster. Then, during the scenes we shot in Saugerties in August, the sax had a shiny golden look. The difference was that, in between those two performances, Sonny had taken the instrument to be newly lacquered, and as he explained to his wife, doing so can alter its sound in unexpected ways. According to Rollins, at the Opus 40 date, it was sometimes as if he intended to play a vowel, and out came a consonant. In fact, during his solo improvising, this was happening so frequently that he began to have a kind of nervous breakdown. Finally, knowing no other way out of this box he was in, he simply jumped to the level below, breaking his heel in the process. In the most painful of ways, he once again had reached the limits of jazz.

The same afternoon that cameraman Erich Roland, sound man Bill Barth, and I shot and recorded the interview with Sonny and Lucille (Sunday, August 24), we also filmed a group interview with three jazz critics: Gary Giddins, Ira Gitler, and our project jazz consultant Francis Davis. At the time, Gary and Francis were already considered among the top jazz writers of their generation, as Ira was of the generation before. We also had invited African American critic Stanley Crouch, but he failed to show, making our discussion decidedly less diverse. Still, I assumed that at least the generational difference among the three who came would lead to debate, especially since the older Gitler was known to prefer Sonny's earlier recordings. But instead, all quickly agreed that Rollins was one of the greatest artists in the history of jazz, that the quality of his later albums was less consistent than that of his earlier ones, that he was on a lifelong quest to elevate his art to the greatest heights possible, and that his live performances, though dependent on his mood and focus, were as impressive as those of any other living artist. By the end, the discussion had evolved into a Sonny Rollins love fest, perhaps suggesting that an artist of his stature is even beyond the limits of jazz criticism. A saxophone colossus, indeed.

Although I presented the film at the Denver International Film Festival on October 19, 1986, its official world premiere took place at London's Barbican Cinema on November 14 as part of the 1986 London Film Festival. Sonny and Lucille (plus cameraman Chris Li and others) joined me for the occasion, and after the screening, festival director and *Guardian* film critic Derek Malcolm interviewed Sonny and me onstage. Eight months later, on July 28, 1987, Britain's Channel 4 Television presented the film's premiere broadcast, at which time British music magazine *The Wire* published editor Richard Cook's extremely generous interview and summary of my career to date, ending with the welcome words, "Give this man a few million dollars and let him get on with it."

Chapter Three

Hearts & Minds (Soul + Message)

Black Wax (1982)

Gospel According to Al Green (1984)

The Return of Rubén Blades (1985)

F
ive years before I presented *Saxophone Colossus* at the November 1986 London Film Festival, I presented *Sun Ra: A Joyful Noise* at the November 1981 edition, marking the first of my many collaborations with festival director Ken Wlaschin, initially in London and then in Los Angeles (after Ken made the move to LA, he was replaced in London by Derek Malcolm). The film was represented by Angus Trowbridge of TCB Releasing Ltd., who would go on to handle sales of my films for most of two decades (as well as becoming one of my closest friends), and when I arrived in the UK, Angus, who lived in Somerset, not far from Stonehenge, informed me that he had sold British broadcasting rights to Channel 4 Television, soon to be the country's fourth national television channel. More precisely, the film had been purchased by Channel 4's first commissioning editor for music, Andy Park, and I decided this was someone I had to meet.

Fortunately, Andy, a charming and hilarious Glaswegian (native of Glasgow, Scotland), had the time to see me, so we met at his small, crowded, temporary offices (Channel 4 was not set to begin broadcasting for another year), and at some point in our conversation, he placed an LP on a portable phonograph, set the needle to play the final cut on side B, and smiled as pulsating bass sounds slowly filled the room. "That's Gil Scott-Heron," I responded, "playing his new song 'B Movie' about Ronald Reagan from his *Reflections* LP." Having run out of money while producing the Sun Ra film, I had moved back in with my parents in Silver Spring, Maryland. "Gil lives in the Washington, DC area," I said, "the same as I do." At which point Andy announced that, "If someone could make a film about him, I'd pay for the whole thing." No one had ever said such words to me, and I would not let them go unanswered.

After the festival, I returned home and began figuring out how to reach Scott-Heron, the brilliant African American author and singer-songwriter, best-known for his witty and poetic songs about Black life and social justice (many of them cowritten with keyboard and flute player Brian Jackson, until their 1980 split). Eventually, I tracked down his half brother and manager Denis Heron, and he and I began discussing a potential film project. Next, I let Andy know I had made contact, and though he did keep me waiting a few months, he provided funding just in time for me to shoot Scott-Heron in concert on the artist's thirty-third birthday. (And just as important to me personally, the salary I received allowed me to return to Philadelphia, which is where I resided again for the next twenty-one years.)

During the months I was planning this project, Washington, DC's former commercial wax museum was transformed into the Wax Museum Nightclub, and Gil Scott-Heron and the Midnight Band were booked to perform two shows there on Thursday, April 1, each of them preceded by a Black history monologue that Gil had first delivered the previous February, during Black History Month. The club agreed to let me shoot both concerts and monologues, and for the first time, I could afford to hire a twenty-four-track music recording truck, which meant the music could be properly mixed during postproduction. However, audio director Bill Barth would still oversee all music recording for me. Also for the first time, I could afford to shoot a performance with four cameramen, three of whom would be Washington, DC-based Chris Li and two of his friends, all shooting from tripods. But the fourth cameraman—and once again, my director of photography—would be Larry McConkey, using his shiny new Steadicam to achieve the most fluid possible handheld cinematography.

Director of photography Larry McConkey and director Robert Mugge set up to shoot Gil Scott-Heron's birthday concert at Washington, DC's Wax Museum Nightclub. (photographed by Robert Caldwell, 1982)

Larry's Philadelphia-based friend Garrett Brown had only just invented and released the revolutionary Steadicam in the mid-1970s, and first used it to spectacular effect on Hal Ashby's 1976 Woody Guthrie portrait, *Bound for Glory*. Larry, dazzled by this invention and already known as the "human dolly" (for his unfaltering handheld camerawork), had quickly mastered the device and acquired one of his own. Viewing this as an incredible opportunity, I asked Larry to use it throughout our concert coverage, as well as for all other scenes, and this was not a decision I made lightly. Earlier political documentaries had typically been shot in black and white and *cinéma-vérité* style, meaning lots of ragged handheld footage, clumsy zooms, and shots going in and of focus. As a result, this approach had become equated with a kind of "authenticity." However, I decided to go the opposite direction, shooting in gorgeous color (thanks to the latest 16mm negative film stocks, beautifully processed and printed by my new film lab, Commonwealth Films, Inc. of Richmond, Virginia) and with every image shot so smoothly that the film would be the visual equivalent of what Erica Jong, in her 1973 novel, *Fear of Flying*, had called a "zipless fuck," meaning one in which the participants are so enraptured that they do not even notice their clothes falling away. In other words, contrary also to Bertolt Brecht, who periodically forced audience recognition that its members were watching a play (so that they would fully engage with his political messages, and not merely be sucked into mindless entertainment), I chose to *seduce* audience members into accepting political discourse that otherwise might have put them off. If you like, call it a "zipless flick," utilizing a nickname for movies that is not so common as it once was.

Another first for this film, as far as my own work was concerned, was that I would be able to rent a communication system that allowed me to speak to the four cameramen and the audio team, more easily directing their responses to what was happening onstage, and coordinating their actions. In addition, a few days before the big shoot, Larry ordered a giant digital clock for me with an LED display of hours, minutes, and seconds. For years to come, we would hang that clock somewhere near the performing musicians so that each camera could shoot it at the beginning or end of every film magazine, thereby allowing me more easily to sync up many hours of concert footage for editing. Every second of film consists of twenty-four frames, and the ability to get picture and sound within, say, a half-second of each other before having to resort to eye and ear is a huge time-saver, especially during long instrumental sections, which are more difficult to sync, absent the singing of distinctive song lyrics.

Gil Scott-Heron and his Midnight Band perform at Washington, DC's Wax Museum Nightclub. (photographed by Robert Caldwell, 1982)

As to the shows themselves, Scott-Heron was fantastic. His witty, opening monologues combined poetry, personal recollections, political insights, reflections on African American history, and more. Then, after a brief break, each was followed by a full concert featuring his superb, ten-piece Midnight Band (soon to be renamed the Amnesia Express). Together, they performed varying combinations of soul, funk, jazz, reggae, and salsa, all setting off prominent and incisive lyrics. Gil's subjects included poverty, racism, drug abuse, political oppression, guns on the American streets, apartheid in South Africa, the aspirations of illegal immigrants, the joys of Black music, the difficulty of classifying his own multi-dimensional songs, and the aforementioned "B Movie," that satirized the politics, governing style, and associates of President Ronald Reagan.

Beyond capturing Scott-Heron in performance, I wanted to do what I had done for Sun Ra, which was create opportunities for him to express more of his personal philosophy and political beliefs without resorting to stereotypical interview situations. With that in mind, during a preproduction visit to the nightclub, I learned that the museum's life-sized wax figures were still in the building, wrapped in plastic and gathering dust in a huge storeroom and former staging area. Therefore, with permission of the owners, two days before filming the monologues and music sets, Bill Barth, Larry McConkey, Larry's assistant Tass Michos, and I took all of those wax figures out of their giant plastic bags, retrieved some of their former backdrops and props, and created a surreal set through which Gil could walk and talk, working off what he later termed "ghosts of America's past."

The day after that, Gil posed with the wax likenesses of US presidents, movie stars, astronauts, figures from early American history, giants of Black music, and members of the Harlem Renaissance, while Larry followed along with his Steadicam-mounted camera, and Bill with his portable recording equipment. Among the many improvised comments and snatches of poetry Gil delivered in this setting were his poem "Whitey On The Moon" (about the shifting of national resources to space travel rather than the needs of inner cities), directed at the figure of astronaut Neil Armstrong, now floating overhead in his space suit and holding an American flag; his poem "Black History," recited in front of a group of African American historical figures; and his interactions with Ronald Reagan and John Wayne figures in our mockup of a Western saloon, which I would later interject into his climactic performance of "B Movie."

During one particular break in that day's shooting, Gil told me about a song he was in the midst of recording for his forthcoming *Moving Target* LP. Titled "Washington, DC," it was a catchy, though biting celebration of the culturally vibrant, yet frequently impoverished Black sections of the city, contrasted with the wealthy white ruling class that occupied shiny white government buildings and constructed monuments and memorials for its own glorification. He then pulled out an audiocassette of what he had recorded so far, which included some basic instrumental tracks and a faint vocal "guide track." Gil then suggested that perhaps I could use it on the film's soundtrack. But instead, I asked if he owned a boom box for listening to music on the street. And when I learned that he did, I asked him to bring along both the box and the tape to our planned shoot on the streets of Washington.

Two days later (Friday, April 2), Gil and his brother Denis met us in downtown DC, and we proceeded to film Gil in various situations around the city. Using the Steadicam, we shot him reciting his poems "Paint It Black" and "Billy Green Is Dead" while walking through Black neighborhoods; shot him in front of the U.S. Capitol Building and Washington Monument discussing the rally his friend Stevie Wonder had staged on the National Mall in support of a Martin Luther King Jr. national holiday (which had not yet been enacted); shot him walking in front of the White House with his two-year-old daughter Gia (as none-too-subtle Secret Service agents positioned themselves along the way); and shot him pretending to fall through a city sidewalk, à la Alice and her "looking glass," so that he would end up in our wonderland of wax figures.

Finally, I had Gil place the audiocassette of "Washington, DC" in his boom box and rest the box on his left shoulder. Then, I had Bill Barth attach a small microphone to Gil's shirt so that we could record him singing along with the audiocassette. As he sang, we shot him walking along the Tidal Basin in front of the Jefferson Memorial, through the campus of Howard University (Washington's historic Black university), and up the hill toward the Washington Monument:

Symbols of democracy are pinned against the coast.
The outhouse of bureaucracy, surrounded by a moat.
Citizens of poverty are barely out of sight.
The overlords escape near evening; the brothers own the night.
Morning comes and brings the tourists, straining rubber necks; perhaps a glimpse of the cowboy making the world a nervous wreck.
It's a massive irony for all the world to see.
It's the nation's capital, it's Washington, DC.

Certainly, this 1982 film bears a connection to my earlier 1978 one, *Amateur Night at City Hall: The Story of Frank L. Rizzo*, the theme of which was *politics as show business*, and my later 1988 one, *Entertaining the Troops* with Bob Hope, the theme of which was *show business as politics*. But in the case of Gil Scott-Heron, I preferred to show him in the long line of folk and popular singers who had added a social and political message to their emotionally affecting music—for example, Woody Guthrie, Paul Robeson, Billie Holiday, Pete Seeger, Ronnie Gilbert, Odetta, Bob Dylan, Joan Baez, Bob Marley, and Nina Simone. These artists wanted not only to entertain their audiences, but also to enlighten them; they created songs both for the heart and for the head. And because I, too, had lived for many years in the Washington, DC area, heavily influenced by its potent Black culture (even if such culture was admitted only hesitantly to the largely white suburb of Silver Spring, Maryland where I grew up), it was a pleasure for me to join with this present-day poet-singer-songwriter in portraying a city we both loved, in spite of the ironies and inequities that haunted its past and its present. (Note: In my 2005 film *Blues Divas*, Odetta would sing Lead Belly's 1937 classic, "The Bourgeois Blues," about discrimination and segregation in the DC of years past).

Ultimately, I named this film *Black Wax*, the title referring not only to the wax figures that Gil addressed throughout the film, but also to LP records, which were sometimes called "wax" (as in the nostalgic movie *American Hot Wax*), and to the historical Black artists, writers, composers, musicians, dancers, and more whose heritage Gil had drawn upon and successfully made his own (tipped from the beginning of the film as he takes a lit cigarette from a wax figure of poet Langston Hughes saying, "Oh, thank you very much. Needed that."). Of course, as an inescapably white American of German heritage, I could never claim lineage from the likes of Louis Armstrong, Duke Ellington, Bessie Smith, and Billie Holiday the way my new friend Gil Scott-Heron could. But simply working with someone like Gil, and facilitating the wider spread of his music and his message, made me feel even closer to the steady stream of African American artists and musicians who had enriched my life.

Then, in the months to come, I was touched by the warm embrace the film received from turn-away crowds of largely African American Gil Scott-Heron fans at the AFI Theater at the Kennedy

Center, at the Filmex Festival in Los Angeles, and at the theater of the School of the Art Institute of Chicago. Of course, on those occasions when I was not introduced until after the screening, as happened at the two showings in Chicago, a gasp would go up from the crowd, in sudden recognition that the very Black film they had just witnessed was, in fact, directed by a white filmmaker. In fact, at one of those Chicago screenings, the first audience member to rise, ostensibly to ask a question, was a Black woman who exclaimed, "I *knew* a white boy directed this film!" And even though, admittedly, I was gratified when other Black audience members hissed her back to her seat, I knew that no response of mine could ever satisfy everyone. Still, I did my best to explain that, as with my previous portraits of George Crumb and Sun Ra, my goal had been to construct a frame through which the art, the life, and the personality of Gil Scott-Heron could be fully appreciated. Or put another way, as I saw it, my race, gender, religion, and political views were irrelevant, because whatever creativity I brought to this project was there in service of my subject's own, and that would be true for all of my future subjects as well.

***

Andy Park was pleased with *Black Wax*, as well as with its world premiere at the London Film Festival on November 22, 1982, a couple of months before its broadcast premiere over the UK's newly operational Channel 4. Over the past year, Andy and I also had become close friends and wished to work together again. Hoping to make that happen, Andy suggested I produce a film on bandleader Andraé Crouch, who was then prominent in the African American gospel scene. I was okay with the idea, but proposed another option.

During the early 1970s, Hi Records producer Willie Mitchell had convinced a young Black singer named Al Green to move to Memphis, and then to soften his naturally powerful voice, emphasizing its more seductive qualities. The combination of Green's sweetly soulful vocals, Mitchell's masterly production, a talented pool of local studio musicians, and the refined songwriting of Green, Mitchell, and drummer Al Jackson had resulted in some of the most popular soul and pop songs of that era: "Let's Stay Together," "Love and Happiness," "Tired of Being Alone," "I Can't Get Next to You," "Call Me (Come Back Home)," "Sha La La (Make Me Happy)," "I'm Still in Love with You," "L-O-V-E (Love)," "Take Me To The River"; the list can appear endless.

Yet, starting in mid-decade, Green's life and career began to unravel. In 1974, when he refused to marry an already married girlfriend, she scalded him in the shower with a pot of hot grits, then shot and killed herself with his handgun, leaving a suicide note in her purse. Other incidents followed, including a 1974 civil suit charging that he beat a female assistant; a 1977 marriage that produced three daughters, repeated divorce filings, and mutual charges of violence; and a 1979 fall from a stage in Cincinnati. In 1976, amid these and other troubling situations, Green founded a church in Memphis, installed himself as pastor, and eventually committed himself to performing and recording only gospel music, which largely ended his partnership with Willie Mitchell, but did lead to multiple Grammys in the Soul Gospel Performance category. Al's self-produced 1977 *The Belle Album* was the first to signal his transformation, especially in the title cut where he sang, "You're the one I want, but *He's* the one I need." Although he was still singing love songs, they now were love songs directed to God.

In 1982, with Green's transition to full-time gospel preacher complete, I began contacting his Memphis office and engaging in a long-running dialogue with his assistant, the appropriately named Hattie Angel. Over a period of thirteen months, I traveled twice to Memphis to meet with Green, and once to New York City, seeing him at his hotel during his teaming with Patti LaBelle in the Broadway production of *Your Arms Too Short to Box with God*. Park and I even traveled to New Orleans together to try and meet with him during his 1983 appearance at the annual Jazz & Heritage Festival, but we failed to make contact (even though having a good time on our own). Still, the courtship continued, with Al never quite saying no to my proposal, yet never quite saying yes.

Then, in December of 1983, knowing that Green was scheduled to celebrate the seventh anniversary of his Full Gospel Tabernacle

Church the Sunday before Christmas—and knowing also that the seventh anniversary, known as the "pastor's day," was considered a big deal in Southern fundamentalist churches—I felt I had to get this project in gear. During the year that Andy had waited patiently for me to close the deal with Green, I actually had shot, edited, and released a feature-length reggae concert film, and our combined patience was now running low.

Fortunately, Al did finally agree to my idea of documenting the primary three-hour church service that would mark his big day (Sunday, December 18, 1983), but not before some intense, last-minute negotiation. And by the time he actually did sign my agreement, I had only days to go before a large crew and I would need to gather in Memphis.

That December, my longtime director of photography, Larry McConkey, was unavailable, because he was assisting Steadicam inventor Garrett Brown with his new invention, the Skycam, which, once perfected, would transport cameras on cables high above televised sporting events and concerts. In the meantime, cameraman Erich Roland had acquired a Steadicam, Brown's original device that permits the smoothest possible handheld camerawork. So, he was the logical choice to replace Larry as my new project's director of photography and Steadicam operator. Unfortunately, Bill Barth was also unavailable, so I hired sound man Terry Hillman out of Nashville, which is where I also found Johnny Rosen and his twenty-four-track mobile recording truck. And rounding out our crew were cameramen Chris Li and Peter Gilbert, plus a number of Memphis locals, including musician and filmmaker Joe Mulherin, who easily opened doors for us on both sides of a stubbornly segregated city.

The worship area of Green's church proved a challenge, because the walls and tall ceiling were rounded, leaving nowhere to hang lights and few places to position them on stands out of sight of our cameras. We also guessed that aisles would grow too congested for use of Erich's Steadicam, meaning that all three cameramen should use tripods until, and unless, I okayed them to go handheld. In addition, having seen Al race into the audience during *Your Arms Too Short to Box with God*, I asked Johnny Rosen to place a second microphone on Green's suit coat (in addition to the one attached to his pulpit) so that, even when he took off running, his voice would still be recorded. As always, we did our best to prepare for the worst.

For two-thirds of Green's Sunday afternoon service, he mostly allowed others to take the lead, whether an associate pastor reading scriptures, an organist leading hymn singing, church officials taking up collections, or a visiting choir performing from seats usually reserved for Al's own choir. However, after two full hours of both the sacred and the mundane, it finally was "star time" at the Tabernacle.

Rev. Al Green begins preaching on the seventh anniversary of his Full Gospel Tabernacle church in Memphis, Tennessee. (photographed by Chuck Cooper, 1983)

Wearing a tan suit and red reading glasses, Reverend Green took his place in the pulpit and, smiling broadly, declared that "Jesus . . . turned water . . . into wine." With that, he began to improvise a spoken sermon that, over time, grew steadily in volume and intensity. The congregation's ritual responses, along with those of several hyper-focused musicians, pushed him to greater and greater heights until, eventually, he was screaming at the top of his lungs, racing around the room, and sweating profusely. One after another, approving female church members rose to their feet as well, filling the aisles with their own sense of abandon.

After reaching a well-earned emotional climax, Green worked his way into song, beginning with slow, blues-like numbers "Too Close" and "When the Gates Swing Open," before accelerating into a forceful, fast-paced "The Lord Will Make a Way." Accompanying him as he sang were the congregation, the organist, the visiting choir, the Full Gospel Tabernacle's own choir, as well as a drummer, a bass player, a keyboard player, an electric guitarist, and three backup singers who worked with Green in the studio and on the road.

Ultimately, the song grew to a roar, echoing off the round walls as more congregants stood, clapped hands, danced in place, and sometimes swooned to the point where they were assisted by nurses in white uniforms. Then, once the music had reached its highest volume and emotional peak, Al gestured for the singing to stop, leaving only his musicians playing quietly in the background as he drank a much-needed glass of orange juice, asked who was "ready to come to Jesus," and then welcomed a weeping man named Calvin "into the Full Gospel family." After that, the instruments grew louder again, and the renewed singing of "The Lord Will Make A Way" rocked the building as before, until gradually running its course.

Suddenly looking both dazed and exhausted, Reverend Green raised his arms to shut down the music, leaving in its place only the sounds of gentle sobbing and moaning around the room. Next, Al lurched as if a spirit were entering his body, then began to babble, suggesting that he was speaking in tongues. Soon thereafter, still focusing inwards, he went on to witness his faith with increasing fervor, and finally strolled around the room, singing almost distractedly, with quiet accompaniment from the organ. Then, as if regaining his strength once again, he sang out, "I was healed, healed, healed . . . by the wound . . . in his . . . side." And with that crescendo fully resolving, he signaled that the service, too, was over, and smiled sweetly into one of our cameras.

I had agreed, in advance, not to bother Al on Monday, December 19, because he reportedly would need that day to recuperate, especially since he planned to conduct a *second* three-hour service Sunday evening. Certainly, no one could accuse Green of having left the music business over a distaste for hard work. But with the reverend unavailable, I took my greatly reduced crew of cameraman Erich Roland, sound man Terry Hillman, and camera assistant Barbie Collins over to Royal Recording Studio, the converted movie theater where Hi Records producer Willie Mitchell had produced countless hits for the likes of Otis Clay, Ann Peebles, Syl Johnson, O. V. Wright, and, most famously, Al Green.

Mitchell, a true Southern gentleman, showed us around his studio with the sloping movie theater floor, graciously pointing out where Green had stood when recording there, and the microphone Al had used ("number nine"). He also told us about meeting Green, encouraging him to move to Memphis, persuading him to soften his approach to singing, and experimenting with "jazz chords" for the song "Let's Stay Together." But the most moving part of our session was when he sat in his office—the wall behind him covered with gold records, "Let's Stay Together" playing on his phonograph—and recalled how painful it was when Green suddenly announced that he no longer would record anything but gospel music, effectively ending his partnership with Mitchell, at least for the foreseeable future.

In retrospect, I believe this scene was at least partially inspired by the pivotal one in Sam Fuller's 1953 *Pickup On South Street*, where the lovable stoolie played by Thelma Ritter listens to a haunting French tune on her small record player, refers to herself as "an old clock runnin' down," and refuses to reveal the whereabouts of pickpocket Richard Widmark, whereupon Commie agent Richard Kiley shoots her just as her record finishes playing. The sense of loss evoked in the two scenes is similar, though, admittedly, Mitchell's real-life situation was far less final than Ritter's fictional one.

The following day, we showed up at Green's offices, expecting to pick up where we had left off with him. However, Al had grown flighty again, first refusing to see us, and then saying he was not in the mood to be interviewed. Eventually, though, I convinced him to let us film a quasi-rehearsal there in his personal recording studio. Taking the cue, Al's house engineer Paul Zaleski, and his bass player

Reuben Fairfax, called in as many musicians and backup singers as they could reach. At the same time, our crew began setting up lights and Erich's Steadicam, and Terry patched into Paul's mixing board in the adjoining control room, all so that we could film and record Al and his musicians pretending to be rehearsing.

From the beginning, Green had declared he would only perform gospel music for our film, and that is what he and his musicians proceeded to play. However, with the Willie Mitchell interview, I had established a theme about Green essentially breaking Mitchell's heart when he switched to singing gospel, and that theme was tied to their most famous collaboration, which was "Let's Stay Together." So, after we filmed Al performing several gospel numbers, supported by two female backup singers and musicians playing an electric piano, a B3 organ, an electric guitar, and drums (but no bass, since Reuben Fairfax had forgotten his), I told Green how much I loved "Let's Stay Together" and wondered if he might play a few bars. To my surprise, he agreed, but first had to teach his backup singers their parts, since they had not been with him during his soul and pop days.

The performance was golden, of course, leaving everyone exhilarated, including Memphis guitarist Larry Lee, who had performed at Woodstock with Jimi Hendrix's original Band of Gypsys. Sharing that exhilaration was Green himself, who suddenly called out, "You wanna do your interview?" Naturally, I was thrilled. But I asked his indulgence as we reset our lights, reloaded our film magazines, and touched base with Paul in the control room, who would again give Terry a direct feed to his recorder.

While waiting for us, Green sat in a chair and picked out chords and melodies on an acoustic guitar. But within minutes, Erich had enveloped him in film noir-like lighting, and Terry had centered a studio microphone above his head. As for myself, I pulled up a chair directly across from him, signaled everyone to begin recording, and waited as Barbie positioned her slate just in front of his face, clapping it in such a way that I would later be able to sync up picture and sound.

With Barbie out of our sightline again, Al and I began one of the most intimate conversations I have ever witnessed, much less initiated. He spoke about growing up in Arkansas and Michigan, with his father permitting only religious music in the house; about performing in a family gospel group; about touring as a young soul singer; about meeting Willie Mitchell in Midland, Texas; and about agreeing to join Willie in Memphis where they would devise some of the most glorious soul and pop music ever envisioned. In addition, Green discussed various songs he had recorded, and to my great pleasure, performed parts of "I Can't Get Next to You" by the Temptations, which he had covered, and his own early composition, "Tired of Being Alone." Together, these samples gave me more of what I needed to portray the hugely commercial career he had left behind.

Midway through, Al was joined by legendary Memphis guitarist Mabon "Teenie" Hodges, wearing a multicolored hooded sweat suit. Ever ready to improvise, Al encouraged Teenie to take a seat behind him, handed him the guitar, and suggested he pick at it through the rest of the session, which he did.

All in all, over a two-hour period, Green and I discussed his musical role models, his increasing success, and the ways in which his soul and gospel music had influenced one another.

But the interview truly caught fire when he addressed how his growing obsessions with women, drugs, and alcohol began to damage his life and career, and how his emotional collapse drew him back to religion. For instance, he recalled how, in 1973, he was "born again" after a midnight concert at Disneyland, and how that started him on his road back to the church:

About 4:30 that mornin', man, I woke up praisin' and rejoicin', and I had never felt like that before, and I never felt like that again. I felt, man, so many things were changing so fast. And I had this input, you know—it's like a charge of electricity, you know—to create a new "person-all" . . . and I said, "all." Okay, to actually . . . [suddenly lurching back and sucking in air] . . . wpppphhhhhhewww . . . come in and just change your whole personality, you know. And I said, "Man, I don't understand." So, I ran into the bathroom. My girlfriend is knockin' on the door, wonderin' what's happenin', what's happenin'. I'm saying,

"Thank ya, Jesus. Hallelujah. Praise God." I said, "Huh! I never said that before." I ran to the bathroom. You know, I tried to cover my mouth . . . [briefly placing his hands on his mouth to muffle his voice] . . . tryin' to keep from sayin' all these things, 'cause she's gonna hear me, right? And I heard this voice sayin', "Are you ashamed of me?" And man, I had to come out of there. [laughing] I came out of there sayin', "No, I am not ashamed. I am not ashamed. And I never will be ashamed." And I kept . . . I was feelin' so good, I tried to keep that feelin' for as lonnnnggggg as I could.

As Green made clear, in Southern Black tradition, one could not walk with both God and the Devil simultaneously, and that was particularly true when it came to "God's music," which obviously meant music of the church, and the "Devil's music," which included blues, rhythm and blues, soul blues, and rock and roll. In other words, the spiritual dissolution of Green's life had caused him to make a choice, and that was to turn entirely toward the church. In fact, likely referring to rock stars such as Jimi Hendrix, Jim Morrison, and Janis Joplin, all of whom had died in 1970 at the age of 27, he stated the following in our discussion:

No, you have to be illuminated . . . enlightened. You have to be spiritually uplifted . . . to take a million- or multimillion-dollar career . . . and say, like this guitar: "Okay, if I make it, fine . . . if I don't make it, fine . . . but I'm gonna do it because I *believe* in what I'm doing. So, if I must set it down—my career, and the money, and the popularity, and the ladies—then I will leave it here." But . . . you must do what you are given to do. You must do what's right. There are a lot of people that are not here, that did not do what they were supposed *to* do.

He then spoke of his 1976 purchase of a church building, and how that had changed his direction forever.

For me, the real suspense of the interview was whether I could get him to discuss the infamous hot grits incident which, in 1974, became the biggest sign for him that he needed to change his life. To date, he had never spoken of this in public, and I had spent months wondering how to broach the subject with him. Somehow, though, he became comfortable enough that, once it came up, he felt as natural discussing that as anything else:

> I went over, after being full of grits, and jumped in the shower because I ached all over, and I called this girl from next door over to help me, because I'm in total . . . you know. And man, I've got these big boils on my skin, and like, man, I'm tellin' ya, I'm in total pain; I can't believe the pain. All of a sudden, you hear "tphoo-tphoo" [holding his right hand as if a gun firing twice]. And that was the end of that. You hear something hit the floor. Boom! [Slapping his hand against his leg.] And that was the end of that. I said, "What's that noise?" She said, "Sounded like gunshots." I said, "It can't be, Babs. Come on. This is ridiculous. This thing is goin' crazy." I go over here. Boom. Here this lady is lying on the floor. Here this pistol is in her hand. I'm sayin', "Oh, my God. What in the world? Call the police." She said, "But this is crazy." I said, "Call the police." And we called the sheriff's department. That's all. You know, I said, "Hey, man . . . just get me to the hospital." I said, "I am hurtin'!"

Ultimately, of course, the entire interview was a performance, as finely crafted in the moment as any of Green's riveting musical performances, whether in church or on a concert stage. Throughout our time together, he created a compelling image of himself as a talented and ambitious young man who had lost his way, openly sinned, wrecked his life, and then found himself again in the loving arms of God. In that context, admitting to the torment of the hot grits incident was perfectly natural, because the stock in trade of every fundamentalist preacher of note was to offer up his or her former depravity as a warning of human frailty, with the attendant promise of redemption, but only through acceptance of Jesus Christ and ongoing support for the church.

What was unique about Green's situation was that, in symbolic terms, it was so much bigger—so much more resonant—than the typical fall-from-grace story. That is, a young woman, responding to the "love and happiness" Al had implicitly offered to all women through his public persona wanted it on the personal level as well. And when he refused to narrow his love to her alone, she responded with violence against him, and then even more so against herself.

By this point in his career, Green had become a kind of Icarus figure, unleashing forces that he ultimately could not control, and that incinerated not only himself, but also many of those around him. As I often have said when introducing screenings of my completed portrait, which I ultimately titled *Gospel According to Al Green*, "This is a film about love, about the connections between soul and gospel, and about a man who flew too close to the sun, got his eyeballs burned, and has been singing ever since with fire coming out of his mouth."

Thanks to Al's conversion, the voice that Willie Mitchell had helped transform into an instrument of seduction had, within the more protective walls of the church, been fully unleashed at last. As Reverend Green said in the film:

Well, I took what I learned from the rock and roll: the ingenuity, the class, the charisma, the steps, the movement, the hesitation, the wait to be . . . curious . . . very curious; to create an atmosphere of curiosity . . . to be, yes! You take all of this, that you learn in pop, rhythm and blues, and you use it to your best advantage. But it doesn't give you the fire. You can't create the charisma for fire. Either you have the fire, or you don't have the fire—the spiritual fire.

To Al's way of thinking, God had given him a sacred talent which, within the commercial music business, became a highly destructive tool of the Devil. Only in the church could his power be controlled, even when fully unleashed and utilized for good.

As the interview came to a close, Green reclaimed his guitar from Teenie Hodges and offered to perform something on his own. Naturally, we were thrilled, and once camera and recorder were running again, Al improvised the sweetest little soul tune that, for the record, I later titled "I Love You," in light of its key recurring phrase. Of course, for safety's sake, Erich suggested we film another take, and Reverend Green graciously complied. The big surprise was that, once again improvising, he created a second version every bit as beautiful as the first, yet also fundamentally different. In fact, the most obvious difference was that his first version was a love song addressed to a woman, whereas his second version included the words, "Oh, Savior," thereby transforming a love song into a gospel song, yet one even more seductive than the first. Still again, Green had epitomized that key transition in his own personal and professional life, which I, too, emphasized by opening the film with his initial take, and closing it with his second.

After our several days in Memphis, I had fully enough material to edit a first-rate portrait. And yet, I also wanted to film a straight-ahead Al Green concert to contrast with his Memphis church service, even if he now performed gospel in concert as well. Fortunately, I had budgeted enough money to do so, and I soon learned that Green would be performing at the Bolling Air Force Base Non-Commissioned Officer's Club in Washington, DC, which appeared to be entirely African American. The concert would be in February of 1984, which gave me plenty of time to hire Erich Roland, Chris Li, David Sperling, and Joe Meccariello to shoot, Bill Barth to oversee audio, and Johnny Rosen to drive his multitrack music recording truck up from Nashville.

Although the concert did feature many of the same gospel numbers Green had performed for us in Memphis, it also included a smattering of the semi-secular, such as his own "Free at Last" and Curtis Mayfield's "People Get Ready." In addition, Al showed that he could lose himself almost as completely in a concert as he could in church, which was especially evident in his medley of "Amazing Grace" and "Nearer My God to Thee." As the medley progressed, his eyes shone as if he had fire behind them. And yet, in this small, all-purpose auditorium, fancied up with white table cloths and vases of red roses on every table, such serious moments were balanced by the military honor guard that walked Green to the stage, and by the dazzled wives and daughters of military men, each wearing her Sunday best and hoping for contact with the sexiest preacher ever to saunter seductively through their midst, a microphone in his hand, and a come-hither smile on his face.

Admittedly, though, even this was not enough. From my point of view, the one thing left to shoot was Ken Tucker, a respected music critic, speaking about Green's appeal as both soul and gospel performer, and about spirituality in popular American music: "That's the essential argument of this," Ken said, "the dichotomy between the spiritual and the sensuous sides of pop music; something that Al Green really holds within himself." But back in London, Andy Park, an experienced composer, musician, television producer, radio executive, and now commissioning editor in his own right, wanted all the films he commissioned to push the edges of traditional TV programming. And two things he wanted from this particular "programme" (as the Brits spell it) were as follows: First, for me to appear in the film myself, so that the viewer could experience the story through me; and second, for me to explore any connections I could find between Al Green's religious music and hundreds of years of European Christian art. Andy even gave me a book on the history of Christianity—basically a book about the European history of Roman Catholicism—and asked me to read it, which I did.

So, in the hope of giving Andy what he wanted, Erich Roland, Bill Barth, and I shot interviews with two Howard University professors—Dr. J. Weldon Norris, who was director of the Howard University Choir, and Dr. Henry Justin Ferry, who was an associate professor of Church History—and also shot me at my film editing table, observing images of religious paintings from throughout European history, and doing my best to compare what Al Green was doing with what artists of the Middle Ages, the Renaissance, and more had done. In other words, whereas my goal for the film had been emotional depth, Andy's equally legitimate (if extremely challenging) goal was relevance for a European general audience.

In visual terms, I had continued to emphasize the noirish lighting ("film noir concert," I liked to call it), which Erich and I were employing to illustrate Green's emotional torment while passing from a popular career to a religious one. We also had emphasized the color red wherever we could find it, or else impose it, if only because Green had long been known for tossing red roses to his fans at the end of concerts, which clearly signified affairs of the heart, and possibly female sexuality as well. Yet, I had a deeper reason for this obsession, which was that, after Swedish director Ingmar Bergman created his 1972 masterpiece, *Cries and Whispers*, he claimed in interviews that his recurring use of red in the film was because he believed it to be the color of the human soul. Now, of course, I was completing a film about two kinds of soul: so-called soul *music* on the one hand and human spirituality on the other. So, I decided to spotlight red in my own film as well, from the scarlet carpeting at Al Green's church, to the red-rimmed glasses he wore as he began preaching, to the red carnation in his lapel, to the red roses on the tables at his concert, to the reddish light in the background during his interview. This was red as the color of romance, red as the color of human anguish, and for Green, red as the color of wine, which, in Holy Communion, symbolized the blood of Christ's own sacrifice for believers.

Once the film was completed, Andy and I introduced its world premiere screening at the 1984 Munich International Film Festival (Filmfest München) as part of a four-film retrospective of my recent work. There, German audiences who had sat patiently through years of often slow-moving and heavily symbolic New German Cinema also sat respectfully through our own 105-minute *Gospel According to Al Green*. However, only days later, on Friday, July 13, I screened the film twice more in a packed Nuart Theater as part of Filmex in Los Angeles, the director of which was now Ken Wlaschin, who previously had hosted several of my films at the London Film Festival. As the first screening began, the anticipation was palpable, and so long as Al Green was on the screen, the crowd was mesmerized. Thoughtful music criticism from journalist Ken Tucker also won its respect. Yet, when the two Howard University professors tried to intellectualize Al Green's emotional appeal, or when I began to expound upon presumed connections between Green's gospel music and traditions of European painting, we were met by scattered hooting, which grew with each new offending segment.

By the end of the screening, it was clear that the audience was pleased overall, and yet, I had learned my lesson, and I immediately made that known. "Thank you," I said. "You have shown me exactly which sections need to be deleted, and I promise to comply." Indeed, that following Monday morning, I contacted Andy in London to tell him what had happened, and being quite a smart fellow, he removed the problem sections before premiering the film over Channel 4 on February 2, 1985. Naturally, I made the same changes in my own copies before showing the newly abridged film at numerous other festivals, including the January 1985 US Film Festival in Park City, Utah, the forerunner of Sundance. And of course, by October 25 of that year, when Al and I helped to kick off the film's weeklong theatrical premiere at Justin Freed's Coolidge Corner Moviehouse in Brookline, Massachusetts, its more modest form was set in stone. However, what made opening night so special was Al Green himself walking onstage with a guitar after each of the night's screenings and inexplicably performing solo versions of his biggest hits; something he had largely refused to do during the making of the film.

Robert Mugge (right) introduces a live performance by Al Green after the theatrical world premiere of Gospel According to Al Green at the Coolidge Corner Moviehouse in Brookline, Massachusetts. (photographed by Justin Freed, 1985)

Still, regarding those cuts, there was nothing at all wrong with the onscreen contributions of Dr. Norris and Dr. Ferry. The real problem was trying to graft erudite analysis onto a film that already offered inherent messages within an emotional presentation. In other words, exactly as Gil Scott-Heron had created music for the heart, then grafted on messages for the head (in his case, social and political ones), Al Green, too, had created soulful, and even sensual music, then added messages of his own. This time, of course, the messages were religious, rather than political; lyrics asking listeners to consider their options (as in sin versus salvation), yet grafted onto songs that made them *feel* the choice.

It was a neat trick, combining the physical with either the political or the spiritual. But it did not mean we could do Green one better by lecturing the audience on what he was attempting. Viewers wanted to hear Al sing, and they wanted to hear Al talk, because he was their chosen storyteller, and Andy and I were not, except in so far as we packaged his own communication. On the positive side, the audience was saying to continue doing what I had thus far done (chronologically speaking) with George Crumb, Sun Ra, and Gil Scott-Heron, which was to give *them* the means to speak and perform for themselves. If we, the filmmakers, wanted to include a message, it needed to be subtle, delivered largely between the lines and between the frames—not between the eyes. And going forward, including with my new ninety-four-minute cut of the Al Green film, that was exactly what I did.

***

Beginning early in 1984, before even completing my Al Green portrait for Andy Park at Channel 4, I struggled to find a third subject I felt could work as well and, above all else, one that Andy could approve. I already was running out of time, because Andy was now planning to leave Channel 4 for other challenges back in Glasgow, Scotland, where his family had remained during his past few years working in London.

First, I tried to arrange a film about George Clinton, the consummate practitioner of funk music. I loved the idea of rounding out a trilogy, with the Scott-Heron film representing Black music and politics, the Al Green film representing Black music and religion, and a George Clinton film representing Black music and celebration. But ultimately, George's manager informed me that, due to personal excesses of Parliament-Funkadelic (the dual manifestations of Clinton's audacious musical identity), I probably could not trust them to show up in a particular city on a particular date, which would leave me paying out a great deal of Channel 4's money for crew and equipment, yet with nothing to show for it. Andy would not have been pleased.

Next, I read that peerless composer and lyricist of modern musicals, Stephen Sondheim, was deep into rehearsals of a show to be called *Sunday in the Park with George*, in preparation for a run on Broadway. I contacted him and asked if I could shoot some sort of "making of" documentary during these final stages, which initially was fine with him. Unfortunately, as we began making plans together for how we would go about it, with Stephen even mailing me copies of previous programs he had liked about his work, he suddenly informed me that we had to cancel. Apparently, tensions had emerged among key members of the production team, as so often happens during theater rehearsals, and he felt the presence of cameras would prevent those involved from speaking honestly to one another, which he considered to be vital to the project's success. Naturally, I was sad about losing such a unique opportunity, and all the more so when I saw the eventual show on Broadway, which not only was extraordinary, but focused on many of the same art-related issues that interested me.

With time growing even shorter before Andy's imminent departure, I heard, and was quite taken with, the latest Rubén Blades album, *Buscando América* (in English, *Searching for America*), which was thrilling his core audience of Latin music fans, drawing raves from rock critics, and crossing over from salsa stations to so-called progressive rock ones. In particular, I loved how Blades had utilized musical styles from assorted Latin American countries, combined them with social and political Spanish lyrics, and infused the finished product with energy enough to fuel a stadium rock show. This, I thought, could be music of a newly diverse and multilingual American future, and I convinced Andy, practically out the door by early 1985, to let me reach out to its creator.

What I learned was that Blades was preparing to graduate with a Master of Laws degree from Harvard Law School, that he was preparing to record a Spanish-language duet with rock star Linda Ronstadt, that he was reading Hollywood scripts for future TV and movie roles, and that he was strongly considering returning to his native Panama to run for president. Hearing all of this, as well as Rubén's music, Andy, too, was sold on the choice. In response, he authorized the project only weeks before leaving the channel, then asked Mike Bolland, the commissioning editor for youth programming, to oversee its completion in his absence. Much later, in the film's closing credits, I would affectionately refer to the two of them as "The Creature with Two Heads."

Ultimately, the making of this film involved five shoots: one in Cambridge, Massachusetts; two in New York City; one in Los Angeles; and one in Panama City, Panama, which seemed appropriately varied. However, just before shooting began, I made a quick and largely unexpected trip to the Cannes Film Festival. It turned out that my New York-based producer's rep of the time, Films Around the World, was paying to screen two of my recent films, *Gospel According to Al Green* and *Cool Runnings: The Reggae Movie*, in Marché du Film, the commercial film market attached to the festival, in the hope of attracting theatrical and TV buyers in various foreign territories. Naturally, I considered this a rare opportunity to attend the world's preeminent film festival, while also promoting my recent work, yet was not sure I could afford the costs involved. Happily, my good friend Richard Peña, then the film programmer for the School of the Art Institute of Chicago, offered me space in his tiny hotel room, thereby enabling me to apply my meager resources to roundtrip airfare, local transportation, food and drink, and the purchase of a tuxedo, without which I would not be admitted to the star-studded evening events.

That year, 1985, the festival ran from May 8 (my thirty-fifth birthday) through May 20, but I only flew there for the first few days, which is when my own films were screening in the market.

However, during my brief stay, I did manage to catch the official premiere of Héctor Babenco's *Kiss of the Spider Woman*; to meet journalist Louis Skorecki, who wrote a rave review of my Al Green film (the first of several such raves he would write for my work) in the French publication *Libération*; to walk past the great French auteur Jean-Luc Godard, right as he was struck in the face by what appeared to be a pie (the New York Times later reported that, with typical cinematic deception, it actually had been a cake topped with shaving cream); and finally, to rent a car for my return to Nice Côte d'Azur airport, making possible a leisurely spring drive through the alluring vineyards lining the shore of the Mediterranean.

Arriving home again, I returned my focus to the filming of Rubén Blades, meeting him for the first time at his graduate commencement ceremony. It was a beautiful spring day, and cameraman Larry McConkey, sound man Bill Barth, production assistant Christine Zeller, and I accompanied him to the following locations on campus: (1) the Harvard Law School's general outdoor ceremony, where a student onstage wore a Roman toga and made well-received jokes in Latin; (2) the graduate school's smaller outdoor presentation of diplomas, which its head agreed to repeat privately so that Larry could use his Steadicam to follow Blades through the process; (3) a nearby table where Rubén, his proud Cuban mother Anoland Blades, and some fellow graduates gathered to celebrate; and (4) an intimate conversation with Dean Frederick Snyder, Rubén's key professor, who resembled a late sixties California rocker, though wearing an academic robe, just as did Blades and assorted other faculty members and graduates. It was a joyous afternoon, made that much more satisfying for Rubén in that his new degree conferred the kind of prestige he hoped would help to elevate him to the presidency of his native country.

From left, record producer George Massenburg, singer-songwriter Rubén Blades, singer Linda Ronstadt, and director Robert Mugge chat during the recording of the Rubén Blades number "Silencios." (photographed by Patricia Saperstein, 1985)

Soon thereafter, we flew to Los Angeles to document Blades recording a duet with hugely popular and perceptive singing star Linda Ronstadt. The song they sang over his prerecorded instrumental tracks was "Silencios," or "Silences" in English. As Blades would later explain to us in New York, "It's about a couple that is breaking up. They can't accept the fact that it's over." Or as he said in his translated lyrics, "To live in silence is another way of dying. Something that starts with joy, at its end, brings agony."

Ironically, the collaboration with Ronstadt was exactly the opposite of what the song described. Instead, it was the coming together of two probing, musical minds, each of them trying to reach across an arbitrary cultural divide of language and ethnic background. For Rubén, this was a further attempt to move his passionate Latin American songs into the US mainstream, whereas, for Linda, it was a chance to practice singing in Spanish as she, herself, prepared to record the songs her Mexican father had taught her as a child. The respect and affection each expressed for the other offered hope, and a kind of blueprint, for greater racial and ethnic diversity in American popular culture. As Rubén stated in their joint interview: "We shouldn't be alienated into corners: white music in this side, Black music here, Latin music over there, you know. I think it's music in general, and we should all be together and work together. So, it was a great opportunity to do so."

Our next stop, on May 30, was at SOB's (Sounds of Brazil) Club in New York City, where Rubén and his seven-person ensemble, Seis del Solar, performed two lively sets for a combination of longtime Latin music fans and newer rock fans, including his new close friend, British rocker Joe Jackson. Somehow, Larry managed to squeeze his Steadicam into the crowded club, while Erich Roland went hand-held, and Chris Li and Dave Sperling worked from tripods. Since Johnny Rosen had a conflict, multitrack recording was provided by New York-based Effanel Music, with Bill Barth once again supervising on my behalf.

Over the course of the two sets, Blades performed thrilling versions of songs taken from his recent *Buscando América* album, as well as popular past songs created during his partnership with New York-born Puerto Rican salsa star Willie Colón. The ones I wound up using from the concert were title cut "Buscando América," "Tiburon" (about imperialism in Latin America), and "Pedro Navaja" (a Latin update of "Mac the Knife"), all written by Blades; plus "Todos Vuelven" ("Everybody Returns," about returning to your roots), written by Cesar Miro, and "Muevete" ("Move On," which was Cuban dance music written by Juan Formell, with new lyrics by Blades addressing apartheid in South Africa).

Two weeks later, Larry, Bill, and I returned to New York City in order to film an interview with Rubén in his apartment, as well as an outdoor conversation between him and his friend Pete Hamill, the prominent author and journalist. Together, Blades and Hamill discussed the evolution from early Afro-Cuban music and Latin jazz to the salsa Blades was currently creating, the Mexican tradition of social and political lyrics versus the Cuban preference for dance music, and Rubén's goal of using music to document history and, as he said himself, "To make people know they are not alone." On his own in his apartment, Blades expanded on such themes: "The majority of my songs describe situations that occur in Latin American cities in general. They're songs about love, songs about problems in the street, problems in life, relationships; some are funny, others are tragic. But I mean, I'm doing like an urban chronicle type of music. Basically, it's like musical journalism—reporting the city folklore."

With his song "Todos Vuelven"— again, actually written by Peruvian songwriter Cesar Miro, but heartily embraced by Blades—he prepared us for accompanying him later that summer on a trip to his home country of Panama. That is, he translated some of the Spanish lyrics as follows: "Everyone returns to the land where they were born. To the incomparable bewitching attraction of its sun. Everybody returns to the place from where they came, where perhaps more than one love blossomed. Under the solitary tree of yesterday, we dream over and over. Everyone returns to the root of memories, but the time of past love never comes back."

For Blades, the root of his own memories was Panama, where he had lived with his Panamanian father and Cuban mother until his parents eventually split. In Panama City, the capital, we spent time with him in his new high-rise condo overlooking the city; joined him and his father, Rubén Blades Sr., for a tour of their former neighborhood; visited a branch of the Panamanian bank where Rubén worked after graduating from law school, but prior to emigrating to New York City (where he swept floors at salsa label Fania Records till becoming one of its biggest stars); convinced him to express his longterm goal of returning to Panama and running for president; and walked with him along the Panama Canal as he discussed the Panamanian sovereignty which he and fellow citizens had long sought.

Sometimes, of course, scenes take on unexpected meanings. For instance, the digging of the Panama Canal, a U.S. project in Panama, had brought together two halves of the world, East and West (whatever long-running political differences also resulted between the two countries directly involved). Now, Blades was seeking breakthroughs of his own, not only for himself (in music, movies, law, and politics), but also for those with common backgrounds and aspirations. As for me, the time spent with Rubén in Panama inspired my title, *The Return of Rubén Blades*, because his was a classic variation of the heroic myth, as outlined by Joseph Campbell in his book *The Hero with a Thousand Faces*—that is, a hero who abandons home and hearth, pursues something of value, succeeds in the quest, then returns to share the fruits of that success.

I should note that, when we visited Panama in 1985, it still was controlled by strongman Manuel Noriega, whom President George H. W. Bush would later humiliate, depose, extradite, and imprison in the United States. Probably as signs of that control, soldiers were a common sight on the streets, and there seemed to be few pollution controls, because exhaust fumes could be overwhelming. The soldiers, in particular, became an issue for us because, on the occasion of some recent press in the Village Voice, my photo had been taken by a gregarious young female photographer, and I had decided to hire her to document our efforts in Panama. However, after we arrived at the airport in Panama City, rented a minivan, and started driving on the highway into the city, we were unnerved by all the open-air trucks on the road filled with large numbers of armed soldiers. In fact, right as one such truck passed by us, the photographer in the back seat opened her window, inexplicably stuck her upper body out through it, and started waving her arms and shouting at the soldiers. Absolutely livid, and fearing her manic behavior would put us in jeopardy, I immediately ordered her back into the vehicle, and as soon as we reached the hotel, I arranged her return to New York City on the next available flight.

Director of photography Larry McConkey and audio director Bill Barth pose beside the Panama Canal during production of The Return of Rubén Blades. (photographed by film crew, 1985)

Nevertheless, once this unfortunate episode was resolved, our time in Panama was a delight. For instance, the fresh fruit was delicious, and we got to see Panamanian boxer Roberto Durán entering the casino beside our hotel. In fact, perhaps our sweetest memory was driving back from the Panama Canal with Rubén when he suddenly pointed out an Indigenous Kuna woman on the side of the road selling hand-made mola textiles. For me, many of the images superficially resembled simple art works we created as kids, drawing with colored crayons on paper, covering over the colors with black crayon, and then scratching away parts of the black to reveal a rainbow of colors underneath. Really, though, this far more intricate style was derived from body painting which preceded it, later combined with European fabrics brought by Spanish colonizers. But whatever their origin, the textiles I purchased were gorgeous, abstract images of birds and fish, which I framed and hung above my living room fireplace, plus shared with my parents.

Our time in Panama ended with Blades on the balcony of his high-rise condo at dusk, discussing how every day includes two twilights: one in the evening and one in the morning. As he saw it, twilight represents both endings and beginnings, with his emphasis now on the latter. In other words, as we filmed Rubén at home in Panama City, thousands of miles from his secondary home in New York City, he was bridging old with new, past with present, male with female, East with West, North with South, Spanish with English, and music with politics. It was a story sure to please even Channel 4's "Creature with Two Heads," who scheduled the film's broadcast premiere for Sunday, May 18, 1986 across the U.K. However, as with so many of my films, the world premiere actually took place at Ron Henderson's Denver International Film Festival (October 19, 1985), followed a few months later by a screening at the pre-Sundance US Film Festival in Park City, Utah.

Chapter Four
Tropical Visions

Cool Runnings: The Reggae Movie (1983)

Hawaiian Rainbow (1987)

Kumu Hula: Keepers of a Culture (1989)

n many respects, *Cool Runnings: The Reggae Movie* was a project built upon sand. Certainly, it started out with great promise, and overall, was a grand adventure. But money (or the lack thereof), ganja (a Sanskrit word for hemp, which became the Jamaican word for marijuana), and Jamaican culture proved its undoing. Perhaps the film's title was even part of the problem, because even though "cool runnings" (usually pronounced with a silent "g") essentially means "go in peace," it has, rightly or wrongly, come to suggest to me the kind of lethargy I associate with another ironic Jamaican phrase, "Soon come, mon."

In the spring of 1983, Gil Scott-Heron, the subject of my 1982 film *Black Wax*, was booked to perform at Reggae Sunsplash, the annual Jamaican music festival, which that year would take place at the Bob Marley Performing Arts Center in Montego Bay, Jamaica, rather than at its usual home in Kingston. A British company that had documented the previous year's festival as a television series planned to shoot there again, and Gil, along with Paul Zukowsky, one of his managers, suggested I be hired to direct. I had already spent months trying to persuade Al Green to work with me on a film for Channel 4 and seemed to be getting nowhere. So, when Paul suggested I come to New York City for the May 2, 1983 press conference at which Tony Johnson, director of Synergy Productions Ltd., would announce his festival's coming lineup, I readily agreed.

Tony, a born salesman, conveyed irresistible enthusiasm for reggae music, Jamaica, and especially that year's Sunsplash festival, set to take place from June 28 through July 2. Although largely featuring top reggae acts from Jamaica and elsewhere, Tony and associates Ronnie Burke and Don Green had booked Scott-Heron to perform, not only because of his growing popularity worldwide, but because Gil's late father had been a Jamaican soccer star. At any rate, thanks in large part to Gil's endorsement, Tony and I hit it off, and he therefore put me in touch with a middle-aged Englishman named Stephen Michael Williams who was busy raising funding to shoot the festival. Stephen's intention was to use the same British production company as the year before, but if it made the festival promoters happy, he had no problem with my serving as director. In fact, he asked me to call and introduce myself to Debbie Harry of the rock group Blondie, who was set to host his new series, which was a pleasant task, indeed.

The funny thing about Williams was that, even over the phone, he had an upper class accent and a jovial, somewhat bumbling personality, not unlike the way Nigel Bruce played Watson to Basil Rathbone's 1930s film version of Sherlock Holmes. Over the weeks to come, however, Tony and I both began to realize that Stephen was failing in his efforts to raise funding, which threw into question the entire project. Although I was scheduled to fly to Jamaica on Saturday, June 25, and then to work with the British crew, I heard from Johnson the night before that the effort had collapsed. At that point, I asked if he could quickly pull together enough cash for me to organize a crew of my own, fly them down later in the weekend, and shoot the festival on 16mm film, which we could later blow up to 35mm. I knew that Synergy already had arranged for stage lighting, a PA system, and multitrack recording. So, all we needed now were crew members who owned their own camera and sound equipment; a communication system; film stock from Kodak; local Jamaicans to act as assistants; and food, hotel rooms, and minimal salaries for the bunch of us. If Tony could raise money to pay for all this, we could document his performances for far less than the British company would have charged, and we could put off postproduction costs until later. Moreover, with this scenario, we would create a film for theaters rather than a series for television, and Synergy would own the final product.

"Yeah, mon! Let's do it!" Tony replied. So, while he started arranging Air Jamaica tickets and rooms at a Montego Bay resort, I called director of photography Larry McConkey, audio director Bill Barth, and cameraman Chris Li. Fortunately, all were available, as were cameramen Dave Sperling and Erich Roland, two friends of Chris Li who would go on to work with me for years to come. By one o'clock in the morning, everything was arranged, and just a few hours after that, I set off for Montego Bay, Jamaica, with the others following a day or two later.

No sooner had I retrieved my bags at the Montego Bay airport on Saturday, June 25 and headed outdoors than someone tried to sell me ganja. This was just as illegal in Jamaica as it was in the States, so I politely declined and watched for my ride to the resort hotel where we were to stay. Normally, a resort with swimming pool and beachfront would have been a treat, but I knew that, over the next week, we would have little time to relax. Sure enough, before I could even settle in, John Wakely, a fourth member of the Synergy team, picked me up and drove me on one of the most harrowing, two-hour rides of my life. As we raced around mountain roads at night, featuring only one lane in each direction and zero visibility beyond the next curve, John would simply lean on his horn and race toward whatever awaited us.

The drive was from Montego Bay, on the northwestern end of the island, to Kingston, on the southeastern end. Tony Johnson wanted me to come there so that I could show him and Ronnie Burke my detailed budget and discuss our respective plans for the coming days. It was a productive meeting, even though, my entire time with them, I was dreading the ride back to Montego Bay.

After my crew flew in from DC, Philly, and Newark, we had just that one evening to look around, eat an actual meal together at our hotel (as opposed to grabbing festival food as we worked), and drink a bit of Jamaican rum and the best pineapple juice I had ever tasted. Among our other uniquely Jamaican experiences were purchasing so-called jerk chicken and jerk goat on the side of the road; having paramilitary police stop and search one of our vehicles for drugs; seeing dreadlocked drug dealers swim up to our hotel's beachfront, thereby evading security; sampling a bit of local ganja, which was some of the strongest we had tried; and in my own case, getting stuck in a roundabout late at night, because I had not yet mastered driving on the left side of the road and manual shifting with my left hand.

We also eased into working early in the week, including checking out the outdoor concert site during the day on Tuesday, June 28, and shooting a festival-related outdoor fashion show that same evening. In addition, Larry McConkey, Bill Barth, Larry's Steadicam assistant Tass Michos, and I filmed Scott-Heron and his brother, Denis Heron, on a beach with their Jamaican uncle. Then, we drove Gil and Denis out to the waterfall at Ocho Rios and tried to film Gil walking and talking there, much as we had done with *Black Wax*. The idea was for him to provide commentary about Jamaica, Jamaican music, the African slave trade (which had helped to populate the Caribbean), and more that I could use throughout the film. Unfortunately, in the year since we had worked with Gil, his drug use had grown more serious, and he was no longer capable of improvising on the level he had before (at least while high).

Wednesday afternoon, we finally took on the primary job we had come there to do, which, to begin, meant hauling our equipment to the festival site and setting up for that evening's filming. We had been warned that performances would go on all night, finishing sometime the following morning. So, we were as rested as possible as we settled in for the first long night of shooting and recording. More specifically, Bill took his place in the multitrack recording truck that Artisan Recorders had brought by boat from Florida and then parked behind the stage, with cables snaking their way to all relevant instruments and microphones; Larry and his assistant, Tass, set up Larry's Steadicam on the edge of the stage, so that they could move in and out among the performing musicians; Erich set up his own camera at stage right, which was also where we placed my communication system and video monitors on a large table; Chris took a position in front of the stage, just to the left of center, where he could shoot good close-ups of singers or soloists; and Dave set up on one of the tall light towers that had been erected some distance in front of the stage, in order to capture the wider perspective of the densely packed audience.

Yet, despite preparations, opening night proved to be our baptism by fire. So many stoned Rastas climbed onto the light tower with Dave that his camera was constantly shaking, which made his footage largely unusable. Ultimately, we agreed that he should join us onstage, taking his place stage left, which was open. Of course, there were issues on the stage as well, with fans sometimes sneaking around security and trying to take seats at my table. At one point, security summarily removed a young woman from one of my seats, much to the irritation of a group of men who were smoking ganja and shouting from below the edge of the stage just behind me. For a time, I felt as threatened as Dave had felt when confronting fans who were shaking the light tower on which he was trying to shoot. Then again, we were guests in their country, so we tried to take such matters in stride.

The next revelation came when we did not make it back to our hotel rooms until noon, knowing we would have to pack up and return to the site again by late afternoon. Factoring in eating, bathing, dressing, and the rest, we realized we would not get more than two hours of sleep, whether in our actual beds or sprawled like typhoon victims on beach chairs beside the pool. We also knew the cycle would repeat itself day after day until Sunday morning, at which point we would finish shooting the last night of performances, then collapse for the final time.

Yet, our rudest awakening came the second night of shooting when our camera batteries ran out of power more quickly than we could replace them with fresh ones. On location shoots such as this, the idea was always to plug in our large battery belts—usually three per camera—in our hotel rooms overnight. That way, they would all be fully charged again for the following day's shoot. However, in Jamaica, we were not in our hotel rooms as long as we would have liked. And on top of that, the electrical current proved to be weaker than we had expected. Still, once we recognized the problem, we improvised some solutions, just as we always have to do on location, especially in countries with less dependable utilities.

As for the music, it was outstanding. I wished we could have utilized every act we shot. But we never could have fit them all into a single film less than two hours long. In addition, certain acts, including reggae and dancehall star Yellowman, would not permit us to shoot them. And three of the top acts at the festival—Third World, Steel Pulse, and Black Uhuru—each insisted on being headliners for the film or else we could not film them, either. It was a tough call, but Tony was close with Third World. So, they became our choice, which I still believe was a good one.

Two more acts whose performances made the final cut were the Skatalites, newly reunited, and Alton Ellis, legendary stars of, respectively, ska and rock steady, two Jamaican musical styles that had preceded reggae. Other stars of the film included family members of the late Bob Marley, including his wife, Rita, and four of their children, who were performing as Ziggy Marley and the Melody Makers. Also featured were Bob Marley backup singer Judy Mowatt (a past member of the I-Threes, along with Rita Marley and Marcia Griffiths); comical singer-songwriter Sugar Minott; younger Jamaican band Chalice; British teen sensations Musical Youth, performing their global hit "Pass the Dutchie"; dub poet Mutabaruka, performing at night in slave chains with an expressive female dancer; politically astute Anguillan singer Bankie Banx; stoned balladeer Gregory Isaacs singing his sultry hit "Night Nurse"; and Gil Scott-Heron performing a masterful version of his classic song "The Bottle."

Our chosen headliners, Third World, gave the final performance of the festival, not coming onstage until mid-morning on Sunday. By that point, the sun was beating down and reflecting off the surrounding bay; the site was still packed with colorfully dressed festivalgoers pressing tightly against the stage; and film crew, stage crew, and fans alike were now fully awake and exuberant over this being the final act of the final night, and a great one at that. Although the band performed a full set of their biggest hits, in the film, I could only fit two of their best: "96 Degrees in the Shade," which perfectly fit that bright, sunny morning, and "Try Jah Love," their biggest hit of all, which had been written for them by Stevie Wonder and now had the honor of closing out the festival. The performance of both songs was sensational, and inspired by the band, our crew summoned newfound energy of its own, including Larry's most dazzling Steadicam shots of the week. Sadly, though, somewhere between the festival stage and my film lab in Virginia, the Steadicam footage for "Try Jah Love" was lost, which meant I only had shots from the other three cameras to use in reconstructing the moment. And yet, Chris, Dave, and Erich worked so hard as well that the cut scene ended up no less buoyant with just three camera views.

Larry McConkey uses his Steadicam to shoot a performance by Third World at the Reggae Sunsplash festival in Montego Bay, Jamaica. (photographed by Rosi Thielen, 1983)

At some point during our stay, desperately sleep-deprived, yet knowing Gil was not in shape to provide connective tissue for the film's disparate scenes, I wrote a poem about reggae that Tony Johnson could deliver onscreen, and Larry, Bill, and I filmed him reciting it on a rooftop with Larry MacDonald, Gil's dreadlocked Jamaican percussionist, playing bongo drums behind him. Then, at dusk on Sunday, Tony led us to an open-air bar in Negril—the westernmost point of the island—so that he and MacDonald could repeat the end of the poem-plus-percussion against a spectacular Jamaican sunset reflecting on the water. Unfortunately, by that point, the sky had grown overcast, and a light rain was falling, thereby wiping out any chance of a sunset. But the scene still proved an effective close for the film, leading into a rousing encore of "Try Jah Love," plus a rhyming festival wrap-up from emcee Bagga Brown.

Third World performs at the Reggae Sunsplash festival. (photographed by Rosi Thielen, 1983)

After making sure that all of my crew members caught their Sunday afternoon or evening flights home, I returned alone to our resort hotel and passed out in my bed, knowing that Tony and I would meet the following morning, discuss how everything had gone, and make plans for the future. For now, I at least could relax again and get my first full-night's sleep in several days. However, to my surprise, my hotel room phone rang at three o'clock in the morning, and when I answered it, I heard only silence at the other end. In response, I hung up the receiver and returned to sleep. Then, perhaps fifteen minutes later, there was a loud pounding on my door.

In Jamaica, even with air conditioning, there was no escaping humidity, so I always slept without covers or clothing. Awakened once again in the pitch black room, I walked to the door without dressing, opened it a crack, and looked out at a pair of uniformed guards, each of whom was armed and holding the leash of a German Shepherd.

"Why are you here?" one of them asked. "And how are you going to pay for your room?" Realizing how vulnerable I was, standing naked behind the door with a small supply of illegal ganja in my closet, I explained calmly that Tony Johnson of Synergy was paying for my room, and that if he had neglected to arrange payment for this additional night, he would do so tomorrow.

"No," one of them replied. "Everyone's gone. You're not supposed to be here. How are you going to pay for tonight?"

The exchange went on this way for some time, growing increasingly heated from both sides. In fact, I began to suspect that what was really happening here was a shakedown. If they had wanted, they easily could have pushed open the door, searched my room, and then had everything they needed for petty extortion. With that in mind, I finally yelled at them that Tony would be there in the morning, and that if they did not back off this second, as of tomorrow, they would both be looking for work. Fortunately, that did the trick, because I slammed the door and never heard another word from them. Moreover, in the morning, after I phoned Tony to let him know what had happened, he stormed into the hotel and reamed out the management. All just another day of doing business in the so-called Third World.

Over the next few months, as I edited the film in my suburban Philadelphia apartment, I was in regular contact with Synergy's Tony Johnson, Don Green, and Ronnie Burke, and kept them informed of slowly accruing expenses. One day, Don flew in from Jamaica with a suit bag filled with thousands of dollars in cash so that I could pay the film lab. Then, weeks later, when Ronnie Burke and I oversaw the music mix at R. P. M. in New York City, he took care of paying, and when I oversaw the film's final sound mix at Trans/Audio there, a charming man in dreadlocks showed up with a paper bag filled with $13,000 in cash, which was exactly what we owed for the mix. I never asked questions about such matters, but was always happy to see bills getting paid as they were coming due.

Sadly, although you can take a film project (or at least your exposed footage) out of Jamaica, you may not be able to take Jamaica out of the film project. And perhaps for that reason, Synergy's resources ran out before the musicians could be paid and before I could be fully paid myself. To be fair, our hope was that, if I could at least finish the editing, perhaps a future distributor would pay off project bills. Yet, by 1983, two years after the death of Bob Marley, the influence of reggae was fading, and distributors were all too aware. Still, we did manage to complete the film, including blowing it up to 35mm and adding a Dolby Surround soundtrack, just in time for a delightful world premiere at the London Film Festival on Friday, November 18, 1983—followed by the US premiere at Filmex, a festival in Los Angeles, on Friday, July 13, 1984—both of them hosted by my friend Ken Wlaschin, who changed festivals between the two screenings. Those premieres were followed by lots more festival screenings around the world, as well as a modest theatrical release in the US, conducted enthusiastically, but unsuccessfully, by my friend Michael Jeck and his R5/S8 Presents. Again, the unfortunate truth was that, by the time our very good film was released, reggae's time in the sun had passed.

Five years later, I packaged six of my feature-length music films for a national PBS series that I titled *Summer Night Music*, and included an eighty-five-minute version of the 105-minute *Cool Runnings: The Reggae Movie*, along with edits of similar duration for *Black Wax*, *Gospel According to Al Green*, *The Return of Rubén Blades*, *Saxophone Colossus*, and the newly completed *Hawaiian Rainbow*, with the programs screening weekly throughout the summer of 1988. Then, almost five years after that, an attorney from the Walt Disney Company called to say that they were making a film about the Jamaican national bobsleigh team, wanted to call it *Cool Runnings*, and were willing to pay for clear use of the title. So, I passed the guy on to Tony, and he and Synergy finally made a little money, which they elected not to share. Yet, as I say, I did complete the film, which has to count for something, with a project built on sand.

***

In May of 1986, after filming Sonny Rollins in Japan for a week, I tore ligaments in my right knee while attending the Vancouver International Film Festival (actually, while walking endlessly around Vancouver's 1986 World Expo), then spent almost three weeks visiting Australia on crutches. The trip consisted of nearly a week each at the Sydney Film Festival and Melbourne International Film Festival, plus a full week of relaxing in Cairns, Australia, which is in the tropical north. While in the country, I hoped to develop a film about Aboriginal music, but friends there warned me that the Aboriginal community was going through a stage of political activism wherein they would not welcome a film made by an outside filmmaker. So, I dropped that idea. However, as it happened, on my way home, I was scheduled to spend two days at a hotel in Honolulu, Hawai'i, and it was there that I found subjects for two of my next three films.

Everywhere around me were sights and sounds, tastes and smells, that went far beyond what years of promotion had led me to expect. Even the commercial luau I attended with reluctance featured live music and dance I found electrifying. Therefore, before flying home again, I bought audiocassettes of local music and listened intently for the rest of my trip.

A few months later, as I was completing the Sonny Rollins film, I received a call from Ann Brandman, film programmer for the Honolulu Academy of Arts (later renamed the Honolulu Museum of Art). By the end of the call, I had agreed to return to Hawai'i that coming February (1987) and screen a week's worth of my films. But the best part, which I would not know until I arrived, was that, over the course of that five days of screenings, Ann would introduce me to J. W. "Jay" Junker, a public radio deejay and budding academic with a Hawaiian music show; Dr. Ricardo D. "Ric" Trimillos, an ethnomusicologist teaching at the Manoa campus of the University of Hawai'i; Vicky Holt Takamine, a *kumu hula* (master teacher of Hawaiian dance) and instructor at the same campus; and Dr. Neil Abercrombie, a former state legislator who recently had run for Congress and lost, then become an education consultant to Governor John S. Waihe'e, Hawai'i's first native Hawaiian governor.

Later, Abercrombie would become a member of the Honolulu City Council for two years, Honolulu's US Congressman for nine years, and Hawai'i's governor for the next four. But at the time, he

was a highly energetic and well-connected politician with unexpected time on his hands, and learning I was anxious to produce a
film about the diverse traditions of Hawaiian music—with Junker,
Trimillos, Takamine, and Brandman willing to assist—he quickly
raised the bulk of needed funding from his former colleagues in the
state legislature. Largely for appearances, the money would be ad-
ministered by Hawai'i's State Foundation on Culture and the Arts,
which I weathered well enough.

In preparation for the coming project, Jay Junker gave me a long-
distance course on the Hawaiian Renaissance of the 1970s, which
had brought renewed interest in the music, dance, art, literature,
language, and politics of native Hawaiians, as well as an update on
the current music scene. Then, based on the amount of money raised,
I concluded that filming would have to be restricted primarily to
the island of O'ahu, and especially to the state capital of Honolulu.
With that in mind, Dr. Ric Trimillos (now my music consultant), Jay
Junker (now my music coordinator), and I decided to stage one big
outdoor concert at Andrews Amphitheater on the Manoa campus of
the University of Hawai'i, then determined which artists should be
filmed there and which should be filmed elsewhere. Those selected
for the all-day event included Vicky Holt Takamine and Pua Ali'i
'Ilima (Vicky's *hālau*, or hula school), who would perform ancient
Hawaiian chants and dances; the Ho'opi'i Brothers, who would utilize their "high falsetto" voices (*leo ki'eki'e* in Hawaiian) in playing
songs native to their island of Moloka'i; Hawaiian Renaissance favorites the Mākaha Sons of Ni'ihau, performing the sweetest of political
songs; slack-key guitar virtuoso Raymond Kāne; and a Hawaiian su-
pergroup made up of powerhouse vocalist Auntie Genoa Keawe, nostalgic performer Violet Pahu Liliko'i, one-handed steel guitar master
Billy Hew Len, and upright bass player Val Kepilino. But that concert
would not take place until our last full day in the islands, and we
would have plenty to shoot before then.

Production was now slated for the first two weeks of July, during which time I checked myself into the Kaimana Beach Hotel (at
the far end of Waikiki Beach, near Diamondhead), and brought in
crew members as I needed them. My first few days back, I worked

with Jay, Ric, Vicky, and Ann to nail down the shooting schedule and all related arrangements. Then, on Saturday, July 4, I was joined by director of photography and Steadicam operator Larry McConkey, second unit cameraman Erich Roland, and audio director Bill Barth, and introduced my mainland collaborators to my local ones.

Our first day of shooting—Sunday, July 5—involved our accompanying kumu hula Vicky Holt Takamine into a dense forest in a mountainous section of O'ahu. There, we filmed her sharing myths and legends of Hawaiian culture, demonstrating an ancient Hawaiian chant, and showing four of her female hālau members how to gather and identify leaves and flowers used in ceremonial performances. In her words, "All of these things are placed on the altar, or *kuahu*, as it is called, in the process of studying the hula . . . the dance of the Hawaiian people." Then, we arranged Vicky and her students in tall grass where they performed a traditional *hīmeni* (a Hawaiian song influenced by the hymns of foreign missionaries) with female harmonies as lush as the foliage around them.

The Ho'opi'i Brothers had created a spirited song titled "Hawaiian Rainbow," and I decided not only to open the film with them performing it, but also to borrow its title for the production. The lyrics of the song mention many varieties of flora native to Hawai'i, establishing, in the process, both the beauty and the diversity of the islands. Therefore, on Monday, I asked Erich to fly to Maui and film a great many flowers for use in illustrating those lyrics. I also asked that he film *paniolo* (Hawaiian cowboys) which I could use to accompany one of Raymond Kāne's slack-key guitar songs. Then, from Maui, I asked that he fly to the Big Island of Hawai'i, meet up with Vicky Takamine at dawn on Tuesday, and film her dancing atop the volcano Kīlauea, home of Pele, goddess of volcanoes and fire, and the mythic creator of the Hawaiian Islands.

On those same two days, Larry, Bill, and I carried out multiple shoots of our own on O'ahu. For one, we filmed elderly Hawaiian singing star and *'ukulele* whiz Andy Cummings, as he performed Hawaiian-themed Tin Pan Alley hits from the late nineteenth and early twentieth centuries. We also shot long interviews with our music consultant Dr. Ricardo D. Trimillos, and with native Hawaiian historian Dr. George S. Kanahele, author of the encyclopedic *Hawaiian Music and Musicians*. And finally, we visited the rural taro fields of the Ka'ala Farm cooperative in Wai'anae, Hawai'i where we filmed Michael Kahikina, wearing little more than a traditional loin cloth as he tended the water-filled taro fields and sang a reggae-influenced song about the first Hawaiians. While there, we also filmed poet Puanani Burgess explaining the collective's concept of reconnecting with the *'āina* (land), and reciting a poem about her "three names" (representing her competing Hawaiian, American, and Japanese family heritage).

As Robert Mugge looks on, audio director Bill Barth places microphones on slack-key guitarist Raymond Kāne and his wife Elodia Kāne prior to their performance at Lanikūhonua on the island of O'ahu. (photographed by Dr. Ricardo D. Trimillos, 1987).

After Erich's return on Wednesday, he, Larry, Bill, and I filmed Jerry Santos and Haunani Apoliona in an updated version of Jerry's Hawaiian Renaissance band Olomana that, since its creation, had evoked the sweetness of late sixties hippie band The Youngbloods. The performance and interview took place in the luxuriant gardens of Queen Emma's Summer Palace. Next, on Thursday, we filmed guitarist Raymond Kāne at Lanikūhonua, the site of the Paradise Cove Luau, as he explained how Hawaiian guitarists developed their technique of "slacking" guitar strings (*kī hō'alu*), thereby creating chime-like effects, and performed a vocal duet with his wife Elodia. Then, on Friday, we stopped by Hawaiian radio station KCCN and filmed deejay Brickwood Galuteria on the air as he interviewed both Hawaiian diva Auntie Genao Keawe and Israel Kamakawiwo'ole, the very talented (and very large) lead singer of the Mākaha Sons of Ni'ihau.

By Friday evening, we had been joined by cameraman Chris Li, as well as by Randy Ezratty and Mark Shane of Effanel Music, who had boxed up and shipped by air most of the recording and mixing equipment they normally moved by truck. We also had received our communication system from Virginia, hired additional crew members from the area, and for Sunday only, rented HMI lights and a tent to house our music recording equipment. As a result, we were fully prepared for the shoots that remained.

From the beginning, I had hoped to film musicians and dancers in an intimate club, and to do so on Saturday afternoon, July 11. Yet, finding the right venue was tough. Finally, though, Larry Johnson, the manager of Hula's Bar & Lei Stand in Waikiki, offered us a dream situation. As it happened, Hula's was a gay bar. But to us, it was just a lovely, tropically themed venue, essentially open-air, yet protected from the elements. In other words, it was perfect.

From left, audio director Bill Barth, cameraman Erich Roland, director of photography Larry McConkey, and director Robert Mugge prepare to shoot a pre-performance interview at Hula's Bar & Lei Stand in Waikiki. (photographed by film crew, 1987)

And so, on that sunny and bright Saturday afternoon, we filmed a performance by the Sam Bernard Trio featuring Kaulana Kasparavitch on upright bass, Clyde Lono on acoustic guitar, and Sam Bernard on 'ukulele. All three sang, of course, but it was Sam's soaring "closed falsetto" that dominated both sweet Hawaiian ballads and more upbeat material. Also, for the occasion, they were accompanied by female dancers from Kaulana's own Lehua Dance Company. Although various songs brought out women of different ages, the most popular was a group of young girls (*keikis*, as children are called in Hawai'i), whose proud parents watched and applauded from nearby tables, and four songs in particular—"Kuhio Beach," *"Pua Mamane,"* "Aloha Kaua'i," and *"Ke'ala O Ka Rose"*— wound up forming the climax of the film.

Moving on to Sunday, we now faced our most demanding shoot of the trip, which was the afternoon of performances at Andrews Amphitheater on the University of Hawai'i's Manoa campus. With four cameras (one of them attached to Larry's Steadicam), twenty-four-track recording equipment protected by a large tent, HMI lights on very tall stands, a PA system strong enough for outdoor listening, my communication system and video assist monitors, and a large crew, we prepared to capture a varied and colorful group of Hawaiian performers.

Over a period of several hours, we filmed and recorded the following, more or less in this order: Vicky and a younger female assistant chanting and playing drums as several young women performed synchronized dances in front of them; the Ho'opi'i Brothers performing mostly fast-paced songs that emphasized "open falsetto" harmonies and cowboy-like yodels; emcee Brickwood Galuteria announcing Raymond Kāne's recent National Folk Heritage Award, then Kāne performing several moderately paced numbers, including a Spanish song Hawaiians had learned from Mexican vaqueros brought to the islands to control the cattle; singer Auntie Genoa Keawe, singer Violet Pahu Liliko'i, steel guitar player Billy Hew Len, and bass player Val Kepilino performing together, with each of the first three taking lead on at least one song (including Keawe belting out one of her classic hits with striking breath control); and the Mākaha Sons of Ni'ihau employing Crosby, Stills & Nash-style harmonies as they raised cultural and political issues through song. To our great relief, Hawaiian deities appeared pleased because, aside from a brief period of midday showers (typical for tropical climates), all went stunningly well.

As planned, we spent most of our time in the islands capturing the elegant melodies and varied rhythms of Hawaiian music, set against colorful local landscapes. And yet, this was also a film of ideas. Therefore, with the help of Ric Trimillos, George Kanahele, and Vicky Takamine, we established how ancient Hawaiian chants and dances offered an early oral history of the Hawaiian people; how, again, Hawaiian harmonies and part-singing called hīmeni were derived from the hymns of American missionaries; how Mexican vaqueros introduced the guitar; how Portuguese sailors imported a small, stringed instrument that became known as the 'ukulele; how Hawaiians themselves devised slack-key guitar methods and invented the slide guitar (which involves running a bar over guitar strings to alter their sound); how Hawaiian music migrated to the American mainland and elsewhere during the first decades of the twentieth century; and how the importation of assorted regional genres, from Cajun to reggae, led to newer musical hybrids played and recorded by younger Hawaiian artists. Trimillos underlined that final point when he said the following:

At present, the Hawaiian music scene is really quite complex. Because of the younger generation's interest in the past, you have the preservation of older styles and older repertoire as one aspect of that rebirth or reinterest. You also have new pieces being composed in the old style. And on top of that, you have pieces which are being composed and performed that partake of rock, and jazz, and even country [and] western that are really part of the mainstream idea of Hawaiian and American mainland music together.

The completion of *Hawaiian Rainbow* was also aided by money from three sources. First, a new company called Sony Video Software purchased US home video rights; second, Rounder Records purchased rights for two LPs, one a soundtrack of the overall film, and the other a live Raymond Kāne album (both of which I produced, with the assistance of Jay Junker and Ric Trimillos); and third, the Corporation for Public Broadcasting purchased broadcast rights so that the film could be included among six of mine that I packaged into my aforementioned public television series titled *Summer Night Music*.

Yet, almost as quickly as *Hawaiian Rainbow* was finished, it was previewed at Ron Henderson's Denver International Film Festival on October 14, 1987, then celebrated with a big, invitation-only screening on Wednesday, November 11, 1987 at the Academy Theatre of the Honolulu Academy of Arts, followed by four more days of public screenings. Governor Waihe'e was present for the premiere, as were many of the film's participants, some of whom performed live at the accompanying reception.

Less than two weeks later, on Friday, November 27, 1987, the film was officially world premiered at the London Film Festival, once again programmed by director Derek Malcolm. The London screening included a live performance by the Sam Bernard Trio with dancers Vicky Holt Takamine and Glen Pasadaba, all of whom also performed at a local music club called the Rock Garden. Although the club mostly featured punk bands at the time, its regular patrons were transfixed by these talented Hawaiian performers in their colorful outfits. Similarly, in the spring of 1988, slack-key guitarist Raymond Kāne and his vocalist wife Elodia performed after screenings at the AFI Fest (American Film Institute) in Los Angeles and at the Sydney Film Festival in Australia, courtesy of directors Ken Wlaschin and Rod Webb, respectively.

***

With *Hawaiian Rainbow* finished and going into distribution, I next had to complete *Entertaining the Troops* (my documentary starring Bob Hope and others who had supported Allied war efforts in World War II) and assist PBS with launching it as a national pledge special in May of 1988. As I wrote earlier, because this was not, strictly speaking, a music-related project, I am not addressing it here, other than to mention how it overlapped the making of my two Hawaiian films, one of which was about music but included dance, and the other of which was about dance but included music.

Nonetheless, as I awaited the national premiere of *Entertaining the Troops*, Vicky Holt Takamine and I discussed the idea of producing a film on Hawaiian dance that could serve as a companion piece to *Hawaiian Rainbow*. Knowing what a great collaborator she had been on the first project, and that I could not produce a worthwhile film on the larger subject of Hawaiian dance without her knowledge and connections, I proposed that we produce the new film together, with me once again directing and editing and Vicky serving as offscreen interviewer and dance coordinator. In principle, she was fine with the idea, yet she also believed that, to do such a film correctly meant filming on all six of the primary Hawaiian Islands. Of course, doing so would require a much larger shooting budget, and we both knew that only one man would be capable of raising what was needed.

Predictably, our good friend, Dr. Neil Abercrombie, was just as enthusiastic as before, and immediately set about finding the money we needed for such an ambitious undertaking.

However, while waiting on Neil to work his magic, I was pleasantly occupied elsewhere. First, on January 24, 1988, my first wife gave birth to the first of our two sons, Robert Marvin Mugge, named after my sociologist father, Dr. Robert H. Mugge, and our longtime family friend, architect Marvin R. A. Johnson, FAIA. At around the same time, I was asked to return to the South of France and show a week's worth of my films at Rencontre Cinematographique de Digne, a festival held every April in the lovely town of Digne-les-Bains, perched among mountain peaks and lush forest in the region of Provence-Alpes-Côte d'Azur. Because my then wife was employed as a flight attendant, which allowed family members to fly for free, I could afford to bring her and young Rob along for the week, which also led to the novel experience of having a passport photo shot of our two-month-old son.

As it happened, the festival was held during rabbit hunting season, which meant that, at the official festival restaurant, every evening meal was somehow built around that local meat of the moment. Otherwise, I was treated extremely well by local press and audiences, all of whom forgave my inability to speak a word of their native language. And yet, my most vivid memories of the week are of a day trip to Nice, where we explored the Musée National Mark Chagall, holding Rob up to take in one gloriously colorful Chagall canvas after another, then dining on profiteroles in a cafe overlooking the Mediterranean.

Meanwhile, back in the Pacific region, Dr. Abercrombie convinced the Hawai'i State Legislature to appropriate $360,000 for our proposed film on Hawaiian dance traditions. This gave us enough money for Vicky to stage a two-day hula festival at Lanikūhonua on O'ahu, which we would film and record in its entirety; for us to take a substantial film crew to other major islands where we would film additional hālau; and for us to pay all the groups who would perform for us, whether at the festival or elsewhere. The only catch was that, on behalf of the state, the project was to be "overseen" by Roy Tokujo's company, Cove Enterprises, which operated the Paradise Cove Luau at Lanikūhonua, but that largely worked out fine as well.

Knowing from the start that I would need an especially large crew for filming Vicky's festival on Oʻahu, that I would also need to transport eleven persons to each of the five additional islands, and that I would have to engage in continuing diplomacy in order to keep production funding flowing, I realized that, for the first time, I would also need to hire a full-time line producer (much the same as a production manager). For all of my previous projects, I had spent as much time dealing with production as with direction. But this time around, directing would mean focusing all of my attention on dozens of crew members and hundreds of musicians and dancers and, therefore, I would need someone else to help with ordering equipment and supplies, purchasing air tickets, renting vehicles, reserving hotel rooms, booking restaurants, organizing laundry services, writing checks, preparing reports, and more. For that reason, I called upon my longtime friend Bob Maier, who had served such roles on many large-scale productions, from ambitious public television series to feature films directed by John Waters, and who, not surprisingly, was happy to join me in Hawaiʻi.

Of course, as the project began, some may have assumed the legislature had underwritten an extended vacation for Bob and me, if only because we made a preproduction trip to Honolulu in July of 1988 which seemed to include as much time in the ocean as it did taking meetings and making preparations. Yet, in fairness, we already knew that, when we returned in September for nearly four weeks of intense production, we could end up with no free time at all. And as it turned out, that was exactly what happened.

By the time Bob and I returned during the second weekend of September, Vicky had completed arrangements for her first Kamokila Campbell Hula Festival at Lanikūhonua which, again, was also the site of the Paradise Cove Luau. Included among her preparations was booking eleven top kumu hula and their respective hālau to perform at the festival, and several more hula schools for us to film on their home islands. Meanwhile, Bob and I had arranged for Larry McConkey, Erich Roland, Chris Li, and Dave Sperling to fly in to shoot the festival, Bill Barth to oversee general audio recording, and Randy Ezratty and Mark Shane of Effanel to record music and audio associated with festival performances. In addition, we had hired a large local crew to support our efforts, booked HMI lights to illuminate the Sunday performances as the sun began to set, and ordered a communication system, film and tape stock, and Effanel's music recording equipment, all of which would have to be flown in.

Early on, Vicky and I decided that the focus of the film should be the kumu hula, or master teachers, who had been creating and passing along traditional chants and dances since 500 CE, when the first Hawaiians migrated to Hawai'i from Tahiti. For this reason, I decided to title the film *Kumu Hula: Keepers of a Culture*. Vicky also explained that there were now two kinds of hula: *kahiko*, made up exclusively of ancient chants, which served as an oral history for the Hawaiian people, accompanied by traditional dances intended to illustrate their meanings; and *'auana*, which was the name for more modern songs, including those dating from the mainland popularization of Hawaiian culture in the early twentieth century, that inspired more varied forms of Hawaiian dance.

The primary thing to know was that the ancient chants and dances (kahiko), which had been passed along intact for as long as a millennium and a half, were not to be changed in any way, because they represented the earliest flowering of Hawaiian culture. Indeed, they had even managed to survive through the period of approximately seventy-five years when US marines, acting on behalf of American missionaries and plantation owners, took control of the islands and banned many aspects of native culture. Still today, the credibility of teachers of kahiko is only as good as that of the kumu hula with whom they have studied, and the educational lineage of such kumu hula going back many hundreds of years, even through the dark period when traditions continued underground.

Having seen other musical genres—including jazz, bluegrass, and zydeco—torn between those who endorsed only the earliest styles and approaches and those who believed all arts should continue to grow and transform, I found it heartening—and quite civilized—to see opposing traditions split into separate lanes. The prevailing notion was that any form of kahiko was legitimate, so long as its origins were traceable and appropriate and its key practices had not been altered, whereas anyone wanting to choreograph new dance moves, or compose or adapt new music, could always do so in the context of 'auana, which was the name given to all modern hula. Of course, as will be seen, disputes still could occur when a kumu hula came forward with radically different styles of kahiko chants and dances, allegedly learned on less-populated islands and with murky attribution.

Regardless of such theoretical maneuvering among top kumu hula—all of whom were teachers and artists (whether of the creative or interpretive variety), and some of whom were also cultural leaders and political activists—in that particular moment, my crew and I had a job to do, and our own concerns were therefore of a more practical sort. The first day of Vicky's hula festival, which was Saturday, September 17, was made up of workshops on the subjects of hula dancing (classes for beginning, intermediate, and advanced students), chanting (known as *oli*), drum-making, and lei-making. The teachers included kumu hula Kalena Silver, John Kaimikaua, Lydia Kauakahi, O'brien Eselu, Hu'i Park, and others, and we used a small crew to capture highlights, making excellent use of Larry's Steadicam and Bill's portable recording equipment.

The following day, our small army of technicians converged on the festival site where we once again set up multitrack recording equipment under a protective tent, erected HMI lights on tall stands, established four camera positions, assembled my communication system, hooked in my video monitors (which showed me what the camera operators were seeing), and prepared to shoot a day's worth of large-scale performances. The site was a hula mound—essentially a green hill on which dancers can perform and be widely seen and heard—and our crew was situated close by, with water behind us and audience members mostly seated on the flat grassy area between us and the mound.

Performances began with John Kaha'i Topolinski chanting as he led his hālau of male dancers in a snaking line up to the hula mound where they were the first to perform. After their set was complete, they were followed by ten other hālau under the following kumu hula: Coline Aiu Ferranti, Lydia Kauakahi, Frank Kawaikapuokalani Hewett, Nalani Kanaka'ole and Pua Kanahele, Aloha Dalire, Thaddeus Wilson and O'Brian Eselu, Keone Nunes, Alicia K. Smith, Vicky Holt Takamine, and others. The twenty or more dancers in each group ranged from all female, to all male, to a mixture of the two, and from the very young (keikis) to largely young adult, but with generally older kumu hula as their teachers.

Female dances and costumes tended to express varying degrees of femininity (though no lack of assertiveness), while male dances and costumes were more forceful and masculine, frequently evoking warrior traditions. At the same time, whereas kahiko presentations incorporated chanting and percussion from the kumu hula, the dancers, or both, 'auana presentations utilized modern musicians, usually performing off to one side. Probably the best known of participating ensembles was slack-key guitarist Ledward Kaapana's trio, I Kona, and we also organized a separate slack-key guitar jam featuring Ledward along with Raymond Kāne and George Kuo, but were unable to fit their group performance into the film.

Where I felt it appropriate, I asked Larry to use his Steadicam to give me moving shots or close-up coverage of both the dancers and the musicians. But otherwise, I had all four cameras shoot from tripods in order to provide dependably varied viewpoints that I could later intercut to convey scale, energy, and essence.

Sunday evening, after we had finished shooting, I injured my back while lifting Erich's camera into one of our rented minivans (probably straining my psoas muscle). That put me out of commission for the next two days. Fortunately, though, on Monday, September 19, Bob, Larry, and others were able to handle the returning of rental equipment, the shipping of exposed film stock to my lab in Virginia, and the transporting of several key crew members back to the Honolulu airport. Then, on Tuesday, most remaining crew members—including Bob, Vicky, Larry, Erich, Bill, two camera assistants, a production assistant, and a still photographer—flew on to Moloka'i and began doing some general filming without me. Finally, to my great relief, I was well enough to join them there the following day.

On Thursday, we filmed singing cowboy Clyde "Kindy" Sproat on Moloka'i as he sang traditional paniolo (Hawaiian cowboy) songs, accompanying himself on 'ukulele. His songs also were accompanied by two pretty young dancers from Moana's Hula Hālau, with Vicky quickly teaching them moves for each of Kindy's songs. Despite the heat, Kindy wore cowboy boots, jeans, a colorful Hawaiian shirt, and a straw cowboy hat with a flower-filled band around it, while the two young women wore matching, off-the-shoulder black dresses, decorated with white and brown palm frond designs.

Kindy, who lived on the Big Island of Hawai'i, was scheduled to be away during the time we would be shooting there. So, he agreed to let us film him on Moloka'i, which was a sparsely inhabited island known for its cattle ranches. His deep, masculine singing voice, like Raymond Kāne's, was a major change from the high-pitched falsetto singing we generally heard in the islands, and his folksy, outgoing personality was a treat as well.

On Friday, September 23, everyone traveled to Maui and spent the evening watching the hula show at the Maui Hyatt. In return for an excellent rate on our hotel rooms, we had promised to film the show and try to feature excerpts as examples of commercial uses of hula which, generally speaking, can still be legitimate. Therefore, after relaxing for much of the day on Saturday, we filmed the hula show that night. However, for whatever reason, the hotel provided far fewer dancers on Saturday than they had on Friday, that made the footage less interesting than anticipated, and I did not end up using it.

Kumu hula Elaine Kaopuiki and her Na Hula O La'i Kealoha hālau perform a traditional kahiko hula on the Island of Lana'i. (photographed by film crew, 1988)

On Sunday morning, September 25, we flew to the island of Lāna'i for the day and filmed kumu hula Elaine Kaopuiki and four members of her Na Hula O La'i Kealoha hālau performing both kahiko and 'auana atop large rocks jutting out into the ocean. Lāna'i was another sparsely populated island, this one filled with pineapple plantations. Yet, every island had its own unique personality, whether in terms of topography, local culture, or the people we met. Elaine Kaopuiki, who alternated between percussion instruments and 'ukulele, depending on the type of dance to be performed, wore a white robe, a thick necklace of intertwined yellow and brown beads, and a thick wreath of mostly purple flowers on her head. For their part, her four dancers wore puffy yellow dresses, thick black necklaces, and wreaths of multicolored flowers. The sun was so hot that day that one of the dancers was overcome, though she recovered quickly, and planes flying in and out were so small that two flights in each direction were required to transport all of our equipment. Still, we shot some great performances, barely returning to our hotel in time for a late dinner.

Sticking to Maui once again, we spent Monday, September 26 at Ulu-palakua Ranch with kumu hula Nina Maxwell, her supportive husband Charles, and more than two dozen young women from their hālau, Pu-kalani Hula Hale. The younger girls wore red tops and white skirts, the older girls wore red tops and gray skirts, and Nina Maxwell and her assistant wore more flowing versions of the same. In addition, each of the women wore a yellow necklace and a wreath of green leaves on her head.

Robert Mugge poses with the younger dancers of kumu hula Nina Maxwell's Pukalani Hula Hale hālau on the Island of Maui. (photographed by film crew, 1988)

The spot selected for filming was a hilly, green area high enough above the water to feature breathtaking views of neighboring islands. There, to the rhythmic accompaniment of Nina's and her assistant's chanting and large hollow *pahu* (drums), the young women performed several dances from a standing position, and one from a sitting position, but always with Larry's Steadicam swirling among them. During the three hours of assorted takes, the smoke from burning sugarcane slowly blotted out the sun, until the air grew heavy and the sky gray.

Winding up the day, Vicky conducted interviews with Nina and Charles Maxwell, and the hālau provided dancers and filmmakers alike with a late lunch. According to Charles, "The hula is the most important part of the Hawaiian culture. What we have now are remnants of that past culture. But it's so important, because everything else of the culture has been obliterated by the Western culture, and has been intermingled—has been diluted. So, if our hula is also diluted, then we have nothing pure to go back to."

Tuesday, September 27 was our final day on Maui, though departures to the Big Island were made in shifts. While one camera crew left very early in order to capture local color, the rest of us stayed behind a few hours in order to film Pua Kanahele (kumu hula, along with her sister, Nalani Kanaka'ole, of Hālau O Kekuhi) speaking to her class at Maui Community College. Pua's class was moved outdoors for the occasion, and she spent the entire hour discussing issues of interest to our production. For example:

When you get the title of being a kumu hula . . . I expect you to know all of the deities of the hula. I expect you to know all of the vegetable manifestations of the deities. I expect you to know what kind of dyes you can make from all of these vegetable manifestations. I expect you to know how to make different kinds of *lei* [ornaments worn about the head or neck] and what the different styles represent . . . what the different flowers represent. I expect you to know how to translate those chants, not only at the literal level, but also the *koana* [hidden meanings] of the chants as well. To me, that is a kumu hula.

That evening, crew members were reunited at the Kona Hilton and decided to dine together on the hotel's "Chinese Buffet." Unfortunately, what seemed at first to be a good decision turned very bad indeed when both cameramen, a camera assistant, and I were all stricken with food poisoning. Somehow, the next morning, one of the cameramen and his assistant were able to work with Vicky as she conducted interviews with kumu hula George Na'ope and two others at Hulihe'e Palace, but the other cameraman and I were too sick to leave our rooms. We were still feeling ill by later in the afternoon, though, luckily, we felt well enough to help film groupings of dancers and musicians in a garden just outside the hotel. First came a unique presentation by kumu hula Iris Nalei Napaipai-Kunewa and four young dancers of Hālau O Kaleiho'ohie, and that was followed by kumu hula Etua Lopes, leading George Na'ope's Kona Garden School of Hawaiian Arts.

It took all of Wednesday night for the symptoms of food poisoning to pass. But by Thursday morning, still another problem was revealed. Bill Barth discovered that, during the hectic filming of the afternoon before, he had inadvertently recorded over much of George Na'ope's interview. The crew therefore reassembled at Hulihe'e Palace so that Vicky could conduct a second interview with George. As it happened, the second interview turned out better than the first, which, if I may say so, was at least partially due to the director being present for the second attempt, and we also filmed a lovely chant by George, accompanied on nose flute (played the way it sounds) by Kahea Beckley. Among other things, George said:

> The Hawaiian language, especially in the hula, tells a story, and the important thing is that Hawaiian words mean so many different things. So, one teacher would interpret it to fit him or her, and the other on this way and that . . . They're just doing their own *mana'o* [idea, interpretation] for each dance . . . because the hula, for me, is the ability to create one's most inner feelings.

Another of Pua Kanahele's comments built upon those thoughts:

> I've seen the hula change—you know, the styles of hula change. And of course, you have hula that comes from O'ahu and Kaua'i. You have hula that comes from Moloka'i. You have hula that comes from Hawai'i [meaning, the Big Island]. And all of these hulas are done in different styles, and originally were done for different reasons. And so, you'd expect that our hula would look different.

Happily, we were already shooting all of the variations mentioned and so felt that we were getting the lay of the land. But less fortunately, this extra setup and shooting time meant our crew could not reach its next hotel in Hilo (also on the Big Island) until well after nightfall. As a result, most crew members decided simply to eat dinner and go to bed, because Friday, September 30 promised to be the most demanding day of the trip.

The next morning, we left the hotel at 5:00 a.m., drove roughly an hour to the summit of Kilauea Volcano, set up our equipment beside Halema'uma'u Crater, and filmed Kaipo Frias of the Kanaka'ole hālau as he performed a powerful chant to the goddess Pele. Considering the sulfurous smoke rising all around us, the segment, which I planned to use for opening the film, turned out surprisingly well, made that much more interesting by Kaipo's traditional (and quite minimal) clothing.

After that, we had to return to our hotel again and prepare for filming an outdoor interview and performance featuring four colorfully dressed women representing three generations of the famous Beamer family. The women performed several songs for us, accompanying themselves with small acoustic instruments, and Malama Solomon chanted as her sister, Hulali Solomon Covington, performed a dance demonstrating the "Beamer method of hula." Finally, they discussed how the eldest of their group, Louise Leiomalama Beamer, had served as the dance and language adviser for the 1937 Bing Crosby movie *Waikiki Wedding*, permitting us to rationalize including a scene from that film in our own. But even then, our day was not yet over, because we still had to fly to Lihue, check in at the Sheraton Kaua'i, and prepare for yet another all-day shoot on Saturday.

Somehow, we found the strength to rise again the next morning, drive a couple of hours north to Hā'ene, Kaua'i, haul cumbersome equipment up the steep and overgrown side of a mountain without the help of roads or trails, film hālau Ka 'Imi Na'auao O Hawai'i Nei as its members cleaned up the *hula heiau* (a sacred performance space on a plateau partway up the mountain), film an interview with kumu hula and political activist Roselle Bailey, and finally film take after take of John Kaimikaua's mysterious animal dances in the intense sun. Actually, these unusual kahiko dances, which the very creative but somewhat controversial John Kaimikaua claimed to have been taught to him by a prominent kumu hula, should have been filmed on Moloka'i while we were there. But the dancer Kaimikaua needed for these dances was not available during our initial trip to Moloka'i. So, she and John were filmed on Kaua'i instead, with him telling an introductory story, then chanting and playing a pahu as she performed the accompanying "dog dance."

Next, on Sunday, October 2, director of photography Larry McConkey left for home, as did some of our Hawai'i-based crew members, while the rest of us headed back to Moloka'i for the night. John Kaimikaua had convinced us to shoot at least one of his dances on the correct terrain and assured us that he and another dancer would be waiting for us there. So, Monday morning, we joined him and the dancer on a grassy hill overlooking the ocean. Once again, he provided an introductory story, then chanted and played a large pahu while a slim young woman performed a bewitching dance for the goddess Laka. Finally, our crew returned to the airport and caught a late flight back to O'ahu.

The following day, our remaining crew accompanied Vicky Takamine to her university office. And there, we filmed as she typed an English translation of an ancient Hawaiian chant into her computer, providing a closing image I had imagined for the film. As Sun Ra had done with African American music, bringing the ancient into harmony with the technological present or future, Vicky was doing with Hawaiian music and dance. Of course, as I write this more than three decades later, there is nothing at all futuristic about Vicky's 1988 computer.

That evening, the last of us celebrated the end of filming, and everyone still present was paid. Then, the following day, Bill Barth and Erich Roland returned to the mainland, and Bob Maier and I met again with Vicky Takamine, Roy Tukujo, Neil Abercrombie, and others before leaving, ourselves, on Thursday, October 6.

Back in Philadelphia once again, I began reviewing and editing a vast amount of 16mm footage. As I did, I received occasional visits from music consultant Dr. Ricardo D. Trimillos, dance consultant Dr. Adrienne L. Kaeppler (not involved with the project until this point), and my fellow producer Vicky Holt Takamine, all of whom gave me feedback for my latest edits, while also helping me retain the meanings and spellings of a host of Hawaiian words and names. However, to my great frustration, on March 9, 1989, just before the three of them arrived to give feedback for my completed rough-cut, I went to purchase a case of beer for use in entertaining them, slipped on a sheet of ice, and broke my left leg. This proved a hindrance during my final stages of postproduction, especially music and sound mixes in New York City. But what kept me going through this challenging final stage of the project were inspiring words from kumu hula George Na'ope:

As I said earlier, they can stand on their heads, as far as I'm concerned, in the modern hula. But kahiko, keep it traditional, so that at least we have *something* that still belongs to Hawai'i, you know. And the hula *is* Hawai'i; the hula is the *history* of Hawai'i. Remember, we had no written language. Everything was in the *po'o*, in the mind. You have to remember they handed down, from one generation to the next generation, each chant.

Or as kumu hula Pua Kanahele expressed the same idea: "Even if other things are being introduced which, you know, I don't necessarily like, the continuation of hula is important."

A year after we shot the film, Vicky arranged several days of screenings at Honolulu's Hawai'i Theatre, beginning with an invitation-only world premiere on September 2, 1989, followed by a reception and attended by virtually all project participants (thanks, in large part, to Vicky staging a second annual hula festival at Lanikūhonua, which once again gave her the ability to fly in hālau from other islands). Then, in November of 1989, I showed *Kumu Hula: Keepers of a Culture* as part of a weeklong retrospective of my films at Festival dei Popoli, a documentary festival in Florence, Italy (where I also was thrilled to be a festival juror along with British director Lindsay Anderson and French cinéma vérité pioneer Jean Rouch), and in April of 1990, did the same thing again at Banlieues Bleues, a film festival in the suburbs of Paris, France (highlights of which included my hanging out with a sweat-soaked, tuxedoed Al Green after his unrelated concert in the city, then having my wallet stolen while seated in an outdoor café).

But more important, with $12,000 left in the film's production budget, plus another $12,500 paid for broadcast of an abridged version of *Kumu Hula* as part of PBS's *Alive From Off Center* series (first shown July 12, 1990), I was able to arrange a ten-city tour of the film with live performances by Vicky and four of her dancers. The ten venues, each of which also made contributions to the costs of the tour, included the Pacific Film Archive in Berkeley, California; the Boulder Theater in Boulder, Colorado; the Denver Film Society in Denver, Colorado; the Dallas Museum of Art in Dallas, Texas; Webster University in Webster Groves, Missouri (a suburb of St. Louis); Global Village's Documentary Festival of New York at Joseph Papp's Public Theater in New York City; the Neighborhood Film Project at International House in Philadelphia, Pennsylvania; the American Film Institute Theater at the Kennedy Center in Washington, DC; Hunter Todd's Houston International Film and Video Festival in Houston, Texas; and the AFI/LA Filmfest (American Film Institute) in Los Angeles, California. Because of my screenings in Paris, I could only be present for a handful of dates on the American tour, which ran from April 8 through April 22 of 1990. But I was pleased that the participating venues, most of which had been screening my films for years, were giving as warm a welcome to Hawaiian dancers and musicians as the people of Hawai'i had given to my crews and me.

Chapter Five
Cross Road Blues

Deep Blues (1991)

Hellhounds on My Trail: The Afterlife of Robert Johnson (1999)

or years, I thought about producing a film on Mississippi blues. My interest was stoked by a series of trips to Memphis, Tennessee, during which I visited two close friends, David Appleby and Steve Ross, with whom I had studied in Temple University's MFA program in Documentary Filmmaking. First David, and then Steve, had taken faculty positions at Memphis State University, later renamed the University of Memphis, finding the city a fertile base for their own award-winning productions. Thanks to the two of them inviting me to screen my earliest professional work for their students and, in the process, introducing me to members of the local music and film communities, I was prepared to shoot *Gospel According to Al Green* there in 1983 and additional music-related films as opportunities permitted.

The next such opportunity came in the spring of 1990 when Dave Stewart, half of the hugely popular British rock group Eurythmics, reached out to author and Rolling Stone contributing editor Robert "Bob" Palmer. While Dave was growing up in the north of

England and developing wide-ranging musical interests, his cousin, then a teacher in Memphis, sent him blues records, blue jeans, and other artifacts of the region. These items provided such a profound influence that, once he became a world-famous rock star, he decided to "give something back" to those he felt had paved the way for him. And having been impressed by *Deep Blues*, Palmer's highly regarded book that chronicled the origin of blues in Mississippi and its migration to Memphis, Chicago, Detroit, St. Louis, Kansas City, and other American cities, he asked his chief operating officer, Eileen Gregory, to see if Bob would be willing to help with a blues-related film.

From 1976 to 1988, Bob had also served as chief pop music critic for the New York Times, and in that role, had become a fan of my films on Sun Ra, Al Green, Sonny Rollins, and others which he called "definitive." After leaving the Times, he relocated to Olive Branch, Mississippi, essentially a suburb of Memphis, and when Eileen tracked him down there in 1990, he was fully focused on writing, teaching, and playing music. At first, he showed little interest in working on a film, a related CD, or anything else. But he told Eileen that, if she could get me to direct a film, he would consider collaborating. For this, I shall always be grateful, because soon thereafter, Eileen tracked me down through my then friend and distributor Bruce Ricker of Rhapsody Films, Inc., and we all (Dave, Eileen, Bob, and I) agreed to work together.

The project began with Bob, Eileen, and me planning a weeklong preproduction trip through Memphis and much of Mississippi. The idea was to visit pertinent locations and to meet the artists whom Bob thought should be included in the film, as well as a few of particular interest to Eileen and me. As it turned out, though, Bob had recently begun a personal relationship with a young, Little Rock-based music journalist named JoBeth Briton, and he wanted her to accompany us. Eileen was against it, but acting as intermediary, I convinced her that this was nonnegotiable for Bob. So, our preproduction trio suddenly became a quartet. As with Yoko Ono's presence during recording of the Beatles' *Let It Be* album, having JoBeth around from preproduction through production was never a problem, except that it split Bob's attention between work at hand and the woman on his arm, just as Yoko had done with John Lennon.

Early in October, Eileen and I flew to Memphis where she rented a car for a week. Then she, Bob, JoBeth, and I set out on the prelude to our big adventure. In Holly Springs, Mississippi, we attended a Sunday performance at Junior Kimbrough's juke joint, noting the white lightning (moonshine) being sold in old whiskey bottles; the pig cooking in the ground out back (soon to be reconfigured as barbecue sandwiches); and the two even tinier shacks beyond that, one of which was reputedly used for gambling. We also stopped by the Holly Springs home of R. L. Burnside, who told Eileen and me that he currently had no guitar of his own, but that, if we would give him $150 in cash, he could purchase a guitar, amplifier, and keyboard from a junkie who needed money. Eileen told him to forget it, but I gave him $100 and said just to buy the guitar and amp, because that's all he would need when we returned.

On the same trip, we also visited Jessie Mae Hemphill at her trailer home in Como, Mississippi; Roosevelt "Booba" (pronounced "Booby") Barnes at his Greenville, Mississippi music club; Eugene Powell at his daughter's home in the same city; Big Jack Johnson at his home in Clarksdale, Mississippi; and Clarksdale-based blues historian Jim O'Neal (with his partner, blues-obsessed chiropractor Dr. Patricia "Patty" Johnson) at O'Neal's Stackhouse Delta Record Mart, which loosely resembled a Mississippi riverboat. By the time we drove back to Memphis, we had worked out more or less who would be filmed when and where; what each artist or act would be paid; and other details that determined the size of our crew, the size of our budget, the equipment needed, the amount of film stock to bring, and our overall budget. And yet, in one area, we were not as well-prepared as we could have been, and that was the working relationship between Eileen and me.

In the beginning, although I was in Philadelphia and Eileen in Los Angeles or London, we collaborated well in our general project planning. In fact, she graciously allowed me to select my own crew, which I loaded with longtime business friends and associates: Bob Maier as line producer, Erich Roland as director of photography and

Steadicam operator, Chris Li as second cameraman, Bill Barth as audio director, and Johnny Rosen's Fanta Professional Services to oversee multitrack music recording. She even allowed me to fly in two of our *Kumu Hula* crew members from Hawai'i—cameraman and Steadicam assistant Phil Nordblom, and camera and production assistant Emmett Dennis—since they had served Bob Maier and me well on that recent and somewhat similar production, and accepted suggestions from David Appleby and Steve Ross of two former students, Craig Smith and Quincy McKay as, respectively, camera assistant and grip. These last four were great hires, because Craig and Quincy were both hilarious, which helped to lighten some of our darker hours, and Emmett and Quincy were both African American, which gave us a bit more credibility as we prepared to work almost entirely in Black communities.

Yet, once we got on location, which we did a few weeks later, the relationship between Eileen as producer and me as director began to unravel, which, eventually, would nearly scuttle the production. From Eileen's point of view, she was likely dismayed to have initiated the project on Dave's behalf, and then spent a year conducting research on her own, only now to see actual creative control passing to me. But her frustrations were easily matched by my own, in that I did not have the autonomy I had enjoyed on other projects, and I resented being second-guessed on even the most routine of decisions. As a result, when disagreements arose, we were blessed to have Dave Stewart's easygoing brother John with us as well. John Stewart owned a London-based company called Oil Factory that specialized in the production of music videos for use on MTV and other programmers of video clips, and he agreed to serve as the film's second producer, never realizing that his primary role would be to keep the peace between two rival power centers.

Still a bit naive about the challenges awaiting us, Bob Maier, Eileen, and I flew to Memphis on Tuesday, October 23, 1990 and began working with Bob Palmer on our final preparations. By Friday, we had been joined by John Stewart from London, Bill Barth from Pennsylvania, Erich Roland from Washington, DC, Phil Nordblom and Emmett Dennis from Honolulu, and Louis Skorecki, a journalist friend of mine, from Paris. Since Louis had offered to write a big feature story about the project for his French paper *Libération*, where he already had published raves for past films of mine, Eileen agreed to let him join us, so long as he agreed to reimburse her for his share of location expenses. Also arriving that day via FedEx (or Federal Express, as we knew it at the time) was our communication system.

At eleven o'clock Friday night, after all the new arrivals had settled into our Memphis hotel, the Radisson on Union Avenue, I attended a reunion concert of Insect Trust, which was Bob Palmer's late sixties psychedelic fusion band. My own musical tastes are broad enough that I could enjoy Bob's improvised jazz riffs, even within the context of sixties-style rock, and even coming from his wailing clarinet. Later, though, I would consider this performance to have been a warning, like a train whistle cutting through a late-night Delta mist.

As to Dave Stewart, by this point, he was touring the US with his current band, the Spiritual Cowboys, and despite fully funding our film (aside from a promised acquisition fee from Avril MacRory, Andy Park's successor at Britain's Channel 4), had no interest at all in appearing onscreen. However, in order to tie together all of the disparate material we would be shooting, I had come up with a storyline wherein Dave would travel to Memphis, look around a bit with Bob Palmer, and then ask him to head out across Mississippi, recording a variety of blues acts for a future CD release. In reality, our only plan at the time was to make a film, but I had no desire to create a self-reflexive work on the making of a film. So, I came up with the CD scenario (which stretched the truth only slightly), and through Eileen, asked Dave if, between his tour dates, he could fly to Memphis just long enough to help us establish that narrative. I also argued that, in so doing, he would assure the film's appeal beyond simply hardcore blues fans, in that his presence alone could attract white suburban rock fans to experience richer forms of blues than the basic blues rock that thus far had entered the mainstream.

Agreeing to this plan, Dave arrived in Memphis early Saturday afternoon, October 27, and was driven straight to Beale Street where we filmed him listening to a pair of blues musicians on a corner, staged his initial meeting with Bob Palmer (staged, yet nonetheless real), established the notion of Dave commissioning Bob to record assorted Mississippi blues acts, discussed the Disney-like makeover of Beale (once the heart of the city's Black entertainment district), and stepped into A. Schwab (the family-owned general store and soda fountain in operation since 1876) to learn about its early sales of blues and gospel records and ongoing sales of voodoo charms and potions. Then, later that evening, we drove across the Mississippi River to the West Memphis, Arkansas home of seventy-six-year-old barrelhouse blues piano player Booker T. Laury.

Although Laury had appeared in *Great Balls of Fire*, the 1989 Jerry Lee Lewis portrait starring Dennis Quaid, and was lifelong pals with well-known pianist Memphis Slim, his notoriety was far more regional than that of his recently deceased friend, yet David Appleby had introduced me to him in a Beale Street club in the 1970s. I should also note that, when paying blues musicians for a performance, it was customary to provide a fifth of whiskey as well. So, we did as expected with each new subject. And on this night in particular, as we shot our convivial, bald-headed host performing at home, Palmer and Stewart became his onscreen audience, happily partaking of their host's libation.

The following day would be devoted to filming two giants of North Mississippi hill country blues. Although virtually unknown until our film was released in 1991, followed by albums produced for a new label called Fat Possum Records, Holly Springs residents Junior Kimbrough and R. L. Burnside would go on to attain legendary status. The night before, second cameraman Chris Li had flown in from Washington, DC, and both Johnny Rosen's music recording truck and Mark Tye's lighting and grip trucks had driven in from Nashville. So, we all headed to Holly Springs, roughly an hour from Memphis, though keeping our hotel rooms at the Radisson near Beale Street, and next door to the better-known but more expensive Peabody Hotel where Dave was staying.

Certainly, *Kumu Hula* had been my first musical road movie, albeit one where the greater emphasis was on dance, and where driving from town to town was extended by also flying back and forth among Hawai'i's six larger islands. Yet, this notion of a filmmaking caravan fully took effect with *Deep Blues*, wherein a string of multiple vehicles roamed from location to location, and from one rural motel to another. As partially noted before, these vehicles included cars and minivans for producers and crew, a van for camera and audio equipment, Johnny Rosen's music recording truck, and lighting technician Mark Tye's lighting and grip trucks, which included a large generator for power in isolated locations. The strategy behind our serial excursions was to move as quickly as possible, in that every new day on the road meant significant new production expenses, but not so quickly that, instead of multiple, in-depth looks at talented musicians in exotic locations, we ended up with "drive-by shootings" so superficial that they revealed nothing worth seeing, hearing, or knowing.

Sunday morning, our fleet of vehicles converged upon Junior Kimbrough's tiny rural juke joint in Chulahoma, just east of Holly Springs and—not unlike American soldiers approaching South Vietnamese hamlets with tanks, helicopters, and mountains of munitions—simply overwhelmed it. We were greeted there by sixty-year-old Kimbrough (born David Kimbrough Jr. in Hudsonville, Mississippi) and his friend Sammy Greer who, together, operated the juke (or jook) in a small cabin Sammy had constructed from repurposed cedar logs and named the Chewalla Rib Shack (until a couple of years later, when Greer tired of the juke joint lifestyle, and Kimbrough opened his own better-known Junior's Place, also in Chulahoma). As Kimbrough and Greer once again cooked a large pig in a pit out back and filled used whiskey bottles with homemade white lightning, my sound and lighting technicians set up as best they could in the cramped little building and surrounding woods, and I took a smaller contingent to film Bob Palmer and Dave Stewart with R. L. Burnside.

Executive producer Dave Stewart trades guitar licks with musician R. L. Burnside at Burnside's Holly Springs, Mississippi home. (frame from film, 1990)

To my chagrin, despite the money I had given Burnside to purchase a guitar and amplifier, he still had neither. But fortunately, Dave had brought along two guitars and an amplifier of his own, so we were able to film R. L. performing two of his signature songs ("Jumper on the Line" and "Long Haired Doney"), then teaching Dave the latter one. We also filmed Bob and Dave approaching the two-room shack where sixty-three-year-old Burnside lived with his wife, Alice Mae, and the younger of their thirteen children, then filmed R. L. emerging from his front door to greet them.

Although we had planned to film singer, songwriter, and guitar player Jessie Mae Hemphill, as well as her fife and drum band, in Como, Mississippi on Monday, in order to save time, we decided to have crew members pick them up and bring them to Holly Springs on Sunday. Then, once Erich, Chris, Bill, and I finished shooting Dave and Bob with R. L., we returned to film Jessie Mae's Fife and Drum Band (Napoleon Strickland on fife, Abe Young on snare drum, and Jessie Mae on bass drum) in back of Junior's juke shortly before dusk. And since Johnny Rosen's truck was parked close by, I had him run cables to where we were standing and do a multitrack recording, even though, normally, I might have had Bill Barth record them more simply. Then, with the sun preparing to set, we filmed Bob and Dave conducting an outdoor chat with Jessie Mae before walking her inside. Overall, Dave was so captivated by Jessie Mae's talent and personality that, learning that her trailer had no running water, he paid to have a well dug for her.

Music director Robert Palmer and executive producer Dave Stewart chat with North Mississippi musician Jessie Mae Hemphill outside of Junior Kimbrough's Chulahoma juke joint. (frame from film, 1990)

Meanwhile, I had known since our preproduction trip that lighting such a minuscule concert space as the Chewalla Rib Shack would be a challenge, but director of photography Erich Roland and the lighting technicians supplemented the few lights we could fit by fogging up the windows on either side of the performers and aiming powerful lights in from outside. Then, as dancers and drinkers began claiming their favorite spots around the room, we realized that only two of our three cameras would fit inside with them, along with me kneeling down beside the cameramen and whispering or gesturing instructions. Otherwise, Johnny Rosen and his assistant Bill Saurel set out microphones for all of the musicians, including replacing Junior's personal mike, which they considered to be unusable.

The first artist to perform that day was Leander "Cotton" Howell, a fragile, elderly man who played guitar and sang with a spare, pleasant enough style, but without sufficient energy or magic to warrant his inclusion in the film. Next up was sixty-seven-year-old Jessie Mae Hemphill, and even though she, too, simply played her guitar and sang, her performance was raw, earthy, and hypnotic, somewhat suggesting a female John Lee Hooker, and she capped off my favorite of her songs, "You Can Talk About Me," with a sexy wink at the camera. Finally, we filmed an entire set by Junior himself, backed up by Joe Ayers on electric bass and Calvin Jackson on drums, including one cymbal that stood vertically and completely limp in front of him. What the three played was just as hypnotic as Jessie Mae's performance, and just as elemental, but with a droning, modal quality, and a drive that set the crowded and increasingly inebriated locals to dancing or gyrating in place, with a glow on their faces and electricity crackling through the room.

At that point, Bob Palmer got it into his head that his sitting in on clarinet with Junior would be appropriate for a film intended to document authentic Mississippi blues, the very music he had extolled with such eloquence in his book. Thus started a nightly ritual wherein he would ask if he could join the band while we filmed, and I would convince him that this was neither the time nor the place for a postmodern blending of styles, genres, and instrumentation. Instead, each night, I convinced him that he and JoBeth should join Johnny in the music recording truck where they could relax, offer occasional feedback, and quietly party on their own. Johnny also had a video monitor in his truck that showed the view of his one stationary camera facing the band, so he and those with him did not have to be totally in the dark about what was happening inside.

Ironically, as Junior's set concluded that first night, Dave grabbed an electric guitar and did some jamming of his own with R. L. Burnside and others. As I saw it, that was fine, because it was after the real work of the day was completed, and because a guitar was clearly more fitting than a clarinet for use in this setting. We even shot a bit of their jam, but decided it was better suited to being a home video bonus feature than a part of the film itself.

As our crew began packing up that night, Erich, Bill, and I filmed Dave saying goodbye to Bob Palmer in front of Junior's juke, declaring he would now need to return to his tour with his current band, but encouraging Bob to keep recording great material for what was then still a fictitious record album. Eventually, Dave would, indeed, decide to release a soundtrack CD for the film, and he enlisted Bob to oversee the mixing and sequencing of recordings made by Johnny Rosen and Bill Barth. But for now, it was simply a plot device, as was my plan to have Palmer "report back" to Stewart about each of the acts we would shoot and record in the days and nights to come.

Monday morning, October 29, as Dave departed from the Memphis airport, our caravan drove due south on legendary Highway 61, widely known as the "blues highway." All of us would eventually meet up in Greenville, essentially the heart of the Mississippi Delta. But my own minivan stopped and started along the way so that Erich and I could capture the regional flavor of billboards, bayous, cotton fields, and country stores on either side of the increasingly flat landscape. At one such store, we received a bit more flavor than expected when the owner chose to show us a jar of "peter pickles." Taking a turn viewing the pickles, which he recalls looking "eerily like human penises," line producer Bob Maier rushed directly back to the gravel parking lot and vomited his response.

After checking into our Greenville motel, we set off to film at the home of eighty-one-year-old blues musician Eugene Powell, who had once recorded as Sonny Boy Nelson. Unfortunately, in the few weeks since our preproduction trip, Powell had been plagued by gout and, therefore, could not perform. So, turning our attention elsewhere, we found our way back to Roosevelt "Booba" Barnes's ramshackle Playboy Club where we plotted approaches for the following night.

One of the results of long-term segregation was that many Southern cities had established Black entertainment streets—for example, Beale Street in Memphis and Farish Street in Jackson—usually including prominent music clubs. In Greenville's case, Nelson was the street of note, and the Flowing Fountain its most famous venue. Nevertheless, Booba's Playboy Club had also made a mark, though mostly as a place where Barnes himself could perform. Of course, by this point in Greenville's evolution, Nelson was known more for pimps, prostitutes, and crack dealers than it was for live music. And yet, Booba had managed to stand tall among all of that urban decay, and that was exactly how we planned to portray him.

Our Greenville motel, the Regency Inn, was almost exactly like every other motel in the state, regardless of chain. Its one true distinction was that the water for drinking and bathing there had a dark hue and an oily texture to it, which was unmistakable when showering, and which drove all of us to drink bottled water exclusively. As it happened, though, management was quite aware of this fact, to the point of leaving the following message in every room:

We at Regency Inn welcome our guests
To Delta hospitality you'll find at its best.
But we know you are wondering why the water's so brown,
It's the muddy Mississippi that runs through our town.
You can drink our water and bathe without fear,
For no one lives longer than the folks around here.

I later learned that this was untrue; the water was actually brown because it came from the Cockfield aquifer and was filtered through ancient cypress swamps where it picked up particles of wood and vegetation thousands of years old. Still, I thought it would be amusing to attribute all the special qualities of Mississippi blues to "something in the water" and, therefore, I asked Bob to read the poem aloud and then comment. Admittedly, we did not have the chance to film this until much later in the trip, at which point Palmer added his own unique spin, which was to sing the verses instead of reading them. Yet, again, since all the motels where we stayed had a similar look, both inside and out, we had no problem shooting this several days later and, in the process, suggesting that we were still in Greenville. It was not so much "movie magic" as it was the "art of the possible," under tight budgets and even tighter schedules.

On Tuesday, October 30, we spent most of the day setting up at the Playboy Club. And because of Nelson Street's poor reputation, we pulled all our vehicles onto a lot near the club, forming them into a circle, not unlike wagon trains in old TV and movie westerns. Of course, even here, we would need the generator to power our lights and recording equipment. And though we did not want to "pretty up" the cluttered and rundown interior of Booba's club, we did want to capture everything accurately. So, we spent a good deal of time positioning our lights, running audio cables, setting up microphones, establishing camera positions, and so forth. (Incidentally, Barnes got his distinctive, though misspelled nickname from his brother, who had been in the army and, reportedly, claimed Booba to be "worse than a booby trap.")

Midway through the afternoon, Frank Self, Greenville's friendly, white-haired mayor, unexpectedly stopped by. We later learned that Booba (again, pronounced "Booby") had phoned him that morning and told him to rush over and see what was happening. Learning our plans, the mayor pointed out that, on average, one person per week was killed on Nelson Street, and he therefore offered to send over uniformed policemen to assist our hired security guards in watching our vehicles and equipment. As a thank-you for that much-appreciated courtesy, we invited him to return that evening and be interviewed with Booba between sets. He happily agreed.

Once all was ready for our Tuesday evening shoot, we ourselves rushed off for supper at Doe's Eat Place, a family-owned Greenville institution featuring steaks and hot tamales. There, meat was ordered by the pound, cooked in an old pizza oven in the wall, and served in a crumbling brick building with down-home charm to spare. In later decades, Doe's would be franchised in cities throughout the South. But in our opinion, the original was still the best, if only because of its history as a grocery store that was opened in 1903, a bootlegging operation that started after the flood of 1927, a Black honky tonk that eventually served whites out the back door (in a reversal of the usual "carriage trade" under segregation), and finally a restaurant open to everyone. All of these businesses had been started by Big Doe Signa and his wife Mamie, and it was their descendants who made our crew so happy that particular day in October of 1990.

We had not seen Bob Palmer and JoBeth Briton the entire day, which was fine, since we had mainly focused on technical issues. But they did show up in time for dinner, and for Bob again to ask if he could sit in with the band. As delicately as I could, I asked that, instead, he once again join Johnny in the music recording truck, offering us his all-important "second set of ears," and Bob, generally a sweet and cooperative guy, readily complied. Of course, this was also the day I realized that Bob and JoBeth (Bob's future wife, with whom he was still in the first flush of a new relationship) were partying all night at our motel and then sleeping as late as we would let them. So, from that point forward, I allowed them to sleep as long as I could, after which we would shoot any stand-ups or interviews with Bob that required daylight. As Palmer's friend and fellow author William S. Burroughs (*Naked Lunch*) also demonstrated, sobriety, regular hours, and conventional morality were not prerequisites for creativity, but they could make one a more reliable collaborator.

Regardless, after devouring stunningly large and juicy steaks, we hurried back to Nelson Street for the night's entertainment. For the first time on this project, we had room in a venue for all three of our cameras, as well as for my rented communication system and video monitors, so that I could see what each of my cameramen was shooting and convey what each of them should do next. I also was happy to be joined by Patty Johnson, who knew all the local artists, their music, and their stories, which proved extremely helpful that night, as well as for days to come.

Fifty-four-year-old Booba was more than ready for us, of course, bedecked in a bright red suit, comically oversized gold jewelry, a modified afro, and whiskers. Throughout two fiery sets, he and his band of local musicians (including talented younger guitarist Lil' Dave Thompson, then a regular in his band) alternated between driving and smoldering numbers, many of which he had polished during several years of residency in Chicago, continued to develop upon his return to Mississippi, and recorded for his 1990 album, *The Heartbroken Man*, on Jim O'Neal's Clarksdale-based Rooster Blues label. But perhaps the most dramatic moments of the night were when he played his guitar strings with his teeth, likely showing why the top front ones, usually hidden by his upper lip, had turned completely black.

Between the two sets that night, we arranged a table and three chairs where we could film Bob interviewing Mayor Self together with Booba Barnes. Perhaps the most startling moment of this joint interview was when Mayor Self declared his intention to "clean up Nelson Street," implying that it could soon go the way of gentrified Beale Street in Memphis. But the most poignant moments came, first, with Booba's admission that local patrons of his club rarely applauded during his shows (though he noted that they had done so that night with our cameras present), and second, with Mayor Self stating what likely no city father had ever said before, which is that they were "proud" of Barnes and "appreciated" what he had done for the city.

If the ongoing presence with us of French writer Louis Skorecki, or the occasional busloads of Japanese tourists that would descend upon Delta hot spots, did not offer ample proof of worldwide interest in American blues, this was also the day we met German photographer Axel Küstner, whom we discovered doing his own documentation of Mississippi blues culture. Noting the high quality of his work, John and Eileen invited him to join us for the rest of our trip, asking only that he provide us with production stills for each of our remaining concerts. This, then, is how we ended up with professional-quality, black-and-white photographs for the Greenville, Clarksdale, and Bentonia performances. (Note: Ironically, the same thing had happened while we were filming in Jamaica in 1983, at which point we found German photographer Rosi Thielen shooting beautiful photos of Sunsplash performances and later arranged to use some of her stills to promote *Cool Runnings*.)

The following morning (Wednesday, October 31), our caravan backtracked, as planned, to Clarksdale, which happens to sit between Memphis and Greenville, and began preparing for a big Halloween concert at the Pastime Lounge. The headliner would be fifty-year-old Big Jack Johnson, known as "The Oil Man," due to his day job delivering heating oil to rural customers of Rutledge Oil Company. So, while most of our group set up lights, ran audio cables, and carved out shooting positions at the Pastime, a few of us met up with Jack, who allowed us to film him driving his oil truck down a Clarksdale street, then, at his home, primping for that night's concert. What was unique about Johnson's house was that, even though it was a single-story ranch, as his wife gave birth to each of their ten children, he kept adding new rooms which, for an outsider, produced a total labyrinth. Happily, though, he not only led us to the master bedroom where we filmed him, but also showed us the circuitous route out again.

On this production, as on all my own, we tried to find enticing ways to feed the crew each night, while not diverting them from essential tasks at hand. Consequently, Eileen arranged for a massive Boss Hogg barbecue smoker to be parked directly in front of the venue, primarily for the purpose of feeding us. Of course, as Erich and I watched smoke churning out of its black metal shell, as from a stationary locomotive (or even some demonic device in a Hieronymus Bosch hellscape), we could not resist filming it as well, along with a long-limbed local gentleman who began dancing beside it.

The audience attending the Pastime was there to see one artist and one artist only, which was Big Jack. So long as we filmed him first, which was our intention, the promoter was fine with us then shooting two other acts in the same venue. One of those would be CeDell Davis—best-known for being a protégé of itinerant blues legend Robert Nighthawk, as well as for playing slide guitar with a butterknife—and the other would be reunited Delta favorites the Jelly Roll Kings, featuring Sam Carr on drums, Frank Frost on harp and vocals, and Big Jack Johnson himself on guitar and vocals. However, this scenario would not go precisely as planned.

According to most sources, sixty-four-year-old CeDell had been born in Helena, Arkansas in 1926. As a ten-year-old child, he had contracted polio, which left him minimal control of his right hand and virtually no control of his left. Yet, by developing his butterknife slide technique, he eventually became a good enough guitarist to play professionally, including for ten years with Robert Nighthawk. Then, while playing a club in 1957, he was trampled during a police raid, leaving both of his legs sufficiently battered that, from then on, he was largely confined to a wheelchair. Still, he continued to perform, and at the time we were ready to film him in Clarksdale, Mississippi, he was living in Pine Bluff, Arkansas, a three-hour drive away. Nonetheless, Bob Palmer was determined to have him in the film, so he and JoBeth drove a rental vehicle to get him.

Certainly, Big Jack Johnson provided such a long and powerful concert (ranging from a spectacular version of "Catfish Blues," a Delta classic reinvigorated by Jack's pyrotechnic guitar playing, to a heartfelt, fourteen-minute version of his own autobiographical soul blues number, "Daddy, When is Mama Coming Home?") that, for a good while, we did not even notice the lengthy absence of Bob, JoBeth, and CeDell. However, once Jack was finished, we *did* notice and grew increasingly concerned until, finally, JoBeth delivered Bob and CeDell to the Pastime Lounge, both of them intoxicated from sharing our gift fifth of whiskey throughout their return trip. Despite our reservations, we then escorted Davis to the performance area where he would be backed by two members of Johnson's Memphis-based pickup band.

CeDell's normal sound, striking because of its subtle flirtation with atonality, had now plunged fully over the edge, resulting in a godawful racket that seemed to please no one except perhaps Palmer, who was too drunk to know the difference. As Davis and his perplexed accompanists went from one song to another, and then another, all equally dreadful (if only because the backup musicians were playing on pitch and on the beat, and CeDell was playing anything but), I also learned from our camera assistants that we were running low on film stock. I therefore rushed to Eileen and told her we needed to cease filming CeDell or else we would soon have to stop for the evening. To my amazement, she refused to believe me, insisting instead that we continue shooting. So, we did continue, and by the end of that set, not only did the camera crew confirm that we had run out of all stock brought to that night's location, but Johnny Rosen informed me that we were out of twenty-four-track recording tape as well.

Next up were the Jelly Roll Kings, but we now had no way to film or properly record them. As a result, I asked Johnny simply to mix their performance live to Bill Barth's two-track audio recorder, which at least meant that I would later able to use part of that recording as background music for the film's entry into the Delta. But I was furious, and when Eileen tried to say it somehow was *my* fault we had run out of stock, I told her that I quit the project.

Frankly, the stress of being second-guessed again and again over the past week had finally taken its toll on me, leading not only to severe pain in my lower back but also to an apparent sinus infection, my immune system seeming to have given up. After that night's shoot, Patty Johnson took me directly to her chiropractic office and rubbed a handheld electronic device back and forth across my lower back until I was numbed into submission, the pain at last reduced to a bearable roar. Fortunately, I next had a chat with John Stewart, who assured me that, henceforth, I could deal with him alone regarding production-related issues. That, along with a decent night's sleep, kept me on the project.

The following day, cameraman Chris Li, camera assistant Craig Smith, and production assistant Quincy McKay all returned to Memphis, and Johnny Rosen and Mark Tye took their respective trucks and assistants back to Nashville. But before Chris flew home to DC, he took a helicopter ride over Memphis and the Mississippi River in order to grab additional shots I needed for opening the film. Meanwhile, back in Clarksdale, Erich, Bill, and I spent the afternoon shooting Bob's interview with Wade Walton, the so-called "blues barber," who told us about shaving and grooming legendary bluesman Sonny Boy Williamson and others, beat out a rhythm with his razor strop, and performed a song while seated in his barber chair. After that, we filmed Jack Johnson being interviewed in a WROX studio by longtime radio personality Early "Soul Man" Wright. Then, we drove our remaining crew to a motel outside of Jackson, Mississippi, the state capital, where we would rest before our final day of shooting, and where, at last, I would capture Bob's thoughts about Greenville water.

Friday morning, we checked out of that latest motel and drove north again to Bentonia, Mississippi, known for its eerie landscape and haunting, minor-key style of "Devil blues," originated in the early twentieth century by Henry "Son" Stuckey, recorded in 1931 by Nehemiah "Skip" James, revived by James at blues festivals in the 1960s, and also practiced for decades by singer and guitarist Jack Owens, often accompanied by the younger blind harp player Bud Spires. Our first stop was the Blue Front Café, a neighborhood juke owned by musician Jimmy "Duck" Holmes, who would, himself, later carry the Bentonia blues torch, and who kindly directed us to the home of fifty-nine-year-old Spires. Then, with Bud onboard, we found our way to the rural, wood-framed home of eighty-five-year-old Owens, who had agreed to play for us on his front porch, which was brightly painted brick red and tan. Devil songs aside, we could not have arrived at a better time, what with it being a beautiful, sunny day, the musicians being in good health and spirits, and the two playing seamlessly together, with unexpected grace, charm, and humor.

Robert Mugge chats with blues singer and guitarist Jack Owens at Jack's home in Bentonia, Mississippi. (photographed by Axel Küstner, 1990)

Later that afternoon, we headed to Lexington, Mississippi where house painter-by-day and bluesman-by-night Lonnie Pitchford lived in a large, wood-framed house of his own with his wife Minnie and their daughter. Although he looked like a man in his twenties, he actually was thirty-five at the time, which still made him the youngest headliner for our project. With obvious irony, we had come there to watch him play the earliest blues instrument, which was the diddley bow, a single-stringed invention brought over from Africa (and the inspiration for rock and roll pioneer Bo Diddley's adopted name). As we filmed Lonnie, he nailed both ends of a piece of broom wire to the side of his house, pulled it tight, and used a crushed soda can to hold it out from the wall. He then plucked at the wire with his right hand while sliding a large, steel socket (made to be used with a socket wrench) up and down the string as he sang a traditional children's song about how "Johnny stole an apple from the apple tree."

Pitchford had been a protégé not only of Eugene Powell, but also of Robert Lockwood Jr., the stepson of legendary Robert Johnson, who had taught him to play many of Johnson's songs. Unfortunately, Lonnie could not demonstrate his guitar-playing prowess that day in that, like R. L. Burnside, he did not currently own a guitar, and Dave had taken away our spares.

After filming Pitchford, our remaining crew returned to Memphis where we spent our final night before dispersing. Then, midday on Saturday, we all met at the historic Peabody hotel for a final lunch together, during which Eileen presented each of us with a souvenir T-shirt which, for me, represented a much-appreciated peacemaking gesture. However, even more surprising was a gift I received at that lunch from Hawai'i-based cameraman and Steadicam assistant Phil Nordblom.

The day we had first entered the Delta, at my request, the minivan in which I was riding stopped so Erich could shoot a billboard welcoming us to Mississippi. There, Phil found a metal, red-white-and-blue map of the state which, presumably, had been attached to the billboard, but which now lay on the ground, a bullet lodged in its center. Then, during the days and nights to come, Phil convinced everyone on the crew to sign it, saying it was a souvenir for himself. Yet, to my surprise and delight, in the closing minutes of our final meal, he presented the flag to me.

Over the next day or so, all of us headed home again. As for myself, as usual with such a project, I would not rest easy till knowing the fate of all processed and work-printed film and transferred audio. And in fact, most of the news was good, though there was one heart-stopping disappointment. A few days after my return to Philadelphia, someone phoned from the lab in Richmond, Virginia and revealed that the Jack Owens and Bud Spires footage had to be seen to be believed. When I did finally receive it, I understood, in that the two men appeared to have been consumed by flames.

With location film shooting, a roll of 16mm stock, lasting ten or eleven minutes, would be loaded into a film magazine, which was then attached to the camera. After the roll had been exposed, the magazine was separated from the camera again and placed inside a black changing bag in which the camera assistant would carefully remove the film, place it in a protective can, bring that sealed can into the light, and write identifying information on its label. The exposed film would remain in that can while being transported to the lab where, in the dark once again, it would be placed on machines for processing and printing.

Most likely, the camera assistant had accidentally exposed the footage to light when removing it from the camera, though he swore he had not. All we knew for sure was that the images glowed as if on fire, and that affixing blame would accomplish nothing, since the footage could not be restored.

Fortunately, Eileen had done something very smart, which was to purchase so-called negative insurance. Such policies (too expensive for me ever to have purchased myself) ensured that, if anything happened to the master materials shot and recorded on location or in a studio (the film's "negative," as it were), the insurance company would pay for restaging and reshooting of whatever was lost. So, after months of editing, I suddenly returned to Memphis, joining Bob Palmer, Eileen, Erich, Bill, Craig, and Quincy for a second drive to Bentonia, and a second try at filming Jack Owens and Bud Spires in performance.

This time around, the day was not sunny as on our previous visit. Instead, it was cool and overcast. As for Owens himself, now he was fighting a cold. Still, he had once again dressed for the occasion. Tall and slim, he wore a blue suit and plaid shirt along with brown boots, brown belt, and brown cowboy hat, while the slightly heavier Spires wore a blue jacket over a white shirt, plus the dark sunglasses typically worn by blind musicians and lovingly satirized by Dan Ackroyd and John Belushi in their tongue-in-cheek Blues Brothers sketches, concerts, and films.

Little had changed about Owens's fenced-in yard, which still contained an abandoned "Delta 88" automobile; free-roaming chickens and ducks; timid, undernourished dogs; and a hog nearly as big as its outdoor pen. Just as before, this seemed the perfect backdrop for country blues, and the musicians themselves did not disappoint, with Bud wryly reciting a tale involving the Devil as trickster figure, that led seamlessly into Jack's version of the local Devil blues. Then, in further tribute to the Bentonia blues heritage, they performed the Skip James classic, "Hard Time Killin' Floor Blues."

A secondary benefit of the original Bentonia screwup, and of the insurance money provided for an Owens and Spires reshoot, was that we now could arrange a follow-up session with Lonnie Pitchford as well. Therefore, after returning Bud to his home, we raced to Lexington, Mississippi where we were once again to film Lonnie, though this time with Eileen's rented guitar in hand. However, when we arrived at Lonnie's house, his wife Minnie said he was out. No explanation was given, but since it was now past dusk, she asked us to go have dinner and promised that, when we returned, she would have him there waiting.

So, we did. We found the rather mediocre steakhouse she had mentioned, ordered and ate as quickly as possible, and rushed back to the Pitchford home again. This time, as predicted, Pitchford was present, though equally vague about where he had been. Seeing no reason to belabor the matter, I asked Lonnie to take a seat in his front parlor, asked Erich to establish moody lighting appropriate for Robert Johnson songs, asked Bill to mike Lonnie's voice and guitar (which usually meant aiming a single mike in such a way that the guitar would not overwhelm the voice), called for silence among the crew and family members standing in the shadows, and signaled

Lonnie to begin. What followed were stunning, crystalline versions of "Terraplane Blues," "Come On In My Kitchen," and "If I Had Possession Over Judgement Day."

Yet, while Lonnie did, indeed, play as if possessed, he struggled to provide coherent introductions for each song. Therefore, again and again, I would help him to organize his thoughts, weeding out extraneous words with each new take, until I finally felt we could use what we had. Afterwards, we drove the couple of hours back to Memphis, used up the last of our stock on nighttime driving shots, spent a final night in the city, and then, the following day, headed our separate ways again.

Several days later, while decompressing at home, I was relieved to hear from the lab that our replacement scenes looked fine. However, there *was* bad news, stemming from the fact that, since we had been given little notice as to when the new shoot would take place, Bill's stereo recorder had been in the shop receiving maintenance, which had forced him to rent another. But what none of us knew, until the lab transferred his quarter-inch tapes to the 16mm mag I used for editing, was that one of this new recorder's stereo heads was misaligned, causing occasional distortion on one of the two tracks. Ultimately, I did manage to edit around the worst of the distortion and minimize more in the final sound mix. Yet, in the end, we could not avoid concluding that, indeed, one should never mess with the Devil in Mississippi (as in Bentonia's classic Devil-centered music). Blues legends Robert Johnson and Tommy Johnson had told us as much, but apparently, we had to learn it for ourselves.

Shortly thereafter, I completed my rough-cut of the film, leaving periodic spots where I wanted Bob Palmer to provide narration: one where he would introduce himself at the start of the film, and others where he would "report back" to Dave Stewart. Bob was suffering from a terrible cold at the time, but he agreed to fly from Memphis to Philadelphia so that Bill Barth and I could record him in a Lancaster, Pennsylvania studio to which Bill had round-the-clock access.

We would be paying for studio time by the hour, so I wrote out drafts of what Bob should say at each point in the film and asked that he turn my skeletal prose into his own scholarly poetry. That way, we could get right to recording the morning after his arrival.

Yet, for whatever reason, Bob did not fulfill his assignment, either at home or on his flight. Therefore, when we got to the studio, we literally waited hours as he wrote a series of essays, when all that we needed, or even could use, were a few sentences for each of the designated spots. Still, once Bob had something on paper, I could help him to edit, while still retaining his personal style. Then, as we began, at last, to record his raspy, flu-inflected narration, and I realized how different he sounded than in his onscreen stand-ups, I had him declare his voice to be "hoarse from yelling in jukes joints," so at least we could justify the difference.

During that same visit, I also showed Bob my cut of the film, which he very much enjoyed. Then, because I knew he had never quite believed me about the quality of CeDell's performance, I showed him an edit of CeDell's entire set so that he could see and hear it for himself. With obvious sadness, Bob agreed that what Ce-Dell had played was not what either of us would call "good" atonality, as he would later capture when recording Davis for Fat Possum Records, but the result of a physical handicap combined with intoxication.

Now nearly finished, the film needed a name. From the beginning, Eileen had wanted to call it *Hard Times Mississippi*, but Bob and I had objected, believing that would emphasize financial struggle over heritage. We also proposed alternatives of our own, but none satisfied John and Eileen. Finally, in desperation, I asked Bob if we could suggest *Deep Blues* as the title. We both knew that Bob's book was a historical study of music of the region, whereas the film was more documentation of musicians currently active there. Yet, both book and film did emphasize the notion of deeper and richer sorts of blues, at least partially the result of African heritage. Happily, Bob was fine with the idea, and so were the producers, since they realized the obvious benefits of cross-promoting the film with Bob's book (and as of October 1992, with the relatively short-lived soundtrack CD as well). From there, the film was completed quickly, with Laurence Dunmore, an associate of John Stewart, creating hand-lettered film titles; Lee Manning, a Los Angeles employee of Dave Stewart, mixing our selected two-track and twenty-four-track music recordings; my friend Athan Gigiakos in New York doing the film sound mix; and my friends at Commonwealth Films in Richmond doing color correction and making 16mm prints.

By mid-1991, *Deep Blues* was in the can, and I arranged several early festival screenings, among which were the following: (1) a world premiere at the Sydney Film Festival on June 10, 1991, which I was unable to attend; (2) an October 8, 1991 screening at the Mill Valley Film Festival, with an accompanying performance by Lonnie Pitchford at the nearby Sweetwater club; and (3) four screenings, January 18 to 24, as part of the documentary competition at the 1992 Sundance Film Festival. The latter screenings were commemorated by my friend Mark Scheerer, a correspondent for CNN's *Showbiz Today*, who intercut brief interviews with Dave Stewart and me regarding the making of the film. Meanwhile, Channel 4, having acquired UK TV rights in advance, chose to broadcast a one-hour version of the film (which, happily, I have never seen) on June 22, 1991, and the producers initiated a couple of early theatrical runs, one of which was a weeklong AFI/USA Independent Showcase presentation beginning November 15, 1991 at Laemmle's Grande theater in Los Angeles, and the other a nine-day release beginning April 1, 1992 at the Red Vic Movie House in San Francisco (one of the independent arthouses around the country where my films occasionally showed).

The early screenings generated almost universal praise. But no one wrote about the film with more poetry than Michael Wilmington in the *Los Angeles Times:* "Robert Mugge's *Deep Blues* . . . is a movie no blues lover, no popular music aficionado, and no devotee of American culture and folkways should miss. It's a genuine document, deep and earthy; a peek into our national soul." He finished with, "And the last few [Robert] Johnson songs, played by young Lonnie Pitchford, show clearly how the blues began, how it lives on, how these bursts of seemingly transient anguish could, indeed, become eternal."

On the strength of those two initial runs, the producers signed with San Francisco-based theatrical distributor Tara Releasing for a modest national release. However, just before that release began, I arranged a five-day, twenty-screening run beginning July 31, 1992 at the Walter Reade Theater at New York's Lincoln Center (thanks to my friend Richard Peña, then program director for the Film Society of Lincoln Center, though formerly programmer for the theater at the School of the Art Institute of Chicago, where we had collaborated many times). Also, Bob Palmer convinced Tramps, the New York City music club, to hold an opening night party for the film and to bring in Junior Kimbrough and R. L. Burnside for two nights of performances, while Tara kicked off its own distribution by moving the film from Lincoln Center to New York's Quad Cinema, immediately after the Walter Reade run.

Of course, one thing about the blues is that it sometimes traffics in sadness, frustration, and disappointment, and that can be true of blues-related projects as well. As just one example, Louis Skorecki, who had said such wonderful things about my work in *Libération*, and for whom I had vouched with the producers, suddenly took off without warning near the end of location shooting, and without paying what he owed for his share of meals and hotel rooms. Then, literally adding insult to injury, after spending all that time with us, he never wrote his promised feature story about our production.

Even worse, Bob Palmer, with whom I had worked so closely throughout the project, waited until completion of the soundtrack album to issue the following statement: "Dave [Stewart] had also started Radioactive, his film production company, and he wanted to send a crew with me on my recording trip through Mississippi, documenting the making of the album. But from the first, we considered the album the whole point and focus of the project, and while I'm very, very proud of the film, I still feel that way." This, and all the rest of Palmer's CD-related press release, was exaggeration to the point of nonsense. At the time we made *Deep Blues*, with my long-standing audio people doing all the recording in the same ways we had done it for every other film of mine, there was no plan to create a soundtrack album, much less a freestanding one. It was only when Bill Barth and Johnny Rosen produced such great recordings that the idea took hold with the producers.

Bob expanded on his fantasy in the CD's liner notes, claiming that Dave Stewart "reached deep into his own pockets to send me out along the highways and back roads of Mississippi, with the aim of recording the music where it lives. We engaged Robert Mugge . . . to make a film of the journey." Somehow, he had come to believe the narrative I had designed to tie together the myriad scenes we were staging and recording, or else he simply took advantage of it in order to posit himself as the star of the venture. Indeed, in those same notes, he went on to claim that our last-minute changing of the film's title to *Deep Blues*, combined with the release of a soundtrack album which, of course, used the name of the film, made them, along with his earlier nonfiction history, "a kind of *Deep Blues* trilogy." Yes, Bob wrote an extraordinary book about Mississippi blues, and he made important contributions to a largely unrelated film that Eileen Gregory and John Stewart produced, and that I directed and edited. But he was just one of many who made lasting contributions to our production, even if some of his were vital to its success.

Ironically, Bob would later admit this in the February 5, 1993 issue of *Goldmine Magazine* (a publication for record collectors), when he said the following to writer Bill Dahl: "The film is really more of a collaboration than anything. It's Mugge's film, and I think he really did a great job on it. The CD I can take responsibility for. I feel really close to the CD." And rightfully so, since, again, Bob supervised Lee Manning's mixing and sequencing of our soundtrack album.

Unfortunately, Atlantic only kept the CD in circulation approximately a year, though hardcore fans hoarded their personal copies for decades to come. Then, in late 2021, after having me supervise 4K remastering of the film in Montreal, and hiring Film Movement to distribute the film worldwide again, Dave finally found the time to remix the original audio tracks and release *them* worldwide as well, this time via online streaming and downloading.

I freely admit that I learned a lot from Bob, and I was immensely fond of him, despite his many eccentricities, or maybe because of them. But this film, like nearly all others, was a team effort, and regardless of Bob's prior claims, it was never intended to be part of some after-the-fact Robert Palmer trilogy. To signal as much, perhaps we *should* have called it *Hard Times Mississippi.* So, sorry about that, Eileen, and for all the rest that went bad between us for a time.

Nevertheless, in making this film, which was envisioned and underwritten by Dave Stewart, our team's primary goal was to bring the deepest and richest blues of Mississippi and surrounding areas onto the world stage, and in short order, we did exactly that, both onscreen and off. And if pursuing this goal too often felt like Joseph Conrad's novella, *Heart of Darkness*—or Francis Ford Coppola's modern film adaptation, *Apocalypse Now*—completion of *Deep Blues* brought almost a religious sort of satisfaction, both for us and for a great many others who would later come to love it

***

In early August of 1998, when the Delta Blues Museum was still located on the second floor of Clarksdale, Mississippi's Carnegie Public Library, I presented a free screening of *Deep Blues* there as part of the Sunflower River Blues & Gospel Festival. As I did, I was introduced to Stephen C. "Steve" LaVere who, thanks to an agreement with a half-sister of legendary bluesman Robert Johnson, had become the quite effective, if controversial, agent for Johnson's music and two confirmed photographic images. To my surprise, the two of us became fast friends and agreed that someone should make a film focused not on Robert's short, productive, and widely mythologized life (which already had been done two or three times before), but on the power of his songs and their influence on both blues and rock musicians. Since there was no known film footage of Johnson, and only the two available photographs, we also agreed that the way to do it would be to film contemporary artists performing as many of his songs as possible. And though I had no idea how such an effort could be organized, much less funded, Steve very mysteriously said he would get back to me.

A short time later, LaVere revealed that he was assisting Robert "Bob" Santelli, then the vice president of education and public programs at the Rock & Roll Hall of Fame in Cleveland, Ohio, who was mounting an ambitious, weeklong tribute to Johnson as part of the ongoing American Music Masters Series. Steve, in his role as a consultant for the Rock Hall's string of events, had asked Bob about the possibility of my filming it, and Bob seemed amenable to the idea, suggesting that Steve have me call him. I did call, learned that this third annual series would be spread among several Cleveland venues (September 20-27, 1998), and promised to try and secure production funding in the brief time left before the events got under way.

At the time, I had just parted ways with Bruce Ricker's Rhapsody Films Inc., which had been my primary US home video distributor for nearly two decades, accepting an offer from WinStar Home Video, a division of the multi-billion-dollar broadband company WinStar Communications and an outgrowth of Fox Lorber Home Video. This new division had been placed in the hands of Michael Olivieri, a longtime fan of Black music (especially blues), and he anxiously gobbled up all films of mine that I controlled myself, before also acquiring *Deep Blues* from Dave Stewart. Although WinStar Communications was badly overextended and would later crash and burn, at the time, they seemed to be rolling in money. So, I contacted Michael about funding the Robert Johnson film, even pushing it as a kind of sequel to *Deep Blues*, in that the previous film had closed with a couple of Johnson's songs and the new one would survey his ongoing influence.

Olivieri quickly signed on, convincing his colleagues to back us and enlisting a WinStar attorney to assist with the effort. However, when I reported Michael's interest to the Rock Hall, executives said they would have to retain ownership of anything involving their programs. So, I worked out a compromise wherein WinStar would control the film for the first ten years, after which rights would revert to the Rock & Roll Hall of Fame. Of course, negotiations carried over until my crew and I had to be setting up in Cleveland, which meant I did not actually receive a fax of the final contract, sign it, and return it again until filming had begun. Such rushed, last-minute dealings had not been a problem with my Sonny Rollins film (likely because of the integrity of my collaborators on that project), but with this one, it led to big issues, indeed.

During those final few weeks, Santelli continued booking artists for shows at three Cleveland venues, and he agreed to include a couple of friends of mine—singer-songwriter Bill Morrissey, who had written and recorded a moving song about Robert Johnson that I had already utilized in my 1994 Rounder Records portrait, and bass player Rob Wasserman, who promised to bring his more famous Weir & Wasserman partner, Bob Weir of the Grateful Dead. We also tried to book slide guitar wizard Roy Rogers and three outstanding female vocalists—Irma Thomas, Marcia Ball, and Tracy Nelson, who were touring together at the time—but they all had conflicts.

Regarding crew, I was thrilled to be able to hire my old friend Larry McConkey as director of photography. We had not worked together since *Kumu Hula: Keepers of a Culture* in 1988, because Larry's peerless Steadicam work was now in constant demand by Martin Scorsese, Brian DePalma, Woody Allen, and other top Hollywood directors. Remarkably, though, Larry was available the week we would be in Cleveland, and for old time's sake, he even charged me his pre-Hollywood rate once again. Naturally, I also brought in audio director Bill Barth, cameramen Dave Sperling and Chris Li, camera assistant Craig Smith, grip Quincy McKay, Greg Hartman with his Big Mo music recording truck from Maryland, and others, mostly local, whom I had not used before. Finally, instead of hiring a full-fledged line producer, I drafted two women who had assisted me on previous projects—Bill Morrissey's wife and manager Ellen Karas and Mississippi blues expert Patty Johnson—knowing that both were smart enough and organized enough to serve as associate producers for the first time, assisting my crew and me to be everywhere at once over a several-day period.

Bob Santelli had scheduled a week's worth of activities, so a few of us arrived early and began filming interviews with knowledgeable guests including record producer and blues deejay Bob Porter, record producer and blues historian Jim O'Neal, and (thanks to intercession from my longtime Cleveland-based friend Nick Amster) Robert Johnson's feisty stepson and musical protégé Robert Lockwood Jr. We also filmed the following: (1) the public renaming of a Cleveland street for local hero Lockwood; (2) the keynote address by music historian Peter Guralnick, who asked how an incomparable talent like Johnson could seemingly arrive out of nowhere; (3) Steve LaVere explaining how he had come to create the Robert Johnson estate, and how money he had placed in escrow would be paid to the eventual, court-selected heir; and (4) a presentation by Santelli, LaVere, and Mississippi attorney Tom Freeland of silent 16mm film footage that had recently been offered for sale by Beale Street merchant Leo "Tater Red" Allred.

Some reportedly believed this footage depicted Robert Johnson performing in front of a Ruleville, Mississippi movie theater, but most conference attendees, including Robert Lockwood Jr., did not. In fact, Steve LaVere effectively shut down debate by pointing out that the film mentioned on the theater's marquee, *Blues in the Night*, was released in 1942, whereas Johnson died in 1938.

After the rest of my crew arrived on Thursday, September 24, we set up to shoot a series of smaller acts, both acoustic and electric, presenting songs by Robert Johnson that evening at Cuyahoga Community College. Among the players and songs which made the film from that night's show were the following: Alvin Youngblood Hart performing "Hellhound on My Trail," Guy Davis performing "Walkin' Blues," Rory Block performing "If I Had Possession Over Judgement Day," Brits Peter Green (of the original blues rock version of Fleetwood Mac) and Nigel Watson performing "Terraplane Blues," Johnson friend David "Honeyboy" Edwards performing "Cross Road Blues," Johnson stepson Robert Lockwood Jr. performing "I'm a Steady Rollin' Man" and "Love in Vain," and Lockwood, Edwards, and Johnson contemporary Henry Townsend performing "Sweet Home Chicago."

A second concert took place the following night at a spacious rock venue called the Odeon Concert Club. Songs recorded there and used in the film included Bill Morrissey's intimate version of his own "Robert Johnson," and then the following Johnson numbers played mostly by larger ensembles: Louisiana's Sonny Landreth (backed by New Jersey's Billy Hector Band) bringing his impressive swamp chops to a second version of "Walkin' Blues"; Joe Louis Walker and Billy Branch performing a soaring, straight-ahead Chicago take on the Robert Johnson/Elmore James classic "Dust My Broom"; Chris Whitley performing a surreal solo interpretation of "Hellhound on My Trail"; Gov't Mule performing a hard-driving, hard rock version of "If I Had

Possession Over Judgement Day"; Philadelphia's G. Love and Special Sauce pouring out a slow-as-molasses rendition of "Love In Vain"; and Bob Weir and Rob Wasserman (backed by Gov't Mule drummer Matt Apts and, eventually, Gov't Mule guitarist Warren Haynes) offering a jam band approach to the project's third version of "Walkin' Blues."

Saturday was set aside for scholarly panels at Case Western Reserve University, featuring Rock Hall programmer (and author) Bob Santelli, Rock Hall curator Howard Kramer, music historians Peter Guralnick and Robert Gordon, and again, record producer and blues deejay Bob Porter. I waited several days for an officious gatekeeper at Case Western to approve my request to film these panels, and when he never got back to me, I simply went ahead and shot them. For a short time, this caused a furor, proving once again that no bureaucracies are worse than academic bureaucracies and that, sometimes, the only way to get anything done is to ignore them.

The final concert was to take place on Sunday, September 27 at elegant Severance Hall, home of the Cleveland Orchestra, and Hall officials had no problem with our crew filming performances there by the Allman Brothers, Taj Mahal, Cassandra Wilson, Keb' Mo', John Hammond Jr., and others. However, they said their union contracts would require us to pay $10,000 for a group of their workers to sit idly backstage throughout the show, while my own crew did the actual work, and there was no way that I could, or would, agree.

For that reason, I began asking singers and musicians scheduled to perform on Sunday if they would allow us to film them in a hotel room Saturday evening. Taj Mahal stopped by, but when I failed to return quickly enough from running other errands, he left again. Fortunately, though, Keb' Mo' showed up after I returned, and we filmed him performing another version of Johnson's "Love in Vain," which I later intercut with the one performed by Robert Lockwood Jr.

By late on Sunday, all our crew members had left, so Larry McConkey offered to fly me back to Philly, and I gratefully agreed. Larry's father, James McConkey, was an esteemed novelist who had taught for decades at Cornell University and whose short stories were routinely published in the New Yorker, and his uncle was a commercial airline pilot. From his parents, Larry had inherited a love of the arts, and from his uncle, a love of flying, which his well-paying Hollywood work now allowed him to indulge.

Certainly, sitting beside Larry as he piloted his own private jet was spectacular, what with the entire horizon spreading before us, plus the chance to catch up with one of my closest friends. And yet, for me, it was just as scary as being driven around those mist-covered mountain roads in Jamaica some fifteen years before. On both occasions, I experienced a sense of awe, but also a fear of the unknown, heightened by a loss of control, and wondered if Johnson felt the same as his wondrous gifts propelled him into uncharted territory. Not that my own abilities compared to his, but perhaps the fact that he and I were born on the same day of the year, May 8, made his choices seem personal to me, as those of Goethe's *Faust* perhaps felt to my German ancestors.

Once I returned home, I quickly received all the processed and work-printed footage from my week in Cleveland, and all of the news was good—all, that is, except what awaited me when finally reading the contract I had signed while in the midst of production. To my utter dismay, the paperwork sent to me by the WinStar attorney, now officially my fellow producer on the project, included budget allocations for everything except my own $50,000 salary. And when I phoned him to complain, his only response was that, if I had thought my proposed salary should be included, I should not have signed what was faxed to me. So, yes, despite having been fully engaged in shooting, which I thought I was doing on everyone's behalf, I should have read the agreement more closely. In other words, I should never have trusted my corporate backers, in that, exactly like Robert Johnson (at least, in the mythic telling of his tale), I had made a deal with the Devil, and now I would pay the price.

Panic-stricken at the thought of having no salary at all for my next six months of work, I tried charm and I tried threats, but nothing seemed to work. Finally, I shared my distress with Steve LaVere, for whom I had already gotten WinStar to commit a total of $55,000 for use of Robert Johnson songs and photos in the film, but for which Steve did not yet have a written agreement. In response, Steve told WinStar that, if they did not pay me at least half my expected salary, he would refuse to sign an agreement with them, and their expenditures on the project to date (including all shooting costs and their payment of $1,000 to each of the performing musicians) would have been for nothing, because they would never be able to release the completed film. It was the most magnanimous act I had ever encountered from a friend or collaborator, and it turned a disastrous situation into one only half as bad.

Consequently, in all the years since, when frustrated musicians, record label owners, film or television producers, music journalists, or rival blues scholars have badmouthed Steve for forging a deal with a Johnson relative and then charging for use of Robert's songs and photos, I have expressed no sympathy whatsoever. This is because, even if Steve sometimes relied on harsh legal language when demanding payments, he mostly did so with corporate music labels, many of which were notorious for their own bullying tactics and for cheating minority artists and songwriters. Moreover, Steve worked tirelessly on behalf of Johnson's legacy, whether overseeing CD and record releases, developing film and theater projects, or just generally working to increase his worldwide reputation, while also earning money for surviving family members.

As just one example, without Steve's creative matchmaking, my own film would never have happened. And if Steve also made money in the process, well, that's the way it works when representing a major artist or the artist's legally recognized estate. That is, the more the artist or estate makes, the more the agent makes as well (fifty percent, I was told, which is what some of my own reps make). And by the time continuing court battles resolved that illegitimate son Claud Johnson was Robert's rightful heir, the artist himself was a household name, and the son and his family were exceedingly well-off. Such happy endings were the work of primarily one man, and like him or not (which I very much did), that man was Steve LaVere.

At any rate, although we had shot much great material in Cleveland, centering the film around the Rock Hall alone felt a bit too institutional. Happily, though, I was able to convince WinStar to fund a quick trip for my crew and me to the Robinsonville, Mississippi area where Johnson had once lived, and to Helena, Arkansas, where the annual King Biscuit Blues Festival was taking place. As a result,

on October 10, 1998, Dave Sperling, Bill Barth, Bob Santelli, and I rushed to Memphis, with Craig Smith and Quincy McKay meeting us there. Next, we drove to Helena, located blues guitarist Roy Rogers, shot a few scenes with him at the festival, and then accompanied him to a nearby motel where singers Tracy Nelson, Marcia Ball, and Irma Thomas were waiting for us.

Robert Mugge supervises filming of, left to right, Tracy Nelson, Roy Rogers, Marcia Ball, and Irma Thomas as they perform Robert Johnson's "Come On In My Kitchen" outside of their Helena, Arkansas motel. In the foreground, grip Quincy McKay uses a reflector to direct light onto the performers at dusk. (photographed by Craig Smith, 1998)

Once there, we gathered in the parking lot outside and filmed Roy backing up the three women as they sang Robert Johnson's "Come On In My Kitchen" for Bob Santelli, all of them visibly fighting mosquitoes. The scene began with Tracy teasing Bob for not having invited them to the recent events in Cleveland when, in fact, they could not have attended due to being on tour. Afterwards, we bid Tracy, Marcia, and Irma goodbye, took Bob and Roy into the motel's lobby, quickly set up our equipment, filmed Roy demonstrating

Robert Johnson's more innovative guitar techniques for Bob, and finally filmed him performing a rollicking version of Johnson's classic song "Ramblin' On My Mind," which I later cut together with scenes we already had shot at the festival.

Not long thereafter, my crew and I were treated to an extraordinary dinner prepared for us by owners of Tunica, Mississippi's Hotel Marie, a two-story brick structure reportedly dating to the 1890s. The couple running it at the time said they only accepted guests when in the mood. But once they allowed you to stay, they loved being able to cook for you in their first floor café. So, I gave them cash, they went out and bought groceries, and then they prepared our small group one of the best steak dinners ever, complete with wine that never stopped flowing. By the end of the night, we stumbled to our rooms upstairs with an increasing affection for the state of Mississippi. In fact, had Nina Simone's classic song "Mississippi Goddam" not addressed the horrors of racial injustice in the Deep South, those could have been our words of appreciation at the end of the meal.

The following day, October 11, we met up again with Patty Johnson and Steve LaVere. Patty had somehow come to know an eighty-year-old man named Willie Coffee who had grown up with Robert Johnson and had wonderful tales to share. With her typical generosity, Patty led us to Coffee's home, where he, too, could not have been more welcoming. And in honor of the way Steve LaVere, Gayle Dean Wardlow, Mack McCormick, and other blues researchers had spent decades doggedly digging up facts about their musical idols, I thought it appropriate to shoot Steve meeting Willie, asking him questions, and showing Willie documents that he and the rest had uncovered.

As it turned out, just as Robert Lockwood Jr. and other Johnson contemporaries had given us important information about the fully formed artist they had known, Coffee told us about Johnson both as a boy and as the talented young man he would later become. In fact, in a telling exchange between Steve and Willie, the Devil myth was laid to rest:

Steve LaVere: When Robert told you that he had sold his soul to the Devil, did you think he was bein' serious?

Willie Coffee: No, I never did think he was serious, because, when he'd come in here with us, he'd always come in with a lot of jive—and you know, joke and crack a lot of jokes like that—and I never did believe in it. And I said to myself, "That's just some stuff he's sayin'; he ain't sold his self to no Devil."

Steve LaVere: Mm-hm.

Willie Coffee: That's what I said to myself. I didn't tell *him* that.

Blues historian Stephen C. LaVere (right) chats and trades guitar licks with Willie Coffee, a childhood friend of legendary bluesman Robert Johnson, at Coffee's home in Robinsonville, Mississippi. (photographed by Craig Smith, 1998)

Coffee also mentioned how Johnson had taught him to play guitar and pushed him to come on the road with him, noting that, if he had tagged along, his own life would have been completely different (and probably much shorter, we thought to ourselves). In addition, when Steve produced the death certificate claiming Johnson had died of syphilis, Willie said he tended to believe it. Of course, this ran counter to the prevailing notion that Robert was poisoned by the bartender husband of a female conquest (a legend even LaVere continued to believe, and which could be true). Regardless, as the interview came to an end, Willie conveyed continuing sadness over the loss of his friend, a living, breathing human being who was then sixty years gone.

Building upon Willie's straightforward reporting, blues historian Jim O'Neal summarized as follows:

A story grew up that Robert Johnson sold his soul to the Devil at a crossroads at midnight in order to become a master of the blues. And he did become a master of the blues and recorded some of the greatest blues ever, and died shortly thereafter. So, I think he got the short end of the deal, if he did make a deal. But that's been an ongoing controversy among blues scholars and fans—whether anything like that really happened, or whether that was just a figurative "sell yourself to the Devil," because the blues has always been known as the Devil's music, and anyone who played it was in league with the Devil. It didn't mean that you had actually gone to the crossroads and actually met a figure who made a deal with you in blood or anything. But I think a lot of people do believe that, or they like to believe it. People are looking for a fantastic myth.

In Ken Russell's 1971 film *The Music Lovers*, the subject was not so much Russian composer Pyotr Ilych Tchaikovsky as it was the friends, fans, lovers, family members, and patrons who tried to possess Tchaikovsky for themselves. These were the ironically described "music lovers." In a similar fashion, I titled my own film *Hellhounds on my Trail: The Afterlife of Robert Johnson*, because, as I wrote earlier, it was not so much about Robert Johnson the man, who was largely unknowable, as it was about his enduring music and his ever-expanding influence after he died, tragically, and in near obscurity. In short, the "afterlife" of Robert Johnson referred to everything that had happened since his death, and the "hellhounds" of the title were *us*—all of us who have loved his work, but who also, for our own assorted reasons, passed along the myths and legends that filled the vacuum where a biography should have been. In other words, it was the mystery, as well as the power of the music, that continued to attract us.

Midway through our project, after the Rock Hall had burned through five executive directors in as many years, former Marvel Entertainment president Terry Stewart became its first long-running president and CEO, and proved to be fully supportive of our efforts. Then, in the spring of 1999, I finished the film, and we world premiered it at Austin's SXSW film festival.

Many of the screenings that followed featured live appearances by participating musicians: Bill Morrissey at the Rock Hall in Cleveland and the Prince Music Theater in Philadelphia, Bill Morrissey and Alvin Youngblood Hart at the Museum of Fine Arts in Boston, Alvin Youngblood Hart and Henry Townsend at the St. Louis Film Festival, and Alvin Youngblood Hart, Roy Rogers, Rob Wasserman, Bob Weir, and others at the Mill Valley Film Festival. But perhaps my favorite premiere was at the Screening Room in New York City where the film ran January 21-27, 2000, along with selected daytime screenings of *Gospel According to Al Green*, *Black Wax*, and *The Kingdom of Zydeco* (see Chapter Seven). During the afternoon of Friday, January 21, my friend Mark Scheerer, who was still a correspondent for *Showbiz Today* on CNN, interviewed me, along with Warren Haynes of Gov't Mule, about Robert Johnson and the making of the film. Then, before the 8:20 p.m. opening night screening, Warren and fellow singer-songwriter-guitarist Chris Whitley sat on stools at the front of the house and, both separately and together, performed Johnson songs live for an enraptured audience. Sadly, less than six years later, Chris would die of lung cancer at the age of forty-five. It happens, of course, with or without a deal with the Devil.

Warren Haynes of Gov't Mule (left) and Chris Whitley perform at New York City's Screening Room on opening night of the film's world premiere theatrical engagement. (photographed by Robert Mugge, 2000)

Chapter Six
Capture & Release

Pride and Joy: The Story of Alligator Records (1992)

True Believers: The Musical Family of

Rounder Records (1994)

Toward the end of 1991, as word got out about our initial screenings of *Deep Blues*, I received a call from someone I had not yet met, which was Bruce Iglauer, the founding president of Alligator Records. Chicago-based Alligator was a so-called "independent" record label, which meant it was not affiliated with any of the larger corporations then dominating record sales around the world and limiting consumer choice in the search for maximum profits. In 1971, after recording an album by Hound Dog Taylor, a personal favorite, Iglauer had started his own label and, out of the trunk of his car, began promoting his one album to radio stations and record stores. Yet, by the time Bruce and I first spoke, two decades later, he had acquired a staff, occupied a small office building, and developed a reputation for having the smartest and most successful blues label in existence. He even was outselling Delmark Records, the older Chicago label run by his friend and mentor, Robert "Bob" Koester, who had been his employer until refusing to record Hound Dog Taylor, which sent his young protégé packing.

This upbeat, idealistic, and assertive head of what was now a small-scale empire was never in business for the money. Like Koester, Iglauer had started his company out of love for the music, and for the people, mostly African American, who made it. Still, in order to pay his staff, to keep lights on in his building, and to continue his recording, promoting, and remunerating of artists he admired, he knew that dollars had to flow *into* his company, as well as out, and for that reason, not all of his decisions could be altruistic.

I knew some of this already, and Bruce later informed me of the rest. However, when I picked up the phone that day, far more characteristically, the first thing he said to me was, "We should know each other." And from that minute on, we very much did.

Beneath Bruce's warm words was a pitch, of course, and I would have expected nothing less, because I spoke that language myself. What he went on to say was that his label was now turning twenty years old, and early in 1992 (just a tad late, of course), he would celebrate with an Alligator Records Twentieth Anniversary Tour. The featured artists heading to clubs and theaters around the country would be Koko Taylor and her Blues Machine, the Lonnie Brooks Blues Band, Katie Webster, Elvin Bishop, and Lil' Ed and the Blues Imperials, with Iglauer himself sometimes serving as emcee.

What we both wondered aloud was whether I could film at least a portion of that tour, then build an Alligator Records portrait around it. I expressed interest in producing such a film, but informed Bruce that I had no idea how to fund it. In turn, he told me that David Steffen, a former big-time executive at A&M Records, but now in charge of BMG's home video division, had expressed interest in recording the tour himself, because he needed product for his new label. Naturally, Bruce and I both speculated whether he might be open to collaboration.

When I reached out to David, he and I bonded as well. However, he did not believe he could afford full funding of a film on Alligator; partial, perhaps, but not full. Therefore, Bruce and I decided our primary goal should be cutting costs to the bone, and the best way of doing that was to film only a single stop on his fifteen-city tour. Each of the four-plus-hour shows would be essentially the same, and since

I and most of my key crew people lived in the Mid-Atlantic region, Philadelphia's Chestnut Cabaret seemed the logical choice. Beyond that, with just three days in Chicago, I figured I could capture the basics of Bruce's story, and could save additional money by using a tiny local crew there. So, with all this in mind, I drew up my smallest budget in years, squeezed as much money as I could out of David Steffen, and then asked Bruce if he could advance the rest, largely as a promotional expense for his label and key artists. After rightly mulling it over, Bruce said yes, and our new project was set.

The Chestnut Cabaret show was number eleven out of fifteen, so I assumed that the musicians would all be well-rehearsed by the time they reached Philly, and not yet succumbing to the unavoidable fatigue of nonstop life on the road. In fact, the opening night show in Grand Rapids, Michigan was February 28, followed immediately by a leap year bonus day show in Chicago, and the Philadelphia show would be March 12. Therefore, Philadelphia was two weeks in, which seemed perfect.

For the big event, I pulled in a few of my regulars: Chris Li as director of photography, Dave Sperling as second camera, Bill Barth overseeing audio, and the Effanel Music truck recording music. The concert lighting team, two additional camera operators, four camera assistants, and a veteran still photographer were all new to me, but all came well-recommended. Beyond that, we had the Alligator Records road crew, the Chestnut Cabaret staff, and Jonny Meister, host of the Saturday night blues show on University of Pennsylvania radio station WXPN, serving as house emcee. So, with me once again manning four video assist monitors and the base of our rented communication system, we were all in position and ready to roll.

In addition to Jonny welcoming the crowd, Bruce spoke briefly about his label, its anniversary, and the tour; and with that, we were under way. First up was Lil' Ed Williams, a senior car buffer at Chicago's Red Carpet Car Wash by day and the look-alike nephew of blues great J. B. Hutto by night, proving convincingly that Hutto's bottleneck boogie style had made it into his own genes as well. Duckwalking swiftly around the stage, and ably assisted by his dexterous Blues Imperials, Ed readily had the packed house writhing on its feet.

Ronnie Baker Brooks, Lil' Ed Williams, Koko Taylor, and other members of the Alligator Records Twentieth Anniversary Tour jam together at Philadelphia's Chestnut Cabaret. (frame from film, 1992)

Next up was Katie Webster, veteran barrelhouse boogie-woogie piano player from South Louisiana. Amazingly, even though singing and playing solo piano in a large hall, she had the audience mesmerized from start to finish. By the age of only thirteen, Katie had been a regular on the "crayfish circuit" between Dallas and New Orleans, and soon thereafter became a respected studio musician, touring and recording with the great Otis Redding for the last three years of his life. She also performed on singles by Louisiana rock and roll artist Lee Baker, Jr., who recorded as Guitar Junior, but whose other gig was playing guitar behind zydeco pioneer Clifton Chenier.

Ironically, in 1959, the legendary Sam Cooke brought this same Lee Baker to Chicago where he fell in love with the blues and changed his stage name to Lonnie Brooks. Now, like Katie Webster, Lonnie was recording for Alligator Records, and the Lonnie Brooks Band was the third act to perform that night, complete with Lonnie's fast-as-lightning son, second guitarist Ronnie Baker Brooks.

The fourth act of the night was well-known singer and guitarist Elvin Bishop, backed up by Lonnie's band and sometimes trading licks with Lonnie's son Ronnie, just as Lonnie did during his own set. Elvin started out as a guitar-playing kid from Oklahoma who, in 1960, enrolled in the University of Chicago, mostly to be near the blues. After playing clubs there for a time, he and harp player Paul Butterfield founded the Paul Butterfield Blues Band, in which Bishop and second guitarist Mike Bloomfield pioneered "extended twin-guitar jamming" (to quote an Alligator tour press release), later practiced by the Allman Brothers and other Southern rock bands. Considered on a par with Jimi Hendrix and Eric Clapton, Elvin would move to the San Francisco area and start his own popular blues rock band, have some national hits with Southern label Capricorn Records, and eventually move to Alligator. Tonight, in typical fashion for him, he was alternating between sizzling blues guitar numbers and self-composed novelty songs featuring the country sounds and humor of his Oklahoma upbringing.

Last up was the uncontested queen of the blues, Koko Taylor, who had been raised on a farm near Memphis before migrating to Chicago where she initially cleaned houses by day while playing South Side blues clubs by night. To her great fortune, legendary blues producer, songwriter, and bass player Willie Dixon took her under his wing and made a star of her at Chicago's famed Chess Records, during which time she recorded multiple blues and R&B hits. However, as that label's dominance began to wane, Koko moved to Alligator where Bruce and his staff brought her years more of recording success. And on this particular night, Koko Taylor and her Blues Machine proved exactly why she was one of the giants of Chicago blues.

Alternating fast-paced and deeply soulful numbers, Koko tore up the Cabaret and even offered some suggestive comic relief with Lonnie Brooks. Then, when all else had been said and done, she kicked off a final, all-out assault on Robert Johnson's "Sweet Home Chicago" during which all five acts joined in, each taking a turn at ramping up the energy until, finally, everyone on stage—and everyone in the audience—was jumping up and down in unison, ecstatic in a way that is unique to blues. It was the kind of show that Bruce Iglauer himself could describe better than anyone:

Blues has this sort of strange power as a music that's real different from any other kind of music I've heard. It kind of reaches in, and it wrings you out. It's like a wet sponge getting squeezed dry. It's not real comfortable when it happens. But afterwards, you feel great. When you listen to blues when you're, like, in a crowd of people and it works, you realize that the things you're feeling are not just what *you* feel; that other people around you— the musicians, you, and the rest of the audience—are feeling the same things, and you feel less alone. Always, when I was younger in my life, I felt real isolated, like I never really was in touch with people. I was walking through the world with nobody quite touching me. And somehow or other, the blues made me feel kind of whole, and like much more a part of being a human.

To be honest, I, too, have had transformative feelings while listening to live opera, jazz, musical comedy (Sondheim, for instance), and gospel, but definitely with blues as well. In fact, as Al Green has pointed out, many modern-day blues and R&B performances derive much of their power from gospel influence. In the Alligator film, Koko Taylor put it like this:

I grew up singing gospel. I grew up in church. And my dad said everybody in his house had to go to church on Sunday. And every Sunday, I'd go to church, me and my sisters and brothers. And on Monday, we'd go to the field to pick cotton, and we'd be singin' the blues amongst ourselves, you know. But I always sung gospel, loved gospel. And even today, when I'm on the bandstand singin' the blues, I have that gospel feeling deep down within, you know? And sometimes I get kind of "happy." You don't know about it, but when I be jumpin' around there on stage, I have that gospel feeling down inside. And I have to catch myself and remember, "You ain't in church now; don't get happy on me!" [laughing] So, I just keep on singin' the blues.

Between sets at Chestnut Cabaret, Chris Li, Bill Barth, and I filmed interviews with Katie, Elvin, and Bruce, yet knew I could leave Koko, Lil' Ed, and Lonnie and Ronnie to be interviewed in Chicago. Tonight, my primary goal was to capture as much amazing music as possible, and among the songs selected for the film were Lil' Ed's "Pride and Joy" (the film's eventual title song) and "Ed's Boogie" (actually recorded in a Chicago studio), Katie Webster's "Pussycat Moan" and "Lord, I Wonder," Lonnie Brooks's "Wife for Tonight" and "I Want All My Money Back," Elvin Bishop's "El-Bo" and "Beer Drinking Woman," Koko Taylor's "It's A Dirty Job" (a duet with Lonnie) and her cover of the Etta James classic "I'd Rather Go Blind," along with the final group performance of "Sweet Home Chicago."

Later that month, I flew to Chicago where I met up with local cameraman Peter Gilbert (who had assisted us at Al Green's church) and audio person Tom Yore. Together, the three of us filmed Bruce giving a tour of his old and new places of business, walking us through his busy warehouse, overseeing a meeting of office staff, joking with his saucy receptionist, looking over alligator souvenirs from around the world, producing Lil' Ed's recording session, reflecting on the joys and challenges of his career, and demonstrating his ability to click his teeth along to music. This latter habit led an early girlfriend to dub him "Little Alligator," which, in turn, led to the naming of his label.

Also in Chicago, as planned, we interviewed Lil' Ed in the recording studio, Koko in the Alligator offices, and Lonnie and Ronnie on the roof of Bruce's building. In addition we interviewed two of Iglauer's longtime friends. The first was Bob Koester who, as previously mentioned, founded independent jazz and blues label Delmark Records, as well as Chicago's Jazz Record Mart, then the world's largest jazz and blues record store. Bob recalled meeting Bruce when his protégé first arrived from Milwaukee, and hiring him to work in the record store. Prior to that, Bob said, Bruce hosted a blues show on his college radio station and simply loved the music. Bruce's other friend we interviewed was Richard "Dick" Shurman, a local record producer, music journalist, and self-proclaimed "blues jack-of-all-trades" whom we filmed at B. L. U. E. S., a bar and music club on the North Side of Chicago. Dick spoke of how he and Bruce "fell into the same sort of social set that was loosely organized around Jazz Record

Mart and *Living Blues Magazine.*" *Living Blues*, America's earliest and longest-lasting blues magazine, was founded by Jim O'Neal and Amy van Singel as editors, and by five others as writers, Bruce among them. Dick went on to say:

> Bruce is the kind of guy—I always knew he would have a good lawyer, a good accountant, a good bookkeeper, and basically have the fundamentals mastered. He was doing this out of love as much as everybody else, but he thought love meant trying to help the artists by putting together some all-around support and actually selling the records and assisting their careers. A lot of other people stopped at the recording, and the rest was painful.

For me, the best part of being in Chicago with Bruce Iglauer was that, every night, he would take me out to hear live music. Wherever we went—bars, clubs, theaters—Bruce was treated like blues royalty: ushered in without paying a cover charge or buying a ticket, and allowed to come and go as he pleased. And because I was with him, I received the same treatment.

Each of the three nights, we heard a major musical act perform, though I can only remember two of the three. One was the great Albert King, performing in a theater; and the other was former Hi Records blues, soul, and gospel singer Otis Clay, who would later appear in my 2007 film *Deep Sea Blues* (see Chapter Ten). At the time, though living in Chicago, Otis was touring with the Memphis-based Hodges brothers who had spent years backing up Al Green, Otis himself, and others in Willie Mitchell's stable of artists. Naturally, when I saw them with Otis, Charles Hodges was playing organ, Leroy Hodges was playing bass, and Mabon "Teenie" Hodges was playing electric guitar, just as he had in the background during my 1983 Al Green interview.

Somehow, despite all this fun, I managed to finish the film in record time, first rolling it out in October and November of 1992, beginning with screenings at three of my favorite festivals. First came the Mill Valley Film Festival where Bruce joined me for the world premiere and celebrities in the audience included Carlos Santana and a very warm Mimi Farina, with whom I chatted afterwards. Next came the AFI Fest in Los Angeles (that year called the AFI/OAS Fest), another of my regulars for the past decade, and then the Denver International Film Festival where, over the years, founding director Ron Henderson showed more of my films than any other programmer. Such festival and museum screenings continued throughout 1993 while, wasting little time, David Steffen released the film on video in the early fall, right as I began shooting three more films with funding from his company.

One of the key themes of my music-related films has been to portray individuals and organizations whose work has helped to protect, preserve, and promote traditional forms of American music. By this point in my career, I already had spotlighted music venues, festivals, radio stations, churches, musicologists, and museums, and now, for the first time, I was fully exploring the efforts of an independent music label. Going forward, I would focus on more of the same, as well as on journalists, folklorists, record stores, blues cruises, and music-related associations and charities. Together, all of these made up support networks for musical styles and genres not typically sustained by the commercial marketplace, but comprising important strands of American and world culture. With that in mind, *Pride and Joy: The Story of Alligator Records* became my first film entirely devoted to the practice of such ideals, and two years later, *True Believers: The Musical Family of Rounder Records* would be my second.

***

David Steffen and I had been happy enough with our working relationship on the Alligator Records film, as well as with the finished product, that we were interested in collaborating again. Yet, we differed as to which film I should make next. As established in my opening chapter, David spent the early part of 1993 communicating with the International Bluegrass Music Association, and he liked the idea of building a film around the upcoming IBMA awards celebration in Owensboro, Kentucky, which would include many of the genre's top musicians. In the meantime, I was hoping to make a film about independent music label Rounder Records, which not only would offer a companion piece to our recently completed Alligator Records portrait, but would also permit me to explore numerous regional American music scenes, all of which were covered by Rounder.

Eventually, I convinced David that, with one big trip through the American South, I could shoot everything needed for a feature-length bluegrass film, and most of what was needed for a Rounder Records film as well. That is, by creating a new caravan—which would, as with *Kumu Hula*, alternate between road trips and plane trips—I could take a crew not only to Owensboro, where we would capture bluegrass performances for use in both films, but also to Memphis, where we would document blues of that city; to Austin, where we would explore both Tex-Mex and a blend of Texas and Louisiana roots music; to New Orleans, where we would immerse ourselves in local rhythm and blues; and to various cities in Southwest Louisiana, where we would focus on Cajun music and zydeco. After that, to complete the Rounder movie, we would still need to film at the label's headquarters in Cambridge, Massachusetts, as well as to shoot a folk music or singer-songwriter performance, probably in New England as well. But the latter could be accomplished with a very small crew and a lot less money.

David liked the idea, but he could not imagine picking up the entire tab for both films himself, which left us in limbo again. By this point, I already had been in touch with the three Rounder owners: Bill Nowlin, Ken Irwin, and Marian Leighton-Levy, affectionately known as "the Rounders." Having founded their label in 1970, apparently just a hair sooner than Bruce Iglauer had founded his, they were anxious to have a film made that could be used to promote their upcoming twenty-fifth anniversary in 1995. And if it were ready in 1994, well, so much the better, because then they could use it while gearing up for their own concert tours and assorted other festivities. Yet, as I had done with Bruce, I now had to make clear to them that BMG Video alone could not pay for the project. So, if they wanted the film to happen, they would have to make a contribution, the same as Iglauer had done with the Alligator Records film.

On his own, David made a deal with The Nashville Network wherein TNN would pay us for an hour-long version of the bluegrass film, which it planned to broadcast prior to the BMG home video release. Meanwhile, Rounder agreed to provide partial backing for its own portrait, which I knew early on I wanted to call *True Believers: The Musical Family of Rounder Records*. For David, the latter would simply be additional programming for his home video company, whereas, for me, it would extend the idea of an independent record label supporting traditional American musicians. In this case, of course, the breadth of Rounder's interests would allow me to engage with a wider range of regional American music scenes, each of which had its own stars, venues, audiences, instrumentation, heritage, and places of origin.

Happily, the assistance offered from TNN and Rounder was sufficient to convince Steffen to move forward with both films. Then, a funny thing happened. As I began working closely with Scott Billington—who, in addition to running Rounder's art department, produced albums for top Louisiana musicians—I realized that the zydeco scene in Southwest Louisiana was so active, and filled with such drama, that it was worthy of a film of its own. Understandably, at the start, David did not wish to hear it. Eventually, though, I convinced him that, for just a small amount of additional money, we could prepare a third film as well, which might even be the most exciting of the bunch.

For a corporate executive like David to come up with even more production money before the end of the fiscal year was no mean feat. Yet, arguing to higher-ups how his new home video label was in need of product to distribute, and that this was a relatively cost-effective way to create three new performance-related films at once, he was able to make it happen. And so, over the coming year, I would be expected to produce, direct, write, and edit a feature-length bluegrass film (see Chapter One), a feature-length portrait of Rounder Records, and a feature-length film about the zydeco music scene of Southwest Louisiana (see Chapter Seven). And so, even though long maintaining that, if funding were available, I could produce more than one feature-length film per year, making these three films simultaneously would certainly be my biggest challenge yet.

As previously stated, *True Believers: The Musical Family of Rounder Records* would essentially serve as my sequel for *Pride and Joy: The Story of Alligator Records*. My plan for this film was to shoot in four Southern cities, and one entire region, during the second half of September 1993, and this meant booking talent, hiring crews, ordering film and tape stock, securing equipment, arranging transportation and accommodations, gaining permission to shoot in appropriate venues, designing three separate narratives, and scheduling everything and everyone needed in order to tell these stories and capture related performances.

In assembling a crew, the first of my longtime collaborators I called were line producer Bob Maier and audio director Bill Barth, each of whom had helped me to survive my two previous road movies, *Kumu Hula* and *Deep Blues*, and who, therefore, were uniquely qualified to assist me with this even crazier undertaking. In addition, I called three cameramen—old standbys Chris Li and Dave Sperling, and newcomer Bill Burke—who would trade off duties and titles from one film to another, and Tennessee-based camera assistant Craig Smith and grip Quincy McKay, who were now full-fledged members of our team. In addition, in one city or another, we would be joined by particular Rounder owners and personnel, plus the most easily available concert lighting and recording people for each location. Otherwise, from within Rounder, Brad Paul would help with overall scheduling and coordination, largely from his office back in Cambridge, while Jake Guralnick, son of my friend Peter Guralnick, would assist with those always pesky music rights.

Production kicked off on Thursday, September 16, 1993, when two Bobs (Mugge and Maier) and two Bills (Barth and Burke) flew to New Orleans and checked out the Lion's Den Lounge, which was owned and operated by Emile Jackson, the husband of singer Irma Thomas. Then, the following day, we welcomed in the rest of our crew and met up with the following: lighting technician Billy Brag and assistants; the Big Mo music recording truck under supervision of original owner Ed Eastridge (supported by future owner Greg

Hartman); Rounder's Scott Billington, who was Irma's record pro-ducer; and Heather West, a manager at Black Top Records, who also had offered to help us throughout the state. Finally, while all of our people were setting up in the concert space at the Lion's Den, a few of us filmed Scott chatting with Irma and Emile about Irma's reputa-tion as the soul queen of New Orleans, and about how her husband's club gave her a consistent place to rehearse and perform.

Later that night, having set up all of our equipment, plus deco-rated the stage with Christmas lights (a juke joint staple) and film lights with colored gels, we shot and recorded Irma, looking stun-ning in an evening gown, and members of her seven-piece band, all of whom wore standard black tuxedos. Although we went on to film her entire set, the one song I selected for the film was "Smoke Filled Room," written by Dan Penn, Jonnie Barnett, and Carson Whitsett. With such a beautiful song performed by one of the loveliest and most soulful singers alive, we could not have had a more propitious start to our project.

Saturday morning, our caravan of cars, minivans, and trucks headed due west, with some of us stopping off in Lafayette, Loui-siana to film Cajun- and zydeco-related scenes at Festivals Acadi-ens, and others heading on to the VFW Hall in Eunice, where we would film an evening concert by young Cajun ensemble Steve Riley and the Mamou Playboys. At the festival, which, years later, would change its name to the more inclusive Festivals Acadiens et Créoles (meaning, both Cajuns and Creoles, rather than just the former), we first found *Bonjour Louisiane* host Pete Bergeron broadcasting from the festival and filmed him conducting an outdoor interview with Rounder owner Ken Irwin for Lafayette public radio station KRVS. The interview concerned Rounder's commitment to recording art-ists from the region, so it certainly fit the dominant themes of our production. After that, we met up with New Orleans-based Cajun artist Bruce Daigrepont, who agreed to perform a song for us right where he and his family were picnicking on the grass. While Bruce sang and played his accordion, his wife accompanied him on triangle and a friend played fiddle.

Next, we headed to Lawtell, Louisiana, where Rounder's Scott Billington introduced us to close friend Kermon Richard (pronounced the French way, with a soft "ch"), owner of the legendary zydeco venue Richard's Club. There, with Kermon standing on one side of the empty club's bar, and Scott standing on the other, the two of them discussed not only the history of the club, but also how it was Kermon who informed Scott by phone that Andrus Espre, known professionally as Beau Jocque, was an artist worth watching. In the time since that call, Scott had recorded the first of what became a highly regarded series of Beau Jocque albums for Rounder.

From there, we continued to Eunice where much of our crew was already setting up for our next scheduled concert. But before we headed to the VFW Hall ourselves, we met the night's performers, Steve Riley and the Mamou Playboys, in front of downtown Eunice's Liberty Theater which, since 1987, had been hosting a Saturday night Cajun and zydeco radio show called "Rendez-vous des Cajuns." With our own show still to film that night, we stopped by merely for the resonance afforded by interviewing the band in front of this beautifully restored building, first erected in 1924 and initially used as a vaudeville theater.

By contrast, the VFW Hall was a bland, single-level building barely noticeable at the side of Ronald Reagan Highway (US Route 190), but perfectly suited to a free-wheeling evening of Cajun music and dance featuring youthful singer and accordionist Steve Riley and his first-rate band. As tended to be the case with Cajun music, the audience, like the band, was entirely white, and the dances seemed more restrained and communal (though certainly still exuberant) than those at zydeco events, where both musicians and crowds tended to be Creole and African American. Still, one of the liveliest songs of that night, which inspired an active dance floor, was Riley's cover of Lionel Cormier and Octa Clark's "Bayou Noir/Back of Town Two-Step," featuring sweet harmonies and some inspired fiddle playing by David Greely.

Sunday morning, a few of us backtracked to Lafayette where we shot numerous scenes for the separate zydeco film, then, by late afternoon, made our way farther west to Lake Charles where most of our crew was busy setting up for a joint Beau Jocque and Boozoo Chavis zydeco concert in the surprisingly spacious Habibi Temple, built and operated by the Shriners. Although I shall deal with this concert at length when discussing *The Kingdom of Zydeco*, I should mention here that, among the interviews we filmed before or during the show was one with Rounder Records founder Bill Nowlin, who emphasized his label's ongoing commitment to Cajun and Creole culture. Also, whereas several songs by each of the two artists performing that night would later be included in the zydeco film, one of the best, "Beau Jocque Boogie," was saved for exclusive use in *True Believers*.

Monday, September 20, as we departed Lake Charles, we said goodbye to our lighting and music recording people, as well as to Scott and Heather, all of whom had been with us since New Orleans, then drove west until we reached Austin, Texas. Although driving for five hours does not equal a day off, at least this was our only commitment for the day, leaving time for Mexican food, beers, and margaritas, as well as some light preparation for what was to come. We also were able to meet up with Rounder's Brad Paul, who had flown in to keep us company.

Tuesday morning, a few of us filmed an interview with Mexican-American singer and guitarist Tish Hinojosa at her home, and then another with blues and R & B singer and pianist Marcia Ball at La Zona Rosa, a bar and restaurant then co-owned by her husband, painter Gordon Fowler. At the same time, the rest of our crew did its best to light La Zona Rosa's vast, adjoining space—a converted warehouse—for that night's concert. Even though, on this occasion, we were forced to do without a music recording truck, we were fortunate to have Walter Morgan, a local recording technician, to record the show for us in-house, while simultaneously providing a flawless two-track mix.

The show that night began at eight o'clock, with a set by Hinojosa and her band, who played a disparate blend of Tex-Mex, pop, and folk songs. However, the song of hers I chose to use in the film was "Dejame Llorar (Let Me Cry)," a beautiful Mexican ballad that she performed as a duet with her superb lead guitarist, Marvin Dykhuis. As she played acoustic guitar and sang like an angel in Spanish, Marvin accompanied her with his own sparkling, Spanish guitar stylings. Both Tish and her songs had a delicacy about them, regardless of language or genre.

After a short break, Marcia Ball's rollicking, Texas-meets-Louisiana blues band took the stage. Then, with Marcia comfortably seated behind her Yamaha keyboard, she launched into a rousing set of originals. Ultimately, the two songs of hers I decided to use were a high-energy, piano-driven, Louisiana swamp rock number called "Big Shot," and a more laid-back, Texas blues tribute to Chess Records legend Willie Dixon, which she titled "Facts of Life." Together, these songs demonstrate how Marcia, who grew up on the border between Louisiana and Texas, brilliantly absorbed the musical traditions of both states.

After filming concerts by Tish Hinojosa and Marcia Ball at Austin's La Zona Rosa, (from left to right) director Robert Mugge, line producer Robert Maier, camera assistant Craig Smith, Rounder executive Brad Paul, cameraman David Sperling, grip Quincy McKay, and cameraman Bill Burke relax with Marcia, whose painter husband owned the club. (photographed by Christopher Li, 1993)

The next day—Wednesday, September 22—we returned our vehicles to the rental company and flew to Nashville where we picked up new minivans, removed their rear seats (as we routinely did to make room for equipment), and loaded them with both people and gear. From there, we drove two-plus hours to Owensboro, Kentucky for the annual IBMA World of Bluegrass events where we would spend the next four days interviewing key members of the blue-grass community, shooting and recording pertinent performances, and attempting to capture the general flavor of rural American culture which, in spite of some early African American influence, had evolved into musical forms performed almost entirely by white musicians for white audiences.

Joining us as a consultant in Owensboro was Deb Sander, a woman who had previously urged me to produce a bluegrass film and even helped me try and raise funding for it, but who, more importantly, was friends with many musicians and therefore a great person to act as artist liaison. In addition, as a wise executive producer, David Steffen had thoughtfully left us alone through the bulk of our trip. However, this particular film was a different matter, because he alone had conceived and nurtured it as a project. So, he rightly chose to join us for a couple of days, basking in the glow of all he had wrought.

For multitrack music recording at the IBMA's awards show and outdoor stage, I called upon my old friend Johnny Rosen and his Fanta Professional Services in Nashville, not realizing that some personal issues had led to the loss of his mobile recording truck. Searching for a substitute that week, he had wound up with a hugely inappropriate semitruck, the trailer for which was enormous. And because of the cost of that truck, he tried to increase what he was charging me for recording performances on Thursday and Friday. However, I replied that there was no way I could afford any increase at all, which he handled with class, still giving me the same great recordings and positive attitude he had in the past.

By design, only a couple of the scenes we shot in Owensboro were intended for use in the Rounder portrait, one of which was an interview with Rounder founder Ken Irwin who, himself, had come directly from our last meeting in Lafayette. He was joined for that session in a mostly vacant hallway of Owensboro's RiverPark Center by two members (Dudley Connell and Eddie Stubbs) of the temporarily reconstituted Johnson Mountain Boys, with all three discussing Rounder's commitment to bluegrass from the earliest days of the label. Then, in the same hallway, we filmed the group in performance.

The Johnson Mountain Boys were devout traditionalists based in the surprising bluegrass hotbed of Washington, DC, also the long-time home of the Country Gentlemen and the Seldom Scene, and Ken had a special affection for the music they created. So, with only two cameras, plus Bill Barth's amazing ability to choreograph the movements of acoustic band members so that each moved forward or backward at just the right times for him to get proper levels on his single stereo microphone, we filmed them performing two lively numbers, both of which were loaded with twang. One was the classic American song "John Henry," and the other was a Hazel Dickens composition titled "My Better Years."

Bill later used the same technique for recording other Owens-boro acts in informal situations, including Russian bluegrass band Kukuruza in a hallway and hotel room of the massive Executive Inn on the Owensboro riverfront. Of course, those other performances were intended for the bluegrass film, as was a third number, "You'll Get No More of Me," performed by the Johnson Mountain Boys with Hazel Dickens on lead vocal.

On Saturday, September 25, several crew members flew home out of Nashville. The day after that, those of us remaining (two Bobs, two Bills, and Craig and Quincy) drove from Owensboro to Memphis, checked into the Radisson, had a relaxing dinner at the Peabody next door, and prepared for our final day of shooting. Then, on Monday morning as planned, we joined Ron Levy—husband of Rounder founder Marian Leighton Levy and head of Rounder blues imprint Bullseye Blues—at Crosstown Recorders, a small studio in the Crosstown section of the city, where Ron was completing work on an album for Memphis-based singer, songwriter, and left-handed guitar player Little Jimmy King. Happily, engineer Rusty McFarland allowed us not only to film Jimmy and Ron duetting on, respectively, electric guitar and Hammond B-3, but also the legendary Memphis Horns (Wayne Jackson on trumpet and Andrew Love on tenor sax) recording their typically soulful horn parts.

Later, we all headed to the nearby (and disturbingly named) White Way Pharmacy, where we filmed newly arrived Marian Leighton Levy at the pharmacy's soda fountain with Ron Levy and Jimmy

King, and then the Memphis Horns as well. Among other things, Marian discussed Rounder's commitment to recording blues, including the creation of the aforementioned Bullseye Blues label; Ron and Jimmy discussed their respective experiences working with blues guitar master Albert King; and Wayne and Andrew discussed formation of their famous horn section, as well as their collaboration with countless headliners, many of them recording for Memphis-based Stax Records.

Once we completed work in Memphis, we flew home again on Tuesday, September 28. However, Bill Barth, Bill Burke, Dave Sperling, and I barely had time to unpack before John Larson and Peter Price, the owners of John & Peter's Place in New Hope, Pennsylvania, gave us permission to film their Thursday evening, September 30 show featuring singer-songwriter Bill Morrissey, a key Rounder folk artist.

Fortunately, this was barely work at all, because Bill's exquisite performance was delivered in the presence of his adoring parents, other proud family members, and a roomful of devoted fans, making it the most intimate of film shoots. Accompanying himself on acoustic guitar, Bill sang such moving, perceptive, and witty songs as "Birches," "Inside," "Robert Johnson," and "Letter from Heaven," three of which I would manage to squeeze into the Rounder movie. I also conducted an informative interview with Bill, and then a sweet one with him and his new manager, Ellen Karas, who had recently become his wife. Sadly, that marriage, like the one between Marian Leighton and Ron Levy, would not last, but Bill and Ellen would remain close friends, as well as business partners, until his death, which arrived much too early. For those of us who came to know and love Bill and his work, his song "Inside" contains lyrics as poignant as our cherished memories of him: "This ain't Hollywood. It never really gets that good. Call it love if you think you should. But no need to explain."

A week and a half later, the two other Bills (Barth and Burke) and I would travel to Cambridge, Massachusetts where we filmed the Rounder owners and staff walking us through various areas of their operations and elaborating on the ideals that had led three recent college graduates to attempt such an ambitious and wide-ranging endeavor. As with the Alligator film, I especially enjoyed meeting all of the key players and learning what each of them contributed to the label's larger mission, which was recording a diverse lineup of traditional American artists, distributing their work, and supporting them as they took their music on the road.

After that shoot, however, David Steffen asked that I put away the Rounder and zydeco films until further notice, because his chief priority was that I rush the bluegrass film to completion. As he was quick to remind me, TNN planned to broadcast its one-hour version in February, which also made it logical for BMG Video to release its longer version at around the same time. In short, that left me until the end of the year to edit the entire film on my 16mm flatbed editing table, plus oversee Rich Adler's music mixes in Nashville in early December. Then, in January, I would need to have the film color-corrected and printed by Bob Koch at my film lab in Richmond, oversee the final sound mix by Athan Gigiakos in New York, oversee a transfer of master film and audio materials to video by Richard Goldstein in North Jersey, create a version of the film less than half its actual length at a post house near Philadelphia, ship that ridiculously short master to TNN for its premiere broadcast on February 23, 1994, and ship David a video master he could use in duplicating the full 101-minute film.

Although all of us were glad to have finished that production by the externally imposed deadline, a kind of pall had covered the project since our return from Owensboro. That was because, in 1993 when we were shooting, Alison Krauss was already the most successful Rounder artist of all time—one who, out of loyalty, had stuck with the label, even after becoming an international star—but she also was the biggest name in bluegrass. So, David Steffen, the Rounder owners, and I were all counting on her appearing in both *Gather at the River* and *True Believers*, because it was her name, more than anyone else's, that promised to make the two projects profitable. And of course, this was why we had filmed Alison during the World of Bluegrass events in Owensboro, both at the awards show where she was co-host, and on the outdoor stage at night, where she performed with her band. But as we later learned, that was when everything "went south," as it were.

We had thought Krauss's outdoor performance extraordinary, and therefore, we expected to use one or more of her songs in both the bluegrass film and the Rounder Records portrait. However, what we later learned from the Rounders, as they learned it from Alison's management, was that the rain that had fallen from time to time during the festival had, she believed, had a negative effect on her voice. Therefore, she was now refusing to allow any of her Owensboro performances to be used in either film.

This was devastating news for all of us, and we scrambled to figure out a solution. Sadly, though, with so little time left for us to complete the bluegrass film prior to TNN's deadline, we would have to release it without a performance from the most commercially successful bluegrass artist in the world. Her absence did not affect the story we were telling, or the overall quality of our finished product, though it did affect the film's commercial potential. On the other hand, the Rounder owners could not imagine releasing a Rounder Records twenty-fifth anniversary film without the prominent involvement of their biggest star. So, they prevailed upon her, and on her multi-instrumentalist band member Ron Block, to fly to Philadelphia where the two Bills and I could film and record them taping a show with WXPN's *World Cafe* radio host David Dye.

This did not happen until Wednesday, June 15, 1994, after I had fully completed both *Gather at the River* and *The Kingdom of Zydeco*. But thanks to the generous participation of David and his producer Bruce Ranes, it was in plenty of time for me to secure good interview and performance sequences for the Rounder film. In fact, what I ended up using in the film was a traditional instrumental titled "Carroll County Blues," featuring Alison on fiddle and Ron on hollow-body guitar, plus Alison's mellow rethinking of "Baby, Now That I've Found You," the 1967 debut single by British pop group the Foundations. As an interesting side note, on this occasion, Alison forgot to insert a fiddle solo in the middle of the song, contrary to what she had done for the forthcoming commercial release. But the important point was that, once again, we had captured an artist both honoring musical tradition and experimenting with new uses of contemporary material.

In closing, I should make two final observations about this unexpected reshoot. First, despite my frustration with Alison's Owensboro decision, in Philadelphia, she proved to be as talented, as professional, as down-to-earth, and as personable as her popular image had led me to expect. Naturally, that is not always the case with hugely successful performers. Second, when Alison sings, which she does beautifully, of course, she does so at a surprisingly low volume, requiring the audio technician to crank up her level. I say this not as criticism, but as a partial explanation, perhaps, for her uniquely soothing sound.

Far less soothing was news in early 1994 that David Steffen planned to leave his position with BMG Video. Reportedly, BMG's corporate heads in Germany had named a new leader for their American operations, and having been through such corporate shuffles before, David decided to jump ship before being pushed. My disappointment was two-fold in that, not only had David become a close friend and valued ally, but his departure would surely affect my remaining dealings with BMG. Fortunately, as it turned out, attorney Neal Edelson, who had negotiated contracts for the four films on which David and I had collaborated, made sure I received the last of my funding. And that, in turn, enabled me to finish my work on the Rounder film, as well as submit my final paperwork for the three latest productions.

Ironically, the real problem happened once all the films were ready for distribution. As so often happens with a change of corporate executives, new management wanted nothing to do with old management's projects. Certainly, they had no problem with honoring my contracts, paying project bills, and allowing the films to be completed. But beyond that, they had no interest at all in seeing them released, even though, for the moment, they still owned a home video division. For that reason, it was fortunate I had retained theatrical and semi-theatrical rights for all of my BMG productions, meaning I would be able to screen all four of them in theaters and at film and music festivals, which also would get them reviewed.

In fact, in October of 1994, I kicked off distribution of the three most recent films by arranging joint world premieres at two of my favorite gatherings—the Denver International Film Festival and the Mill Valley Film Festival. Then, in mid-1995, after I presented all four BMG funded films at several other festivals, my friend David Kinder, former film programmer at Webster University in St. Louis, created Dakin Films, primarily to arrange modest theatrical releases for the four, whether separately or together. And yet, aside from efforts by David Kinder and myself, and home video releases already initiated by David Steffen for *Pride and Joy* and *Gather at the River*, the other two films simply gathered dust on BMG's shelves.

The one exception was that, having invested significant time, talent, and money in the making of *True Believers*, the Rounders insisted they be allowed to distribute free VHS copies of the film in celebration of their upcoming twenty-fifth anniversary. BMG agreed, so Rounder printed up its own posters and video packages, had a great many VHS cassettes manufactured, and sent out packaged tapes to press, media, radio stations, musicians, and other members of their extended musical family.

In other words, thanks to Rounder itself, the film at least was seen by people to whom it would mean the most. And just as I gave Alligator Records owner Bruce Iglauer the final say regarding his label, I should do the same with the Rounders and their own impressive legacy:

Bill Nowlin: I think the overall reason that's kept us together has simply been a love of the music and a belief in what we're doing. We have often said that we feel a kind of mission to the work that we do, and that we really are doing something that we each find very, very valuable. And that means enough to us. It's a bigger thing than just the three of us.

Ken Irwin: To the music and to the artists that, in many cases, become like family to us. You know, we have our family here, the Rounder family. But it's an extended family, which often includes the artists as well.

Marian Leighton Levy: Well, the artists and all of the people who work on the records, meaning, like, other musicians. But also, almost any record that we were to look at, there's like a group; it's like a community thing, in a way, because there are always people from wherever that artist is from who've been pushing us to do it. And of course, you might find it interesting to learn where the name Rounder came from. Ken?

Ken Irwin: We had a little bit of difficulty when we started out, and we needed to come up with a name. And we, sort of had a session where we all threw out names, and the name "Rounder" came up, and we all started free-associating. One of the early influences on us was a group called the Holy Modal Rounders, who did old time music, and introduced us to old time music, and we went back and discovered the people who had been the roots of their music. And then, rounders are hobos, you know; people who are on the road making the rounds. And early on, we were traveling around in our VW bus, or in Bill's VW bus at the time, and hitting festivals, and going places and sleeping in the bus. And we had shared certain experiences, and it felt like we had an affinity with rounders. And of course, records were round. And so, we just kept associating and came up with other ideas.

Marian Leighton Levy: And we always liked that fact that, you know, a lot of songs—blues songs and country songs from the twenties—would say, like, "low down rounders," and refer to, like, "low down rounders stole my gal from me," and stuff like that. They seemed like pretty colorful, interesting people that you'd like to get to know and would have lots of stories to tell.

Chapter Seven

Creole Crowns (SW Louisiana Royalty)

The Kingdom of Zydeco (1994)

Zydeco Crossroads: A Tale of Two Cities (2015)

During a previously described shoot for *True Believers: The Musical Family of Rounder Records*, I asked singer-songwriter Bill Morrissey about zydeco, and in his typically witty fashion, he responded: "I remember, in '73, I guess—'74, '73—I went to Berkeley for the first time . . . Berkeley, California. And I heard Chris Strachwitz's radio show, and I heard this guy named Clifton Chenier playing zydeco. And nobody back east had a clue what that was. And I thought: Well, it's kind of blues, it's kind of French, it's kind of . . . strange!"

This 1993 exchange also returns me to 1989 or so when Ken Wlaschin, my friend at the American Film Institute in Los Angeles, invited me to participate in a small showcase of music-related films in Santa Monica. I attended, of course, and while there, had the pleasure of meeting the delightful Mel Stuart, who screened his 1973 classic *Wattstax*, and hanging out with my friend and obvious influence Les Blank, whom I had first met (along with his engaging partner and collaborator Chris Simon) in January of 1985 when we both screened music-related docs in competition at Sundance (or at least, at the Park City precursor to Sundance which, again, was called the US Film Festival). I no longer remember which film or films of mine were screened in Santa Monica, but I do remember what Les showed, which was his recently completed collaboration with Chris Strachwitz and Maureen Gosling titled *J'ai Été Au Bal (I Went to the Dance)*. I remember because it was, and is, such a charming and informative history of what the filmmakers described as "the toe-tapping, foot-stomping music of French Southwest Louisiana." But even more than Les's wonderful film, which I saw for the first time that day, I remember his reaction when, after the screening, an audience member asked him the difference between Cajuns and Creoles. To say the least, this question annoyed that most imperturbable of filmmakers, and his response was that, by that point in time—and especially fresh off of a screening of his latest film—no one still should wonder what distinguished one Southwest Louisiana group from the other. And yet, to this day, outside of the state, people still confuse Cajun with Creole, whether in terms of race, cuisine, music, or other aspects of their somewhat overlapping French culture.

Part of such confusion comes from varying definitions, even within Louisiana. But suffice it to say that, in Southwest Louisiana, "Cajun" refers to lighter-skinned persons of French ancestry (descendants of Acadians who fled French Canada), while "Creole" connotes usually darker-skinned persons, not only of French and African heritage, but probably of Spanish, Native American, and Caribbean as well. As is often implied, Creoles, in particular, are like the Louisiana dish called gumbo, which can come in either Creole or Cajun variations, but which is always comprised of myriad ingredients. Otherwise, in race-conscious America, people from outside the region are prone to identify Creoles as African American, simply on the basis of their typically darker skin tones.

At any rate, my film *The Kingdom of Zydeco* deals exclusively with the Creole culture of Southwest Louisiana. And just as Chris Strachwitz of Arhoolie Records assisted Les Blank and Maureen Gosling with the making of *J'ai Été Au Bal*, and music writer Robert Palmer assisted me with the making of *Deep Blues*, Rounder's Scott Billington was an incomparable source of information, contacts, and inspiration for my first film produced entirely in Louisiana. Not only was Scott familiar with the region in general, but he also had worked with, and developed close relationships with, all four of the key artists on which the film would be focused, as well as with other influential figures in the community. In other words, his participation gave me the foundation I needed to record performances and to tell an important story, without concern that anything I presented would be inaccurate or, in a sense only locals might detect, inherently untrue. And with the laying of such groundwork, my own story could begin.

During the summer of 1993, after David Steffen of BMG Video had approved the idea of my shooting two films at once—a bluegrass film and a Rounder Records portrait—primarily on a big trip through the South, I began consulting with key Rounder staff members Scott Billington and Brad Paul about which Rounder artists should be included and in which Southern cities we should film and record them. It was at this point that Scott began schooling me on various aspects of the zydeco music scene of Southwest Louisiana, the heart of which stretches from Lafayette to Lake Charles, and on the Creole musical families that produce generation after generation of top zydeco artists. In particular, I learned that, despite my recent experience with enduring musical scenes in Hawai'i and the Mississippi Delta, probably no traditional scene in the US was then more robust than the Creole music community of Southwest Louisiana. More specifically, it was a scene in which older generations of musicians were passing the torch to younger ones; in which musical styles were evolving rapidly, as was the split between traditionalists and new innovators; in which live music clubs—usually dark, smoky, and somewhat cramped—were packed to capacity with dancers, some of whom were periodic visitors from elsewhere in the country; in which Rounder and other labels were releasing new recordings on a regular basis; and in which these CDs, records, and cassettes were receiving radio play, not only throughout the region, but also in New Orleans and parts of Texas (Houston, in particular), where many Creoles had settled after traveling there for work opportunities.

This was a time of flux for artists and fans alike, because the self-appointed yet renowned "King of Zydeco," Clifton Chenier, had died six years before, and his designated successor, Alton Jay Rubin, better known as "Rockin' Dopsie" (pronounced "Doopsie"), had just died as well. These losses had left a vacuum, because the Creole community had come to appreciate the notion of royalty and now was divided as to whom, if anyone, should be considered king number three. Much of that talk surrounded, or rather was initiated by, the aforementioned Andrus Espre, the former air force sergeant and oil refinery worker who now performed and recorded zydeco under the name of Beau Jocque. Certainly, at the age of thirty-nine, he was considerably younger than still-functioning pioneers of the genre such as Boozoo Chavis, John Delafose, Rockin' Sidney, Buckwheat Zydeco, Queen Ida, and Roy Carrier. And yet, he was older than much of the newer crop of artists—Nathan Williams, Terrance Simien, Keith Frank, Chubby Carrier, and others—if only because he had started so much later in life. Still, Beau Jocque's forceful and funk-flavored dance music, coupled with his gruff voice and hard-pumping accordion, had made him the most crowd-pleasing artist currently working.

As mentioned previously, Scott had produced a well-regarded first album for Espre/Jocque, with a second one on the way, and firmly believed that Beau should represent zydeco in our Rounder Records film. I was fine with that, very much liking what the two of them had thus far accomplished, and therefore left it to Scott to make the arrangements. Of course, what happened next would surprise us both, and led me to propose that we make a third film for BMG, this last one focusing exclusively on zydeco.

Scott and I had assumed we would shoot and record Beau Jocque in a smoky nightspot like Richard's Club in Lawtell, El Sid O's in Lafayette, or Slim's Y-Ki-Ki in Opelousas. Yet, ever the self-promoter, Beau Jocque had decided on his own that, number one, he wanted to upgrade the image of zydeco by having us film him in a much larger (which, to him, meant classier) venue; and number two, that he wanted to take on Wilson Anthony "Boozoo" Chavis, perhaps the most respected of surviving zydeco pioneers.

Early on in his musical career, Boozoo had played widely in the region and, in 1954, even recorded "Paper in my Shoe," considered to be the first zydeco recording. Then, in the sixties and seventies, having lost faith in the music business, he stopped recording and performing in public, choosing instead to farm and raise racehorses at Dog Hill, his property near Lake Charles. But in 1984, after seeing another musician using his name and still others appropriating his songs, he returned to performing himself, exciting new generations with his raw, down-home version of their collective music.

Finally, in 1993, with Boozoo looking like the strongest of older contenders for zydeco coronation, Beau Jocque decided the two of them should engage in a public feud, culminating in a widely promoted "battle" for the crown. With perfect timing, Lawrence "Black" Ardoin, a highly regarded member of Creole's first family of musicians, offered to produce a dual concert at the Habibi Temple in Lake Charles that would be billed as the battle to end all battles. And with both Beau Jocque and Boozoo onboard, it was clear that we would have far more drama than was needed simply for a segment in the Rounder Records movie. (Note: Lawrence is the musician son of Creole accordion legend Alphonse "Bois Sec" Ardoin, who was, himself, the musical partner of Creole fiddle great Canray Fontenot and the younger cousin of pioneering Creole vocalist and accordion player Amédé Ardoin. Lawrence is also the father of popular zydeco artists Sean and Chris Ardoin.) At that point, I began doing research of my own in Southwest Louisiana, calling groups in the region with an interest in such matters. In the process, I discovered that the Louisiana Music Hall of Fame, a largely white organization, was making plans to crown Boozoo, claiming authority from the recently deceased Rockin' Dopsie, which, in turn, was angering the Creole-dominated Original Southwest Louisiana Zydeco Music Association. With such information in hand, I contacted David Steffen, letting him know that a cultural powder keg was about to blow, and that, if he could spare just a bit more money, we not only could shoot a third film during our Southern trip, but also one that could be the most exciting of the bunch. After much wringing of hands and gnashing of teeth, David finally agreed, while offering no more money than the absolute minimum I proposed. Still, with Rounder's help, I made do.

Together, Scott and I planned a brutal schedule for the two main days we would be in the region, and I carefully separated out which of our planned scenes would be shot for the zydeco film, and which would be intended for the Rounder movie. As a result, upon our arrival in Lafayette on Saturday, September 18, we filmed a couple of quick scenes at Festivals Acadiens for the Rounder film. Then, he and I raced a few of my crew members to numerous other zydeco-related locations while the rest of my crew set up for the Steve Riley show that night in Eunice.

Kicking things off for the zydeco film, we interviewed local entrepreneur Sid Williams at Sid's One Stop, which was his combination gas station and convenience store. Sid, wearing his signature cowboy hat, told us long, colorful tales about his inspiring life to date, as well as about his guidance of his brother Nathan's zydeco career, at one point revealing the pistol in his belt for effect. Next, we went around the corner to El Sid O's Zydeco and Blues Club, which Sid also owned. There, out in front, we filmed Sid's brother Nathan as he sang and played accordion on a tune of his own titled "Ma pauvre maman (My poor mama)," with his cousin, Mark Anthony Williams, accompanying him on rubboard. After that, we stopped by local radio station KVOL where we filmed zydeco deejay Lester Thibeaux playing a Beau Jocque song, followed by a promotional spot for the Habibi Temple show later in the weekend. Lester then directed us to Houserocker Records, operated by his sister, Irene Hebert, who was as sweet and soft-spoken as Lester was loud and hyperactive. A quick interview with Irene confirmed that, over the past year or so, Beau Jocque had become her biggest seller of zydeco CDs and cassettes.

Leaving Lafayette, we drove to Richard's club in Lawtell where, as previously described, we filmed owner Kermon Richard speaking with Scott Billington for the Rounder portrait, then also filmed him on his own for the zydeco movie. For the latter, Kermon briefly discussed the history of his legendary blues and zydeco club, as well as Beau Jocque's current dominance in the zydeco club scene. From there, we raced to Eunice where we filmed my interview with Steve

Riley and the Mamou Playboys, and then joined the rest of our group for filming Riley's Saturday night performance at the VFW Hall.

Sunday morning, September 19, as the bulk of my crew headed to the Habibi Temple in Lake Charles to prepare for the evening's concert, Scott and I took Bill Barth and Bill Burke to Lafayette's Acadian Village, which offered an idyllic re-creation of the buildings and general layout of an eighteenth-century Cajun community, complete with a small lake. There, in a large, open-air structure, the Louisiana Music Hall of Fame was readying one of its periodic induction ceremonies. I had spent a fair amount of time on the phone with the Hall of Fame's leader, a middle-aged woman named Lou Gabus, who could be alternately warm, abrupt, bawdy, frazzled, opinionated, defensive, overzealous, controversial, and unexpectedly generous. Seeing us arrive, she pulled my small crew and me off into a wooded setting out of earshot of her compatriots inside and said that now was as good a time as any to interview her.

As our camera and recorder rolled, Gabus self-righteously held up photos, letters, official proclamations, and more as she recalled how the great Clifton Chenier, the "king of zydeco," had named Rockin' Dopsie his successor, leading her to crown Dopsie ("my friend!") the king after Chenier's death. According to Lou, later on, Dopsie asked her to crown Boozoo Chavis as his crown prince, and that crowning was to have happened that very day. However, in the meantime, Dopsie, too, had died, leaving Gabus to claim that, at some future date, she would crown Boozoo as the next king. Yes, she said, she knew that the Creole community opposed any such crowning, but for whatever reason, she still felt entitled.

Our second stop of the day was at the rural home of fifty-four-year-old zydeco artist John Delafose, who walked us out back to where he kept doves in a large cage and cows inside a fence. There, he sang us a version of one of his biggest hits, "Joe Pitre A Deux Femmes (Joe Pitre Has Two Women)," while accompanying himself on accordion, and with his grandson Gerard playing rubboard. As an older and more traditional artist, John scoffed at the notion of two of his peers battling to be the new king of zydeco, declaring that, even in death, Clifton Chenier was "the true king." It was a sweet moment, later made bittersweet by the fact that John would pass away in September of 1994, only months after the zydeco film was completed. As so often happens in that culture, John's band, the Eunice Cowboys, would carry on for years afterwards under leadership of his son, Geno Delafose, and Gerard Delafose formed a band of his own.

From there, we rushed to Lake Charles, arriving in the late afternoon. The bulk of my crew was already well into resolving the challenges of lighting a huge room with a high ceiling, shooting musicians as well as a large crowd of dancers with just three cameras, and recording clean sound in a cavernous space. Included in those efforts were Billy Brag's Available Lighting and Ed Eastridge's Big Mo music recording truck, both of which had been with us for our Friday night Irma Thomas shoot in New Orleans and our Saturday night Steve Riley concert in Eunice. The ground we were covering in such a short period of time was astounding.

With Bob Maier, Dave Sperling, and Chris Li in charge of the setup inside, I took Bill Barth and Bill Burke outside to shoot an interview with the six-foot, six-inch Beau Jocque and his much shorter but very attractive wife, Michelle. Beau's powerful presence made it easy to believe he had spent nine years in the air force until an explosion put him in the hospital with temporary amnesia, then years more as an oil refinery worker until an accident left him temporarily paralyzed from the waist down. Yet, it was difficult to picture a happier, friendlier, or more mischievous person with whom to chat, especially as he took every opportunity to rib Boozoo Chavis, saying how much he respected Boozoo's contributions to the music, but how the guy "didn't have a chance" against his own highly popular songs, heavily influenced by blues, soul, and especially funk of the sixties, seventies, and eighties. Certainly, the gentle taunts of this tall, handsome musician evoked those of boxer Muhammad Ali.

Robert Mugge meets Boozoo Chavis, his wife Leona Chavis, and his son Charles Chavis prior to the competing concerts by Beau Jocque and Boozoo Chavis at the Habibi Temple in Lake Charles, Louisiana. (photographed by film crew, 1993)

After that, Boozoo Chavis arrived, still wearing a large, diago-nal sash he had been given by Lou Gabus earlier in the day, and accompanied by his wife, Leona, and his son Charles, who played rubboard in Boozoo's band. Although greeting us warmly, as soon as I asked Boozoo about the competition with Beau Jocque, he began to grow irritated. In fact, the longer he talked, the more upset he got, expressing shock that a newcomer like Espre could even *presume* to challenge a veteran such as himself, and ridiculing, through imita-tion, some of Jocque's crowd-pleasing, onstage antics. I later learned that Chavis's mood had been affected by Lawrence Ardoin informing him that, since Beau Jocque was currently the more popular artist, Boozoo, the veteran, would have to perform first, making him essen-tially the warmup act. Yet, watching the short, feisty musician grow hotter and hotter was not unlike watching Bugs Bunny adversary Yosemite Sam in old Warner Brothers cartoons, because Boozoo was nothing if not equally animated. But eventually, Chavis cooled down again and was just as gentlemanly as he had been before.

Prior to the concert, we also were able to feast on some of the flavorful barbecue chicken that had been prepared in a large, cylindrical smoker while I was interviewing both men. It resembled the one that had been used to feed us at the Big Jack Johnson concert in Clarksdale, Mississippi during the shooting of *Deep Blues*. Then, after eating, we were off and running, with both artists performing long sets on the stage inside, and hundreds of dancers taking advantage of the far more spacious floor than was typically available in zydeco clubs.

Assuredly, no prisoners were taken, because each of the bands "killed it," as fans are known to say, with Boozoo performing such classics as "Do It All Night," "Gilton," "Motor Dude Special," "Dog Hill," "Gone á la Maison," and "Forty One Days," and Beau presenting such recent hits as "Damballah," "Zydeco Boogie Woogie," and the enormously popular "Give Him Cornbread." At least, these are the songs I included in the film, using more by Boozoo, of course, simply because Beau's songs ran longer and were more open-ended. But inasmuch as neither artist was measurably better than the other, we heard no more claims about the show settling anything. Instead, as typically happened on such occasions, the audience felt richly entertained and eventually went home humming. As for our two headliners, they came to see a winning formula in this king competition, and so repeated it again and again thereafter, including at Jazz Fest and the Rock 'n' Bowl, considered the two best spots in New Orleans for live zydeco.

Happily, Lawrence Ardoin had provided a lengthy break between bands, so Bill Barth, Bill Burke, and I were able to conduct additional interviews in the dark, making use of a portable film light. The first was my interview with Rounder owner Bill Nowlin, in which he affirmed his Label's commitment to zydeco, as well as to other aspects of French Louisiana culture. This, of course, was intended for use in the Rounder film. Without doubt, though, my second interview, which was conducted with Wilbert Guillory, Creole president of the Original Southwest Louisiana Zydeco Music Association, and his associate Paul Scott, would prove an effective counterbalance to the statements of Lou Gabus. Their message, delivered with both passion and reason, was that an overwhelmingly white organization like the Louisiana Music Hall of Fame should not be interfering with a non-white art form. From their point of view, the era of Southern white paternalism was still in effect.

Over the next several months, as I edited the bluegrass film, and then the zydeco film, I stayed in touch with Lou Gabus about her plans. Eventually, she let me know that, disregarding the wishes of the Zydeco Association and other key figures in the Creole community, she was proceeding with her plans to crown Boozoo Chavis the king of zydeco and would do so at the next Louisiana Music Hall of Fame induction ceremony on Sunday, April 10, 1994. So, when the time came, Bill Barth, Bill Burke, David Steffen, Scott Billington, and I all flew to Lafayette again, drove to Acadian Village, and met up with Lou, now dolled up in a fancy blue skirt suit with white stripes, collar, and pockets; gold hoop earrings; heavy mascara; and teased back strawberry blonde hair. Back in the same wooded area as before, she briefly defended her decision to move forward with the coronation, despite widespread criticism, claiming she was doing it so that "Rockin' Dopsie will be able to rest in his grave." Then, having said her piece, she raced back to the covered, open-air structure once again, in preparation for her big event.

A short time later, as a formal proclamation was read from the stage, Boozoo Chavis—accompanied by his wife, and looking snappy in his blue suit, turquoise shirt, multicolored tie, and white cowboy hat—stepped out of a white limousine to applause and shouts of "Hail, King Boozoo!" and walked through the crowd to the stage. Then, as a band played behind them, white-haired tourism official A. J. LeBlanc placed a red and gold crown on Boozoo's suddenly bare head, and Lou Gabus placed a scepter in his hands. Next, the three of them posed for pictures from the stage, and seeing our own camera off to one side, Lou directed an open-mouthed expression of glee directly at us, apparently showing both pleasure and relief that she had pulled this off at last.

After the ceremony, we managed to corner Boozoo, now wearing his white cowboy hat again and flanked by two of his sons. The sons held his crown and scepter with appropriate reverence, which allowed Chavis himself to continue holding the Budweiser can from which he had been drinking. Asked to place this honor in context, he summed up the day as follows:

> It's wonderful, and it's a great big pleasure bein' out here, to see each and every one out here, and for me to try to keep up the tradition and the culture. There were Clifton Chenier, and there were Dopsie, but I was there all the time. They just overlooked me; I was kind of short. [Now holding the crown.] It means a whole lot, you know. And when I get to the jazz festival, somebody in front gonna say, "Boozoo, where's your crown?" So, I might get on the stage with it and play a couple numbers. After that, I'm gonna take that off, you know? [Having returned the crown to his son.] Yeah, I can't wear that to church. I ain't gonna bring it with me there. And when I die, I ain't gonna be able to take it there. I can't bring it everywhere I go!

With the Hall of Fame event winding down, our group headed over to see Sid and Nathan Williams at El Sid O's. With a kind of call and response, the two of them collaborated on a message: It was not enough simply to have a king. Instead, there also should be a crown prince, as Dopsie had been; an ambassador, as Buckwheat Zydeco still was; and perhaps even a Duke. Nonetheless, they both offered congratulations to Boozoo, even as they also noted that he had been crowned by "an organization," rather than by "the people."

By a nice coincidence, that same Sunday afternoon, Beau Jocque and his band were performing on a jury-rigged stage outside of Richard's Club, as local Creole families, including small children, enjoyed the spring air, most of them dancing on the grass. Speaking with us during a break, and with no more pretense of an actual rivalry between Boozoo and himself, he graciously extended his own congratulations: "I'm happy for him. I think he deserves it; it's something that he's earned. He's been out there for years, and he's been giving his heart out. You know? And I think it's made him very happy. And knowing that, that makes me very happy. Yeah. I wish him well."

And with that, Beau Jocque and his band started playing again, and people started dancing again, as they always had in Southwest Louisiana, and as they always would, with or without a royal succession or command performance.

Beau Jocque and the High Rollers perform in a Sunday afternoon concert outside Richard's Club in Lawtell, Louisiana. (frame from film, 1994).

***

In June of 1994, New Orleans-based journalist Michael Tisserand secured a promotional tape of *The Kingdom of Zydeco* from David Kinder, my distributor, and wrote an extraordinarily positive review in *Off-Beat*, the essential, monthly music magazine in that city.

This was a surprise because, even though a series of modest theatrical runs had been planned for bigger cities around the country, none was yet scheduled for New Orleans, and none at all would take place before the theatrical premiere in New York City beginning July 1, 1994, which really would be just a handful of midnight and matinee screenings at the Cinema Village. Of course, the larger significance of the New York opening was that it would take place a week after New York's first Beau Jocque vs. Boozoo Chavis battle of the bands, which was scheduled for June 25, also the birthday of the late Clifton Chenier.

Happily, my buddy Mark Scheerer was able to use that opening to profile me on CNN's *Showbiz Today* again, and other friends, including WBGO-based deejay and record producer Bob Porter, were able to promote the film by interviewing me on their blues radio shows. But with no screenings scheduled for the Crescent City before the New Orleans International Film Festival premiere in late October, the *OffBeat* rave was that much more gratifying, especially since it would be read by many of those most likely to care about such a film. And when the key New York reviews also turned out to be raves (especially Gene Seymour's piece in *New York Newsday*), the *OffBeat* piece looked, in retrospect, like a very good omen, indeed.

Michael and I would go on to become close friends, with zydeco a continuing part of our connection. In fact, because Michael was hugely knowledgeable about Southwest Louisiana and its music (having covered it continuously in the press), early the following year, I paid him to accompany me on another trip to the region as I gathered facts for a screenplay titled *Zydeco Rose*. My plan was to base it loosely on the life of female zydeco artist Rosie Ledet, with parts written for other key zydeco musicians as well. Unfortunately, although I did complete the feature-length screenplay, I never raised the funding needed to turn it into a film. Meanwhile, Michael went on to write the most exhaustive study yet of the genre, and when it first came to be published in 1997, he asked permission to borrow the title of my film for his book, which I told him would be an honor.

Later, although I would also include zydeco performances and interviews in a more general Louisiana music film, *Rhythm 'N' Bayous: A Road Map to Louisiana Music* (see Chapter Eight), which I shot in 1999 and briefly released in 2000, I would not devote another film exclusively to Creole music in Southwest Louisiana until 2014, when I was asked to create a film as part of Zydeco Crossroads, a multileveled project developed and overseen by Roger LaMay and Bruce Warren of Philadelphia, Pennsylvania public radio station WXPN, and underwritten by a generous grant from the Pew Center for Arts & Heritage. As part of that project, WXPN would bring zydeco artists to Philadelphia for concerts; would co-sponsor events with Philadelphia's Cajun and zydeco dance organization Allons Danser; would produce a zydeco-related radio series hosted by Lafayette-based newspaper journalist and deejay Herman Fuselier; would create a project website and YouTube channel for the posting of relevant photos, essays, and video clips; and would organize an eventual trip to Lafayette by station staff members, during which it would closely collaborate with Lafayette public radio station KRVS. As for myself, in conjunction with my wife and filmmaking partner Diana Zelman (a former Philadelphia-based financial advisor and filmmaker I had met in August of 2005, and with whom I began collaborating soon thereafter), I would document the broad strokes of WXPN's project, while also generating events and activities of my own in order to create what I considered to be a sequel, or at least an update, for *The Kingdom of Zydeco*.

This new production, which I titled *Zydeco Crossroads: A Tale of Two Cities*, carried forward my ongoing theme of individuals and organizations working to support traditional musicians and music scenes, and did so even more overtly than had my previous zydeco film, with its focus on music organizations, music clubs, a radio station, and a record store. On this occasion, I was again spotlighting music clubs and organizations, but my primary focus was on radio station WXPN in Philadelphia as it helped to promote the culture of another region of the country, assisted by an unofficial sister station, which was KRVS in Lafayette. And at least in passing, I should mention that KRVS had assisted with two of the other Louisiana music films I produced between *The Kingdom of Zydeco* and *Zydeco Crossroads*. But more on those films in the next chapter.

The fact that Diana and I now lived in Muncie, Indiana, and not in either Philadelphia or Lafayette, did complicate matters a bit, because it meant long drives to Philly whenever I wanted to cover anything there, as well as the expected flights to shoot in Lafayette. But two things I did not want to miss were artist C. J. Chenier, son of the late zydeco king Clifton Chenier, performing at WXPN's annual XPoNential Music Festival in Camden, New Jersey, just across the Delaware River from the City of Brotherly Love, and WXPN general manager Roger LaMay announcing the sixteen-month Zydeco Cross-roads project from the stage there. Both were happening together on Saturday, July 26, 2014.

With project funding not yet fully in place, I needed to document Chenier's set as cheaply as possible. I therefore asked cameraman Dave Sperling to drive down from his home in North Jersey and bring along three video cameras, one of which he would operate just below the front of the stage, another of which I would operate standing on the left side of the stage, and the third of which we would set up at the back of the stage and leave largely unattended. In addition, WXPN put me in touch with Bob Giardini, who singlehandedly shot many of the XPoNential performances for live webcasting, and he agreed to operate one of his cameras from the top of the hill on which the audience was seated, and to attach an unmanned camera to the right wall of the stage. In this way, we documented C. J.'s entire crowd-pleasing set, as well as Roger LaMay's announcement, late that Saturday afternoon. Fortunately, WXPN also had booked Indre Recording Studio's remote recording truck to do live recording and mixing of all the shows at that year's festival, so concert audio could be broadcast live over local airwaves and via the XPN website, and company owner Michael Comstock was willing to provide a live mix to me as well, for later use in the film.

The two songs from the concert that I ended up using were a pair of classics written by C. J.'s father, Clifton: "Zydeco Boogaloo" and "I'm Coming Home." In addition, before the show, Dave Sperling, Bob Giardini, David Dye, and I took C. J. to a quieter spot by the river so that David could interview him, not only about his famous father, but also about his own decades-long career, and I used portions of that interview to accompany his performance. Interview audio was generously recorded and mixed by *World Cafe* producer Kimberly Junod.

WXPN's plans for a several-day trip to Louisiana centered primarily around a concert it was arranging with KRVS for Thursday, October 30 at Lafayette's Blue Moon Saloon. Two recently formed supergroups, Creole United and Soul Creole, would perform that night, with the concert broadcast live to WXPN listeners. The Philly broadcast would also include a panel discussion featuring *World Cafe* host David Dye, Lafayette journalist and KRVS deejay Herman Fuselier, and Creole musician Sean Ardoin, who was the driving force behind Creole United. Supplementing that show, I arranged with old friend Sid Williams of El Sid O's to pull together a big Wednesday night jam featuring several generations of zydeco artists, and Roger LaMay invited down top station donors to enjoy both shows and related activities. So, we all would have plenty to keep us busy.

Traveling to Lafayette with Diana and me, though from several cities, were director of photography Dave Sperling and additional cameramen Chris Li, WXPN's Bob Giardini, and my former student Joe Sailer, who was quickly becoming a top freelance cinematographer himself. Meeting us there were Southwest Louisiana-based Terry DuPuy to record music and audio for the film; my friend Michael Tisserand from New Orleans to serve as an onscreen music consultant; and key WXPN personnel, including general manager Roger LaMay, associate general manager Bruce Warren, *World Cafe* host David Dye, and *World Cafe* producer Kimberly Junod. The station staff was there mostly to oversee the Lafayette leg of their larger project, but also would assist us with production of the film.

On Tuesday, October 28, my crew and I checked out the two performance venues, had lunch with our WXPN counterparts, and then had dinner at our favorite Lafayette eatery, which was the (admittedly tourist-friendly) Prejean's Restaurant, where we enjoyed eating first-rate Cajun cuisine to the sounds of live local musicians, all while under the gaze of a gargantuan stuffed alligator. Then, the following day, we spent the afternoon lighting the stage and bar at El Sid O's, as well as filming David Dye's interviews with Michael Tisserand and Nathan Williams at the bar. Later, Sid Williams brought us all pulled-pork barbecue dinners in styrofoam containers, and allowed any of us who wanted to try the "possum" he had spent the day cooking in an oversized stock pot there in the room with us.

In addition to hiring a lighting company from the area, having a communication system shipped in from Virginia, and leaving music recording to Terry DuPuy, we paid Nathan Williams, Jr., the musician son of longtime zydeco artist Nathan Williams, to provide backline (amplifiers and PA system). Envisioning this solely as a jam, we also booked core members of Buckwheat Zydeco's Ils Sont Partis Band to back up all of the headliners: the legendary Lil' Buck Sinegal on guitar, the equally great Lee Allen Zeno on bass, Sir Reginald M. Dural (Buckwheat's son) on keyboard and rubboard, and Kevin Menard on drums. However, it proved impossible to stop a few younger musicians from bringing their own bands and then expecting us to pay the uninvited band members as well. To their credit, as well as frustration, Diana Zelman and Bruce Warren spent several hours sorting out who was on stage, who should be paid, and exactly how much they should be paid, as well as getting everyone to sign releases.

Over the course of the evening, we filmed a few songs each by major zydeco artists Buckwheat Zydeco, Chubby Carrier, and Nathan Williams, and a few by Nathan's older brother Sid, with Sid's grandson, Lil' Mike Dugas, playing rubboard. We also filmed a number of younger artists, including Chris Ardoin, Corey Arceneaux, Nathan Williams Jr. (stage name: Lil' Nathan) with his younger brother Naylon on organ, and Rockin' Dopsie Jr. Although most zydeco headliners play accordion, as did the late Rockin' Dopsie, his son Rockin' Dopsie Jr. (real name: David Rubin) sang and played a very aggressive rubboard, while David's brother Anthony played the accordion, his brother Tiger played drums, and on this occasion, Mississippi blues artist Vasti Jackson joined them on guitar. Among the songs performed that night which I used in the film were Buckwheat Zydeco's "Jackpot" (written by him with his manager Ted Fox), Sid Williams's self-promotional "Got A Party Goin' On At El Sid O's," his brother Nathan's "Lookin' For What You're Lookin' For," Lil' Nathan's "That L'Argent," Chubby Carrier's "Tu Le Ton Son Ton" (written by Clifton Chenier), Chris Ardoin's "Back Home," Corey Arcenaux's "Creole Man," and Rockin' Dopsie Jr.'s "Josephine" (written by his father) and "Baby What You Want Me To Do" (written by blues great Jimmy Reed).

During breaks in the nighttime concert, we also filmed David Dye in front of the club interviewing Chubby Carrier, Buckwheat Zydeco with his longtime friend Sid Williams, Lil' Nathan with his brother Naylon, and Rockin' Dopsie Jr. with his brother Anthony Rubin. In addition, we filmed Vasti Jackson, Chubby Carrier, and

Rockin' Dopsie Jr. performing a song called "Zydeco Crossroads," which Vasti wrote especially for the film, focusing on the influence of Mississippi blues on the evolution of Louisiana zydeco.

The following day, we spent the afternoon setting up to film the nighttime show at the Blue Moon Saloon, then spent the early evening in an exterior side area filming David Dye interviewing the following: Sean Ardoin and Andre Thierry of Creole United; Sean's father, Lawrence "Black" Ardoin, producer of the Habibi Temple concert we filmed in 1993; and Lawrence's frequent musical partner, fiddle player Edward Poullard. After that, we filmed the Creole United set, from which I chose two songs for use in the film. One was "Mmm Mmm Mmm," a modern Creole song written by drummer Sean Ardoin and accordion player Andre Thierry. The other was "Les Barres de la Prison," a classic song composed by Canray Fontenot, the legendary fiddle-playing partner of Bois Sec Ardoin, and now performed by Edward Poullard on fiddle, with Andre Thierry on accordion, Lawrence Ardoin on triangle, and Sean Ardoin singing the French lyrics.

Next to be filmed and recorded was Soul Creole, another band revisiting regional musical traditions, this time spearheaded by Cajun fiddle player Louis Michot (a founder and ongoing member of the Lost Bayou Ramblers) and Creole accordion player Corey Ledet (who headed his own zydeco band). After their set, we filmed David Dye interviewing the two of them about the origins of the fiddle in Cajun and Creole music, the influence of blues on zydeco, and the idea of their forming a group to explore the overlap between Cajun and Creole culture. The Soul Creole number I decided to use in the film was an improvised medley of the traditional Cajun song "Madeleine" and Bob Marley's reggae classic "Buffalo Soldiers."

On Friday, October 31, the WXPN people all left for home, as did two of my four cameramen. But Dave Sperling, Chris Li, Terry DuPuy, Diana, and I stuck around to shoot scenes at the first day of the annual Step N Strut, a major trail ride taking place in Opelousas, Louisiana. When making *The Kingdom of Zydeco* twenty-one years before, we had not had occasion to film this essential part of zydeco culture, wherein Creole cowboys and music fans ride horses to a prearranged location, then eat, drink, and dance to live zydeco performances. So, we were pleased to be able to shoot the start of that weekend's events, as well as an interview with Step N Strut Trail Ride organizer Dave Lemelle. However, since our crew could not be present on Sunday for the start of the actual trail ride, my friend and collaborator Vasti Jackson, who was with us at the site on Friday afternoon, offered to return there in order to shoot it on our behalf.

Later that evening, we sought out a chain restaurant called Hook'd Up Bar and Grill in Youngsville, where zydeco veteran Major Handy was performing live on accordion, backed by his lovely wife Frances Ayers Handy on rubboard, along with a laptop on which he had recorded himself playing other instruments. As we filmed, delighted family diners got to hear Major sing his charming compositions, including "Zydeco Feeling" and "Trail Ride," both of which I used in the film. In addition, we conducted an interview with Major in which, with Frances looking on, he discussed how, over the years, he also had performed blues, jazz, and country music, and how he had brought all of those influences to zydeco.

Finally, at the same location, we filmed Vasti Jackson on a blues-friendly steel guitar performing another rendition of his "Zydeco Crossroads" song, with Major and Frances backing him up on accordion and rubboard, respectively, and helping him to emphasize the aforementioned connection between blues and zydeco:

> Down at the zydeco crossroads,
> where the Delta meet the bayou,
> got the gris-gris and the mojo,
> down at the zydeco crossroads.
> We put the rhythm in the blues;
> yeah, we make your body move.
> A little waltz and a two-step;
> we slow drag and shuffle fast.
> Say, we've got some jambalaya mustard greens;
> prettiest women that you've ever seen.
> Louisiana and Mississippi,
> there ain't nothin' missin'.

Vasti Jackson on guitar (center), assisted by Major Handy on accordion and Frances Ayers Handy on rubboard, finishes performing his title song for the film Zydeco Crossroads. (frame from film, 2014)

Two David Dye interviews provided meaningful closing thoughts for the film. First, author and journalist Michael Tisserand noted how people outside of Louisiana (like, for instance, radio hosts, programmers, and listeners from Philadelphia) were bringing overdue recognition to Creole culture: "So, I think that brings a sense of purpose, a sense of self-respect, a sense of realization that we really do have something special here, [and] that, sometimes, it helps to have the outside world validate that for a home crowd." Second, Creole musician Sean Ardoin took such thoughts even further: "It *is* special to be Creole, because my African American experience is definitely, totally seasoned with my Creole experience. Matter of fact, I identify with my Creole experience first, because the Black experience is gonna happen when I walk in the room. The Creole experience is something nobody else has; it's strictly us."

Back in Indiana once again, no sooner did I begin editing than WXPN scheduled another zydeco concert near Philadelphia, which I did not feel we could miss. The featured artist was to be Rosie Ledet, the most prominent female artist in zydeco over recent decades, and one of my own personal favorites, ever since her earliest CDs were released in the mid-1990s and, soon thereafter, I penned my unproduced screenplay, *Zydeco Rose*. Several years later, I also featured her and her former husband Morris in my film *Rhythm 'N' Bayous: A Road Map to Louisiana Music*. Nonetheless, I could not pass up a chance to include her in this latest survey of the Southwest Louisiana Creole music scene. And besides, Dave Sperling and I needed to return to Philadelphia to film introductory and connecting interview sequences for the film, so we decided to shoot those at the station one day, with *World Cafe* producer Kimberly Junod again recording audio, and Rosie Ledet's concert and interview the following day.

As XPN's Bruce Warren made sure I knew, Rosie and her band were to perform at an Allons Danser event scheduled for Saturday, December 13, 2014 at the Holy Savior Social Club in Norristown, Pennsylvania, just outside of Philly. Performing with her at the time were rubboard player and backup singer Lil' Malcolm, drummer Boss Hog, former Beau Jocque bass player Chuck Bush, and New York-based guitarist and band leader Andre Nizzari. Happily, the station had hired Indre Studio's music recording truck for the event, and I booked Dave Sperling, Bob Giardini, and a friend of Bob's to run cameras, as well as operating one myself, and having another hung from the ceiling to the right of the band. I also asked Dave to bring stage lighting, and I hired C. C. Crabtree to provide a house PA system. But to save money, we did not bother with a communication system; instead, I gave instructions to each cameraman prior to the show and, whenever I had additional thoughts, ran over to convey them.

As part of our crew finished setting up coverage for that evening's concert, Dave, Bob, and I raced to a nearby sandwich shop called Lou's Steaks & Zeps. There, we were met again by *World Cafe* host David Dye and producer Kimberly Junod. After clearing a space at the soda fountain and lighting it, we were set to film David's interview with Rosie Ledet using two cameras as Kim simultaneously recorded it. I had filmed Rosie sharing the basics of her story before in 1999. But since zydeco was even more male-dominated than blues or jazz, I thought we should have her unique perspective and biography in this film as well.

As to the concert, Allons Danser events were largely excuses for its members to dance. So, we would have plenty of action on which to focus. Then again, Rosie's music was involving as well, alternating between high-intensity dance numbers and slower-paced romantic ballads, while also including sudden bursts of humor (currently provided by Lil' Malcolm and Chuck Bush) and of sly sexuality (evident even in her earliest compositions, perhaps most brazenly in "Sweet Brown Sugar"). Still another of her early numbers, "You're No Good for Me," at once soulful and gently feminist, was a second of my personal favorites, and the song of hers I chose to include in *Zydeco Crossroads*.

In my opinion, Rosie's overall performance and interview were so good that, once the primary film was almost finished, I decided to combine highlights of the two into a separate, fifty-five-minute portrait film titled *Rosie's in the House Tonight* for inclusion with the upcoming *Zydeco Crossroads* Blu-ray. My friend Steve Savage, based in Northern California, had done a phenomenal job of mixing the music we recorded in Louisiana (assisted by our Louisiana recording engineer, Terry DuPuy), and Michael Comstock had done a first-rate job mixing the C. J. Chenier set. But Rosie's guitarist and bandleader, Andre Nizzari, knew her current arrangements better than anyone, so I asked him to mix her music for both films, and he did not disappoint.

During this same period, I was simultaneously remastering many of my older films for new Blu-ray and DVD releases via my new distributor, MVD Visual, and I had found I could save money by doing much of the work at Technicolor in Toronto. Technicolor's reasonable prices, coupled with the current exchange rate, led me also to complete postproduction for *Zydeco Crossroads* in Canada (thereby symbolically reversing the migration of French-speaking Acadian people from Nova Scotia, New Brunswick, and Prince Edward Island to Southwest Louisiana).

And with that, by early spring of 2015, both the primary film and the Rosie Ledet spin-off were ready to go. However, WXPN's larger project would not run its course until October, at which point they would go out with a bang, including staging a final series of Philadelphia concerts by top Louisiana bands. The official climax was expected to involve a screening of the film on Thursday, October 22; several performances on Friday, October 23 and Saturday, October

24; and a panel discussion on Saturday—all at World Cafe Live, a building that housed a restaurant, two concert venues, and WXPN's offices and studios on the edge of the University of Pennsylvania campus. Thinking our own responsibilities in Philadelphia would be only for that Thursday screening, Diana and I accepted two other invitations: one from our friends Pat Mire, the prominent Louisiana-based filmmaker, and Rebecca Hudsmith, a dedicated federal public defender, to fly to Lafayette and world premiere the film there on Tuesday, October 13, in conjunction with their annual Cinema on the Bayou Film Festival (from which I had previously received a Lifetime Achievement Award); and another from our friend Roger Naber, to leave for Fort Lauderdale on Saturday, October 24, and sail on his Legendary Rhythm & Blues Cruise for a week, on which we would also premiere the film.

It was only then, after we had accepted these invitations, that the Philadelphia screening was moved to Saturday, October 24, which meant that we would not be able to attend. So, the series of premiere screenings went as follows: Tuesday, October 13 in Lafayette, with Diana and me attending and spending a week hanging out with Pat and Rebecca; Saturday, October 24 in Philadelphia, with Roger LaMay, Bruce Warren, and David Dye presenting the film in our absence; two heavily attended screenings on Roger's Blues Cruise, which were Monday, October 26 and Friday, October 30; and a benefit screening on Tuesday, October 27 for New Orleans public radio station WWOZ at the Robert E. Nims Theatre of the University of New Orleans. The latter screening only became possible because the Blues Cruise scheduled a stop in New Orleans that particular day, and filmmaker and professor Henry Griffin offered to host a showing at his university.

In his typically generous way, Major Handy assembled a band to perform at the Lafayette screening, including Major on accordion, Lil' Buck Sinegal on guitar, and Lee Allen Zeno on bass, with other prominent musicians both on stage and in the audience. Similarly, after the screening and panel discussion in Philadelphia, Corey Ledet, Wayne Singleton, and Rosie Ledet performed with their bands, which Diana and I would love to have seen. Next, Vasti Jackson sang and played guitar after each of the Blues Cruise screenings. And finally, for the screening in New Orleans, guitarist Vasti Jackson, bass player Lee Allen Zeno, keyboard and rubboard player Sir Reginald Dural, and Diana and I caught taxis from the ship to the theatre, where we were joined by Major and Frances Ayres Handy. As previously arranged, Major and Frances drove two and a half hours from Lafayette to meet us, perform with us, and contribute a PA system. Then, once the screening and subsequent performance were over, they had to drive all the way home again, so that Major could open his auto body shop again the following morning. But for the several hours in between, all of these artists formed into a single band for a special occasion.

To Major's great frustration, during that final performance, his accordion broke down, and there had been no room in his car to fit a spare. So, at that point, Vasti stepped up, taking the band in more of a blues direction, with no one seeming to mind. Our New Orleans screening and concert also had additional resonance due to the presence of Scott Billington, who had collaborated with me on *The Kingdom of Zydeco*; Ben Sandmel, who had been an onscreen guide and performer (with the Hackberry Ramblers) for *Rhythm 'N' Bayous*; and Michael Tisserand, who had assisted me with *Zydeco Crossroads* and much more. And just in case additional resonance were needed, it turned out to be Scott's birthday, prompting Vasti to lead all in a bluesy singing of "Happy Birthday." Otherwise, taken together, these premieres in Lafayette, New Orleans, Philadelphia, and the Caribbean were the perfect conclusion for a one-of-a-kind story, later reinforced by the Best Blues & Roots Film Award from Roger Stolle's 2016 Clarksdale Film Festival, and then a 2016 Blu-ray release from MVD Visual.

Chapter Eight
American Wellspring (Before & After the Flood)

Iguanas in the House (1996)

Rhythm 'N' Bayous: A Road Map to
Louisiana Music (2000)

New Orleans Music in Exile (2006)

Although my two zydeco films, *The Kingdom of Zydeco* and *Zydeco Crossroads*, and two other films using related footage (*True Believers* and *Rosie's in the House Tonight*), bookended my coverage of Louisiana music, in the years between, I actually made three other films exclusively in the state (the subjects of this chapter) and used Louisiana artists in several films shot outside of it (most notably *Pride and Joy*, *Hellhounds on My Trail*, *Blues Divas*, *Deep Sea Blues*, and *All Jams on Deck*). The enduring appeal of Louisiana—especially its food, its people, and its music—has simply been too great for me to resist.

Of the three more general films I have made there, the first was *Iguanas in the House*, which I released in the spring of 1996. Its genesis came from a week's worth of films I screened at a small New Orleans theater during the fall of 1995. Since I was never paid for these screenings, or for my appearances (as much an ongoing problem for independent filmmakers as for regional musicians), I will not mention the theater or the person programming it. However, one good thing did come of my time in New Orleans, and that was meeting with members of The Iguanas, the outstanding New Orleans roots music group.

They informed me that their band, whose unique blend of New Orleans rhythm and blues, conjunto, jazz, rock, and more (which I had enjoyed hearing over Philadelphia's WXPN) was preparing to record a new CD. They also said that the band would enjoy having the sessions filmed as a means of promoting the album, and that their new label, Jimmy Buffett's Margaritaville Records, might be willing to pay for such a project. Naturally, I expressed interest and was put in touch with Robert "Bob" Mercer, the hugely successful former head of EMI out of the UK who had married Buffett's ex-wife, moved to Nashville, and agreed to run his record label. Perhaps because of my previous work for Channel 4 in London, I hit it off with this affable Brit and eventually convinced him to fund my filming of the Iguanas recording sessions, though only after I agreed to an absurdly small budget.

The band had made a strong impression with their 1993 MCA Records album, *The Iguanas*, which produced the single "Para Donde Vas," and their 1994 Margaritaville Records album, *Nuevo Boogaloo*, which produced the single "Boom, Boom, Boom." Now, they had the green light from Bob Mercer to record their third album, *Super Ball*, at Chez Flame, the home recording studio owned by engineer and producer Keith Keller. It was located on Annunciation Street in the Lower Garden District of New Orleans.

The work had begun on Tuesday, October 10, 1995 in the large front parlor of Keller's Victorian house, and Bill Barth, Bill Burke, and I flew in on Sunday, October 22, rented a car, and checked in at the studio. There, Keith, a large, bald, white-bearded, teddy bear of a man welcomed us with his patented mix of conviviality and acerbic wit. Showing us around the studio, he made a point of railing against all things digital and showing us the huge analog tubes he had installed below the room's polished floorboards. These, he declared, ensured customary analog warmth at a time of frigid digital recording.

Across the back of the room, Keith had created a kind of cockpit, literally surrounding himself with recorders, speakers, mixing boards, a computer monitor, lamps, cables, wall racks filled with tapes, and more, but leaving a space between two wooden towers through which he could see and converse with recording musicians. Directly across from him, in an alcove at the front of the house, was a drum set; at the center of the room were microphones on stands and a device to control them; and along the walls were chairs, headsets, guitars, keyboards, amplifiers, more cables, and assorted piles of studio detritus. Like a field of battle recently abandoned, though without resolution, this room conveyed the echos of past clashes, but also the trumpet calls of those to come.

Speaking of horns, just outside of this central space, and a short distance from the front door, was a booth wherein reeds and brass could be recorded simultaneously with voices or other instruments in the main room, but without intermingling of their separate sounds, thereby assuring sufficient separation for a clean final mix. Like most recording studios, the room was also configured so that individual vocalists or musicians could be recorded to playback in the main room, though with said instrumental playback only heard over singer, musician, and producer headsets.

On Monday morning, October 23, the two Bills and I were joined at Chez Flame by local camera assistant Tony Brignac and local production assistant Kathy Hunter, who were there to help us function quickly and effectively in unfamiliar terrain. We were also joined by members of the band: guitarist, lead vocalist, and key songwriter Rod Hodges; sax player, lead vocalist, and key songwriter Joe Cabral; bass player René Coman; drummer Doug Garrison; and second sax player Derek Huston. In fact, as each of them arrived, we asked him to repeat his entrance so that we could shoot him separately, then later combine their arrivals for the start of the film.

The Iguanas pose in front of Chez Flame, the New Orleans recording studio of producer Keith Keller. From left are René Coman, Rod Hodges, Joe Cabral, Keith Keller, Derek Huston, and Doug Garrison. Seated in front is visiting Mexican percussionist Armando Montiel. (photographed by Robert Mugge, 1995)

Ruling over everything, of course, on behalf of The Iguanas, was engineer Keith Keller, who was producing the new album in collaboration with the five of them. But all were accommodating to our needs, allowing us to position Bill Burke for the shooting of each new take, from one perspective or another, while Bill Barth took a feed from Keith's live recording or mix. In that way, over the course of only two days, we were able to document the full creation of two great new songs, "Is This Love" and "Lupita," the second of which featured added percussion from visiting Mexican drummer Armando Montiel. Armando spoke only Spanish, but that was not a problem, since Rod and Joe grew up speaking it as well.

Both of those songs were said to have been written by Joe and Rod together, with one of them likely contributing more to "Is This Love," and the other perhaps contributing more to "Lupita," just as happened with earlier teams such as John Lennon and Paul McCartney. However, we also filmed Joe Cabral developing a third song with the band, this one titled "Make Time," and taking it through various creative stages. Unfortunately, the band later decided it was not polished enough to include on the album. But I thought it appealing, and also thought viewers would enjoy watching it come together. So, with the band's permission, I built the latter part of the film around it.

On both Monday and Tuesday, at points when Keith was organizing what recently had been recorded, my crew and I took time to explore the city, gathering images that would work as partial illustration of one song or another's lyrical content. For instance, we rode along with a horse-drawn carriage in the French Quarter, then filmed joggers, puppeteers, homeless people, riverboats, buildings, trains, and more. We also filmed signs and odds and ends around the first floor of Keith's house, as well as a large green iguana, which we rented from a pet store, posed around the studio, and then returned at the end of the day. Production assistant Kathy Hunter likely found this a more enjoyable assignment than simply bringing us meals.

On one wall was a photo of the bust of singer Jim Morrison of the Doors that had been sculpted by a Croatian artist, placed on Morrison's grave in Paris's Pere Lachaise Cemetery, and then stolen. Asked about it, Keith said a guy he knew had stopped by one day and asked if he could leave the bust in Keith's storeroom. Keith had told him that was okay, but out of curiosity, shot a photo of it. Then, after a few months, the acquaintance came and retrieved the bust, and that was the last Keith heard of it. I have always been fascinated that certain musicians, like certain religious figures, take on a greater sense of mystery in death than in life, be it Robert Johnson, Sun Ra, or Jim Morrison.

Speaking of which, one day, as we arrived at the studio, Keith was mixing music I recognized as live performances by Sun Ra and his Arkestra. According to Keith, John Sinclair—poet, music historian, political activist, manager of the MC5, and co-producer of the 1972 and 1973 Ann Arbor Blues and Jazz Festivals, and then living in New Orleans—had asked Keith to mix the Sun Ra sets from both festivals, because he was planning to release them. Since it was the late Sun Ra's performance at the first of those events that had convinced me to make a film about him, I found Sinclair's plans of more than passing interest. On the one hand, this appeared to be still another sign that disparate projects of mine are, at heart, all connected, while on the other, it made me view Keith's studio as a sort of interdimensional way station for spiritual artifacts. But those were thoughts for another time.

Now having shot everything we needed, and with Keith promising to send me final mixes for the key musical takes, Bill Barth, Bill Burke, and I flew north again on Wednesday, October 25. In relatively short order, I completed the editing, which included illustrating performances of the two main songs, so that either section of the film could be released as a separate music video. Yet, as much as I liked the final results, it seemed to me a shame to deliver a film only a half-hour long. I therefore asked the band what they thought of my shooting them in concert, then combining that footage with the studio scenes, which would give us a more typical feature-length portrait. They were all for it, so long as Bob Mercer approved. And approve Bob did, though with the proviso that any further funds be considered an advance against the band's future royalties. That, of course, proved a bridge too far for musicians just starting to make a name for themselves, and as much as I regretted not having additional time with them, we would, indeed, work together again, though in unexpected circumstances.

Ironically, once I completed *Iguanas in the House*, Bob Mercer found, as I had warned, that distributing a twenty-seven-minute film can be a challenge. Bob therefore invited me to do with the film as I pleased. So, after premiering it at the New Orleans International Film Festival in October of 1996, I mostly included it with screenings of longer films of mine, and much later, paired it with *The Kingdom of Zydeco* for a Blu-ray release. Yet, regardless of who sees the film and under what circumstances, I love what it shows of an exciting time for a special group of musicians.

***

In 1999, having completed *Hellhounds on My Trail: The Afterlife of Robert Johnson* in collaboration with the Rock & Roll Hall of Fame, I spent much of the year overseeing the early distribution of that film, while also trying to figure out what to do next. At the same time, I remained in touch with Terry Stewart and Bob Santelli, the Rock Hall's president and vice president with whom I had, in the process of our work together, become good friends. In conversation with Bob, I learned that the Rock Hall periodically organized excursions to noteworthy music scenes, much as my friends at WXPN would later do, and they were now preparing for a trip to South Louisiana. In fact, Bob was then arranging activities for New Orleans, but wondered if I could give him advice about things to do in the southwestern part of the state. I was happy to help, of course, but I also wondered if I should try and film the Rock Hall tour, and to use that as a leaping-off point for a film on music of the entire state. Perhaps, I thought, I could pull together a filmmaking caravan through Louisiana, much as I had through Mississippi with *Deep Blues*, and maybe even get the state to pay for it, as I had with *Kumu Hula*. Collaborating with the Rock Hall again could give me credibility with the state, and securing funds to promote Rock Hall activities, as I recently had with WinStar, would surely please Bob and Terry. So, I proposed making a larger film, the shooting of which could also include the Rock Hall excursion from New Orleans to Lafayette, and Bob said to give it a try.

Thus encouraged, I reached out to the state tourism people and, through them, managed to convince Louisiana's Lieutenant Governor Kathleen Babineaux Blanco to put up half of what I needed. At least, I thought to myself, that would be enough to pay for shooting on location, remunerating talent, and doing an initial edit. But while making the film, I would have to continue searching for money, whether from US or foreign television, home video companies, grant-giving organizations, or any other sources that came to mind. Otherwise, the film might never be completed. However, for the moment, it seemed most important to lock down the collaboration with Bob and Terry and get the project started.

My notion of covering the full range of Louisiana music meant not only accompanying the Rock Hall to New Orleans, and letting Bob and Terry accompany me to Lafayette, but also finding collaborators in Northern Louisiana who could help me to document music-making prevalent there. Since that end of the state bordered Mississippi and Arkansas, I figured we would be talking blues, gospel, country, and rockabilly, but I would again need knowledgeable guides who could help me to identify artists, connect with them, and place their work in a larger cultural context. Maybe I was only making a single film this time around, as opposed to the three I had made simultaneously for BMG. Yet, in deciding to focus on three musically autonomous regions of the state, I was once again creating a daunting challenge for myself with only minimal available resources.

My friend Michael Tisserand, though offering counsel from a distance, was now too busy serving as editor of *Gambit Weekly*—like *OffBeat*, another essential New Orleans publication-—to accompany us on location. To my great relief, however, I did find knowledgeable advisers throughout the state, with only one (pushed on me by the lieutenant governor) proving to be a problem. Among those signing on were Ben Sandmel, the esteemed New Orleans-based author of books on Cajun, zydeco, and New Orleans rhythm and blues traditions; Dr. Michael Luster, a respected folklorist, executive director of the Louisiana Folklife Festival in Monroe, and an expert on music of North Louisiana; and Dr. Shane K. Bernard, the author of definitive books on swamp pop and (because he was the in-house archivist for the McIlhenny Company) Tabasco sauce, as well as later books on Cajun culture. Also helping out behind the scenes were Lou Gabus, the Lafayette-based head of the Louisiana Music Hall of Fame, who had been helpful with *The Kingdom of Zydeco*; Lafayette-based El Sid O's owner Sid Williams, who had been featured in the same film; and Maggie Lewis Warwick, a songwriter and musician based in Shreveport, and the aforementioned friend of the lieutenant governor.

Despite the ground we had to cover, I knew I could afford only seven days of shooting. I therefore needed a crew that would be fast and effective, but also remain calm under pressure. After having pioneered several of these musical road movies with line producer Bob Maier (*Kumu Hula*, *Deep Blues*, and the three simultaneous BMG films), I would have expected to work with him again. But by 1999, he had taken a full-time job with Charlotte, North Carolina public television station WTVI. Fortunately, though, I had an excellent alternative in co-producer Tim Healey, a buddy of mine from high school who had spent years guiding Hollywood productions. Otherwise, I raised my comfort level still further by bringing back director of photography Dave Sperling, second cameraman Chris Li, audio director Bill Barth, recording technician Chris Young (Bill's nephew), camera assistant Craig Smith, and grip and driver Quincy McKay. For me, this would again be a family affair, further enhanced by my friend Dave Spizale, general manager of KRVS public radio in Lafayette, who provided Karl Fontenot and Terry DuPuy to handle multitrack music recording on the four occasions we would need it.

In setting the schedule, I could not designate a single day for travel alone. If we had to drive from one city to another, we did that in the morning, knowing we would do major shooting in the after-noon and evening. Also, I knew that the Rock Hall bus would arrive in New Orleans on Thursday, November 18, 1999, then move on to Southwest Louisiana the following day. So, in consultation with Bob Santelli and my assorted advisers, I built the following itinerary: a major shoot in Shreveport on Monday, November 15; several smaller shoots in Monroe and Winnsboro on Tuesday; a major shoot in Baton Rouge on Wednesday; a small shoot in New Orleans on Thursday afternoon, and a bigger one with the Rock Hall group in attendance that evening; a major shoot in Lafayette on Friday evening, with the Rock Hall people invited; smaller shoots in Ville Platt and Mamou on Saturday; and a major, all-day shoot in Lafayette on Sunday, which would close out our production schedule, as well as the Rock Hall's Louisiana excursion.

I flew into Shreveport on Sunday, November 14, picked up the first rental vehicle, finalized hotel arrangements with Casino Magic in Bossier City, and touched base with folklorist Mike Luster who would be our guide through North Louisiana on Tuesday. The rest of my crew arrived in Shreveport via plane or car on Monday, and we immediately started preparing for our big shoot that evening. The plan was to film and record multiple acts at Shreveport's Municipal Auditorium, the recently restored original home of the nationwide *Louisiana Hayride* radio program which, from 1948 till 1960, helped to launch such important American artists as Hank Williams and Elvis

Presley. Maggie Lewis Warwick, a country music veteran, as well as a former *Hayride* regular, had pushed me to shoot at the mammoth auditorium and said she would book talent for the occasion. A number of the acts she mentioned sounded great, but I repeatedly warned her to limit the number of performers or else I would not have the money to pay them all.

Unfortunately, Ms. Warwick was far more enthusiastic than she was reliable. That quickly became clear as we began lighting the mammoth stage, which we would have to shoot with just two cameras, and our KRVS friends made preparations for recording. While we worked, more and more musicians arrived—seemingly all of Maggie's musician friends who happened to be in town—and I tried not to panic. Over a period of several hours, we filmed local country rocker Kenny Bill Stinson and band (including *Louisiana Hayride* veteran Felton Pruett on steel guitar) performing a spirited number of Kenny's own titled "Country Girl"; Maggie and the same band performing something of hers that I chose not to use; country singer Claude King and his group (including legendary *Louisiana Hayride* jack-of-all-trades Tillman Franks on bass) performing King's 1962 country crossover hit "Wolverton Mountain," which I loved as a kid; rockabilly star Dale Hawkins performing his 1957 monster hit "Susie Q," which he wrote with Shreveport guitarist and frequent Elvis Presley sideman James Burton (then touring Australia in support of a Presley hologram), and conveying, with his buddies, the essence of cool at sixty-three years of age; traditional Black gospel quartet the Ever Ready Gospel Singers performing "Jezebel," a gospel standard, with luscious four-part harmonies; and roots rocker Buddy Flett performing a deeply felt solo rendition of traditional prison work song "No More Cane On the Brazos," which is sometimes attributed to Huddie "Lead Belly" Ledbetter.

Admittedly, it was a great evening of music, and the hall was beautiful. Yet, as one group of musicians after another signed releases and requested thousands of dollars in payments—not to mention others who had provided backline and "entertainment technical support"—I grew increasingly angry at the woman who had arranged all of this, when I would have been perfectly happy with a handful of artists performing in a small club.

With that in mind, once we had broken down our equipment, packed our vehicles, and gathered the last of the signed releases, Tim Healey and I headed directly to our minivan. However, as I climbed behind the wheel and started the engine, Maggie and her husband ran up yelling that I had forgotten to pay her. I responded that, after all she had cost me, I had no intention of paying her. Then, as I backed up our vehicle, the two of them grabbed hold of my door, yelling like characters from the old *Dukes of Hazzard* TV show that they would get me for this. Finally, I dislodged the two of them, yanked my door closed, and screeched away, happy in the knowledge I would never speak to them again, though confident Maggie would complain bitterly to the lieutenant governor about carpetbagging filmmakers. Nevertheless, I did give Maggie a credit in the film, acknowledging her organization of our long day's journey into night.

The next day, we were totally in the hands of folklorist Mike Luster, which was a very good place to be. After returning to the Municipal Auditorium, so Mike could provide introductions for each of the acts we had filmed the night before, we drove an hour east to Monroe, where we shot three performances, and then an hour east and south to Winnsboro, where we shot one more. Upon reaching Monroe, we gathered along a bank of the Ouachita River to film biracial blues duo Henry Dorsey and Marlan Wayne Collom (a.k.a., Po' Henry and Tookie) performing "Prison Song" on guitar and harmonica as a train passed over a railroad bridge in the background. At our next stop in the city, we filmed colorful gospel deejay Sister Pearlee Tolliver ("the jewel of the dial") of radio station KYEA as she read her indescribable commercials for bail bondsmen, clothing stores, auto parts companies, and arthritis medications, all of which were a key draw for her shows.

From there, we proceeded to Monroe's Paul Hewitt Music, where the Rev. Gerald Lewis—cousin of musicians Jerry Lee Lewis, Mickey Gilley, and Carl McVoy, as well as preacher Jimmy Lee Swaggart—demonstrated the Ferriday, Louisiana piano style. Connections between gospel music and early rock and roll were especially evident when, assisted by younger pianist Kenny Bill Stinson, Reverend Lewis performed a rousing version of gospel standard "I'll Fly Away."

Finally, after continuing on to Winnsboro, we stopped by the First Zion Baptist Church where young African American preacher Lionel D. Wilson and several of his female congregants, dressed entirely in white, demonstrated the remarkable Easter Rock rituals (musical expressions of faith performed once a year, on Easter Eve, and dating back to the Civil War). In brief, the male preacher, holding a large banner, led the women around a long table covered by a white tablecloth and laid out with such symbolic items as twelve cakes, twelve lanterns, Easter eggs, and red wine or punch. As the procession moved rhythmically along, its members sang traditional spiritual numbers such as "The Rock," about David and Goliath, and the better-known "When the Saints Go Marching In."

Posing with Baton Rouge, Louisiana pianist and blues singer Henry Gray are, from left at the back, cameraman Christopher Li, audio director Bill Barth, director Robert Mugge, recording technician Christopher Young, grip and driver Quincy McKay, co-producer and line producer Tim Healey, drummer Earl Christopher, and bassist Mark Johnson; from left at the front are camera assistant Craig Smith, director of photography David Sperling, and Henry Gray at the keyboard. (photographed by film crew, 1999)

Wednesday, November 17, we drove four hours from the Red Roof Inn in West Monroe to the capital city of Baton Rouge in South

Louisiana, then made our way to the Riverside Pub & Poboys to meet the great blues pianist Henry Gray. Henry had been raised in that part of the state, moved to Chicago for thirty years—where he performed with blues giants Muddy Waters, Elmore James, and especially Howlin' Wolf—and then returned to Baton Rouge after the fading of that original Chicago blues scene. As we finished setting up, Henry gave us an interview and demonstration at his keyboard. Then, with the accompaniment of his standup bass player and his drummer, he performed a full set, including "They Raided the Joint" and "Blues Won't Let Me Take My Rest," two of his signature songs. Finally, after packing up and dining on po' boys and beer, my tired crew and I drove another hour to the (appropriately low budget) Sleep Inn in New Orleans, where we prepared for another full day of musical performance.

Although November 18 would be our only day in the state's most celebrated city, we were prepared to make the best of it. Once on our feet again, we rushed to the Snug Harbor Jazz Bistro on Frenchmen Street, invited by manager (and later owner) Wesley Schmidt to film blind New Orleans pianist Henry Butler in the empty club. There, Henry performed spectacular jazz originals for us. But what I decided to use was his moving rendition of "Deep River," a traditional New Orleans spiritual. With Henry sounding like a modern-day Paul Robeson, the song evoked the storied past of this incomparable river city. In addition, I asked Henry if he would demonstrate styles of earlier New Orleans pianists for us, and he responded with sterling introductions to those of the late Professor Longhair and James Booker.

From there, we rushed to Vaughan's Restaurant where, later that evening, we would meet up with our friends from the Rock Hall in Cleveland, then film the weekly Thursday night performance by popular New Orleans trumpet player Kermit Ruffins and his Barbecue Swingers.

Kermit personified jazz trumpet traditions going back to Louis Armstrong (and perhaps even the unrecorded Buddy Bolden), and he had a similar gift for balancing incisive playing with full-throated and heartwarming vocals. He also embodied the tradition of night-long and year-round New Orleans partying, and he commanded a loyal following that literally followed him from his Thursday night gig to others around the city, whether planned or not.

Vaughan's was short on space and, at night, surprisingly dark. So, in order that we could see the five-piece band—trumpet, trombone, piano, standup bass, and drums—playing at one end of the room, plus the pressed-in patrons who occupied the rest, we had to brighten it considerably, which provoked a chorus of groans from the nocturnal regulars. Still, Kermit and band cast a deeper and warmer glow of their own, which reflected on faces throughout the room and, in audio terms, was handily captured by Karl and Terry from KRVS, joining us for the second of our biggest concerts.

Certainly, everything Kermit played and sang that night was enjoyable. But I chose to use two of his catchiest, most colorful, and most characteristic numbers, which were "Tremé Second Line (Blow Da Whistle)" and "I'll Drink Ta Dat." Those two song titles alone spoke volumes about the experience offered by Kermit Ruffins at Vaughan's.

During the break between the band's two sets, Dave, Bill, and I rushed out front to shoot two pertinent interviews. In one, Terry Stewart told us why he and Bob chose Vaughan's as one of their key stops in New Orleans and how he had grown up in nearby Mobile, Alabama, listening to Louisiana music on the radio. In the other, Kermit told us about his seven years of playing there for loyal followers, and about sometimes bringing a grill on the back of a pickup truck, just as he had that night. His purpose, as we recorded, was the generous feeding of his audience with freshly prepared barbecue.

The following morning, we checked out of our hotel; had shrimp and roast beef po' boys at a favorite eatery, Mother's Restaurant on Poydras Street; then drove two and a half hours west to Lafayette. Upon our arrival, we checked into the Hilton Hotel & Towers, which always gave me great rates and a hot breakfast for my crews. Next, we raced across town to El Sid O's Zydeco & Blues Club, where we began setting up lights, cameras, KRVS recording equipment, my communication system, my video assist monitors, and more in preparation for shooting multiple zydeco acts that night, with the Rock Hall tour group again in attendance.

The first act to perform was Nathan and the Zydeco Cha Chas, essentially the house band, since, again, Nathan was the younger brother of club owner Sid Williams, and other family members were in the band as well. Immediately after Sid welcomed our Rock Hall friends and introduced his brother, the band launched into Nathan's dance-inducing song "Let's Go," which just as quickly brought well-dressed locals and casually dressed Rock Hall members to their feet.

Next up was an amusing young Texan named "Lil' Brian" Terry who, along with members of his band, had driven all the way from Houston so we could sample their hip-hop-flavored zydeco. Brian's madcap song "Party" reflected a theme that we had established at Vaughan's in New Orleans and that he and Nathan reiterated here. Naturally, I selected it for the film.

The last to perform was the lovely and gifted Rosie Ledet, backed by a band comprised mostly of family members and overseen by her husband Morris. At that point in her career, Rosie was so shy that she waited in the family van until it was time for her to perform, at which point she would suddenly blossom. Although I had met Rosie and Morris in 1995, when Michael Tisserand and I sought them out during our Southwest Louisiana research trip, this was actually the first time I had filmed her (*Zydeco Crossroads* still being fifteen years in the future).

Teenaged Cajun fiddle player Alida Viator (left) sits in with zydeco singer/songwriter/ accordion player Rosie Ledet at El Sid O's Zydeco & Blues Club in Lafayette, Louisiana. (photographed by film crew, 1999)

All the self-composed songs Rosie performed that night were engaging, but the ones I chose to include in the film were a fast-paced musical plea titled "I Can't Find Love" and an extended medley of Beau Jocque tunes intended as a tribute to that great artist, who had died from a heart attack just two months before. The latter performance was so electrifying and, with fifteen-year-old Cajun artist Alida Viator sitting in on fiddle, also politically profound, that I used it as the climax of my two-hour film which, by then, I already knew would be titled *Rhythm 'N' Bayous: A Road Map to Louisiana Music*. But more on the Viator family in a moment.

Between sets at El Sid O's, we rushed into the moist evening air and conducted interviews. First up were Sid and Nathan, who expressed gratitude for the influence of Clifton Chenier, Rockin' Dopsie, Buckwheat Zydeco, and others. After that, Lil' Brian discussed his efforts to merge zydeco traditions with hip-hop and blues, and also of how, when the economy turned bad in Louisiana, many Creoles had moved to the Houston area, turning it into "a small Louisiana."

Finally, Rosie and Morris spoke of how, when the two had married, he already had a zydeco band of his own, but that, after she secretly taught herself to play accordion (while he was out working on the family farm), they decided to restructure the band, with him moving to bass, and her taking over on accordion and lead vocals. She also explained how her songwriting had developed from old stories and poems she had written, and even old movies she had seen.

Saturday was not so intense a day, but it was just as productive. In the early afternoon, we met Rock Hall president Terry Stewart at the Ville Platte offices of Floyd Soileau, an influential figure in all genres of Southwest Louisiana music. Not unlike Bob Koester in Chicago, in 1956, after graduating from high school, Soileau had opened a successful store, Floyd's Record Shop, specializing in music of the region. Seeing continuing interest in Cajun French music, he also began producing records and, in 1957, founded a label called Swallow Records to release such material. A year after that, he began his Jin label for the release of popular music records that later would be called swamp pop, and in 1975, he started the Maison de Soul label for the release of Creole and zydeco records. I saw Floyd's story as the perfect way to establish all three genres, and Terry's lively conversation with him brought out everything needed.

Robert Mugge (left) chats with legendary Ville Platte, Louisiana music label and record store owner Floyd Soileau (center) and Rock & Roll Hall of Fame president Terry Stewart. (photographed by film crew, 1999)

At this point, I should mention that, taking a cue from my friend Les Blank, I had decided to contact Ann Savoy on her family's farm near Eunice and see if she and her husband Marc would like to perform and discuss Cajun music in our film. However, Ann informed me that she and Marc would be away the weekend my crew and I planned to be around. I then turned to another family who billed themselves as La Famille Viator and were just beginning to make a mark in local musical circles, yet certainly not receiving the widespread attention enjoyed by the Savoys. At any rate, when I phoned the number given to me by Lou Gabus, the four family members were so welcoming that my crew and I felt we could have moved into their home, and for a day at least, we more or less did.

Étienne and Deborah-Helen Viator owned a beautiful house, modern yet rustic, on a lush piece of property in rural Mamou which, like the Savoy's farm, was a short distance from Eunice, where my crew and I had filmed Steve Riley and the Mamou Playboys six years before. We arrived at their home on Saturday afternoon and rushed to shoot as much as we could outdoors before losing daylight. That included fifteen-year-old Alida and her eighteen-year-old brother Moise performing "One-Step de Choupique," a traditional French-language song recorded by pioneering Cajun musician Dennis Mc-Gee (the key musical partner of Creole legend Amédé Ardoin). Exemplifying the family's devotion to heritage, Alida sang the song in Cajun French, accompanying herself on fiddle, as her brother Moise played along on guitar. With proud parents looking on from a distance, sister and brother stood with their backs to a nearby pond in which could be seen green reflections of surrounding trees and shrubs. For me, Alida and Moise, encircled by nature as they performed a traditional melody and French lyrics, evoked recent history of the region, with Cajuns and Creoles so long isolated from outside influence that they were free to evolve their own language, their own cuisine, their own music, and their own lifestyle, all of which were still practiced, decades after radio, television, commercial airlines, and elevated highways opened them to the world.

Over the next few hours, we filmed various groupings of these four family members. For instance, husband and father Étienne, a commuting law professor at Loyola University in New Orleans, spoke about how, while he was growing up in Southwest Louisiana, "there was music in the air; you just heard music all the time," and how, if you were not playing music yourself, you were listening or dancing to it. He also spoke about the complicated racial and ethnic history of the region and suggested that supposed differences between Cajuns and Creoles were, at best, exaggerated. Finally, he made the fascinating point that, prior to World War II, both white and Black musicians played what was called "French music," but that, beginning at least with the Second World War, Cajuns began hearing country music on the radio, and Creoles began hearing rhythm and blues, and those influences caused the further separation of their music into more distinct genres or styles (a separation which, in truth, had been growing for decades, and which, for myriad reasons, both social and musical, is too complex to elucidate here).

For her part, wife and mother Deborah-Helen described how their two children had been home-schooled, and how that had led to them making their own violins, first as a school project, and then as a family craft led by Deborah-Helen herself. She went on to show how they often built images of native Louisiana birds into their designs, and how handmade violin making, as opposed to manufacture by machine, allowed for an instinctive manipulation of the wood which, in turn, affected the sound of the instrument, referring to the process as "a laying on of hands."

Finally, Étienne produced his steel guitar, sat at the kitchen table and, together with Alida on fiddle and Moise on his hollow-body guitar, kicked off a family performance of a New Orleans Creole song called "Madame Peydeaux." In his introduction, Étienne declared that Jelly Roll Morton spoke of hearing it in Storyville at the turn of the century and said "it was the one that made 'em kick their hats off." For this infectious number, Moise took the lead vocal and also played a brief acoustic guitar solo, while the other three family members sang vocal responses, and Étienne called out the occasional "Eh la bas!" That phrase, "Eh la bas!" was a refrain from a well-regarded Creole song of the same name, as well as a classic Creole greeting.

With completion of this final song, our crew packed up its gear, and the family presented us with an absolute feast, which we would not soon forget. In any such isolated community, there was no greater compliment than being invited into someone's home, and no greater joy than eating sumptuous homemade cuisine, lovingly prepared by one's hosts. Of all the unique gifts we received while shooting this film—both musical and otherwise—none was so special as this one. And it gave me similar joy when, a year later, at film premieres in New Orleans, Philadelphia, and Washington, DC, I was able to include a live performance by Eh, La-Bas!, the latest iteration of the Viator family band.

Yet, before moving on, I should mention another aspect of living and working in such close communion with nature. The pond near the Viator's home was also a remarkable breeding ground for mosquitoes. After shooting Alida and Moise performing in front of it, during which we all were under constant attack, we literally took off running for the house, grateful that the rest of our filming could be indoors. Then, hours later, when it was time to go, our hosts turned on all the lights on one side of their house to attract the mosquitoes, then encouraged us to slip out the dark side, both for the family's protection and for ours. Of course, this plan was not foolproof, because plenty of the insects quickly discovered our escape route, followed us to the empty minivans, and, as we opened the backs to stow our equipment, swarmed in around us.

Naturally, having our vehicles flooded with flying, bloodsucking vermin made the return to our Lafayette hotel, almost an hour away, something of a challenge. In addition, from previous experience in this part of the country, we knew what would await us the following morning, which was hundreds of mosquitoes resting on the minivan's ceiling. So, on Sunday morning, as we reopened both vehicles, we rushed to smash as many as we could before they once again took flight.

Annoying insects aside, we still had one more day of work ahead of us. At my request, my other Lafayette accomplice, the irrepressible Lou Gabus, had organized an extravaganza for us to film and record that Sunday afternoon at Acadian Village, and we had timed it so that the Rock Hall tour could enjoy it as well. Over the course of a single day, we would film two Cajun acts, five swamp pop acts, and a New Orleans rock and roll act, all of which meant that we were ending this latest musical caravan with as demanding a set of performances as we had begun it. And yet, even though still limited to only two 16mm cameras and the modest multitrack recording equipment supplied by KRVS, we knew that we could handle this. Our company of music-seeking road warriors was now rested, battle-tested, and ready to shoot. So, in the immortal words of Louisiana music lovers everywhere, "Laissez les bon temps rouler (Let the good times roll)!"

The one act Lou had not booked herself was the Hackberry Ramblers, a pioneering group founded in 1933 by fiddler Luderin Darbone and accordion player Edwin Duhon and known for combining Cajun music with western swing and country music. Their four surviving senior (citizen) members, which also included James "Glen" Croker on electric guitar and Johnny Faulk on upright bass, were largely able to continue playing thanks to the management and drumming of New Orleans-based music historian Ben Sandmel, who not only kept the group functioning, but also fully participated in their revitalized music. I had contacted Ben in advance, hoping he could serve as my final onscreen guide, and even as he agreed to serve that important role, he also convinced me to include his band in our climactic show. Certainly, I could see no downside to that arrangement, and apparently, neither could Lou, because she readily added them to the lineup.

Introduced by master of ceremonies Bill Best, a longtime promoter of country music in Acadiana, and vice president of the Louisiana Music Hall of Fame, the group exuded major charm, in large part because its four older musicians were such balls of fire. Also contributing to the effect were their matching white shirts, white cowboy hats, and red suspenders, all of which worked well with the American flag and flagpole extending from the top of Johnny's upright bass. In retrospect, my biggest regret of the project was that the only song of theirs I could fit into the film was their short but electrifying "Hackberry Ramblers Theme Song."

Performing next was the Jambalaya Cajun Band, a younger ensemble with similar instrumentation but a more modern approach. Where the delivery of the Hackberry Ramblers was raw and energetic, the Jambalaya Cajun Band fashioned a warm and polished sound that was equally appealing in its own way. On the two self-written, French-language songs I used from Jambalaya ("Le Jig Cadien" and "Merci M. Dewey"), lead singer Terry Huval offered appealing vocals, while sometimes playing the band's second fiddle and sometimes its second guitar. I also found it of interest that, regardless of any musical divergence, in their dress, the younger musicians employed the same basic color scheme as their elders.

Speaking of younger, my parents gave me my first radio at the age of four, and I began watching teen music shows like *American Bandstand* at the age of seven, which gave me an early, if limited, view of musical changes taking place at the time. So, when the song "Sea Cruise" was released in 1958 and attributed to eighteen-year-old white singer Frankie Ford, I was naturally drawn to the spirit of the performance, the romance of the lyrics, the insistent rhythm, and even the novelty sound effects. Yet, as an eight-year-old, I had no idea that this was New Orleans rhythm and blues, and neither did I know that both "Sea Cruise" and its B-side, "Roberta," were actually written, arranged, and performed in the studio by the popular African American artist Huey "Piano" Smith, who had expected to release the two songs as his own next single, until the white owners of his record company slipped in a new vocal for each song by the unknown Vincent Francis Guzzo Jr. (alias, Frankie Ford), and even changed the name of the B side from the Black female name "Loberta" to the white female name "Roberta." Of course, I would eventually learn that, in the 1950s, that was the way even the greatest of African American artists were treated.

Now sixty himself (as of late 1999), and one of the artists Lou Gabus had invited to perform for us, that same Frankie Ford burst onto the Acadian Village stage with much of his teen-idol-for-a-minute bravado, but now in more Liberace-like packaging. He was accompanied by a pair of pleasant-sounding male and female backup singers, and the band supporting them was Kenny & the Jokers, a skilled and highly adaptable group of local swamp pop musicians led by Kenny Thibodeaux, who would also back up all of the artists still to perform. Not surprisingly, "Sea Cruise" and "Roberta" got the Rock Hall people up and dancing, and some even laughed at Ford's nightclub patter between songs. In short, regardless of his slightly troublesome origins, Ford's present-day show earned audience approval, and so did the swamp pop performances to follow.

Note: Just as it took a French film critic to brand shadowy, crime-filled US films of the 1940s and 1950s as "film noir," it took a British music critic in the early 1970s to label South Louisiana popular music of the 1950s and 1960s as "swamp pop." According to Dr. Shane K. Bernard, author of the definitive book on the subject (*Swamp Pop: Cajun and Creole Rhythm and Blues*), swamp pop combined Cajun and Creole music with New Orleans rhythm and blues and a touch of country. With that in mind, after interviewing Shane at Acadian Village, we went on to film four swamp pop acts of note: the legendary Warren Storm performing his 1958 hit "Prisoner's Song"; Shane's father, Rod Bernard, performing his 1959 hit "This Should Go On Forever" and 1962 hit "Colinda" (the former written by Creole artist Bernard

"King Karl" Jolivette and recorded by Rod when Karl's label refused to release his version); Dale and Grace performing "I'm Leaving It Up To You," which I heard repeatedly on Top 40 radio in 1963; and "Little Alfred" Babino who, off and on from 1966 onward, replaced Creole lead singer Huey "Cookie" Thierry in the integrated band Cookie and the Cupcakes, and who performed their 1959 hit "Mathilda" for us. As a further reminder that the 1950s and 1960s were no golden age of racial harmony in Southwest Louisiana, both Shane Bernard and Little Alfred discussed the racist treatment to which Creole swamp pop artists were subjected, even as white swamp pop artists claimed to revere Black ones, and certainly emulated them.

Eventually, the sun set on Acadian Village, the performances came to an end, our friends from KRVS and the Rock Hall departed (by car and tour bus, respectively), and much of our crew began packing up gear. At the same time, Dave Sperling, Bill Barth, and I filmed perceptive introductions by music historian Ben Sandmel for Henry Gray, Henry Butler, Kermit Ruffins, Nathan Williams, Lil' Brian, the Hackberry Ramblers, Baton Rouge blues, New Orleans nightlife, Creole music, and zydeco. Although it was not yet even Thanksgiving, the "cultural park's" elaborate Christmas lights were already up, including a multicolored outline of a Mississippi riverboat that was planted in the lake, and the latter served as the luminous backdrop for Ben's remarks.

Afterwards, we wrapped at last, and our crew raced to Prejean's, our favorite Lafayette restaurant, just in time to be served a final meal together. Perhaps it was not as special as the homemade dinner prepared for us by the Viators, but it was the perfect end for our latest Southern road movie. As usual, Bill Barth and I acted out our comic ritual wherein, regardless of the type of cuisine, he always wished he had ordered what I had. Truthfully, though, what mattered most was the time together, and fulfillment of another mission. And with that concluding meal very much under our belts, on Monday, November 22, most of us flew home, while Craig and Quincy drove back to Tennessee.

Financial woes hindered completion of this film, because I never raised the second half of funding I needed, which led to some belt-tightening for me personally, as well as conflict with the video post-production house that had purchased my Richmond, Virginia film lab. In addition, I could not afford to pay for the songs performed, which kept the film out of general release for many years. However, I still was able to show it at many film festivals, including four in October of 2000 that essentially shared the world premiere: Mill Valley (with Dale Hawkins performing live), Denver (with Dale Hawkins again performing live), New Orleans (with Eh-La-Bas! performing live), and Leeds in the UK, where I showed a number of other films as well. These screenings resulted in a great review by Dennis Harvey in *Variety*, and a wonderful conversation between me and writer Bunny Matthews in New Orleans-based *OffBeat* magazine. In fact, partially acting on advice from Bunny, who had seen the film in rough-cut, I added a small animated map at the beginning of each section so that viewers could follow our caravan's progress.

I also gave introductory titles to the three separate sections: Part One became "Another Country—Northern Louisiana," underscoring that musical traditions in the north are different from those in the south, and also that Shreveport's *Louisiana Hayride* radio program offered the only serious competition to Nashville's *Grand Ole Opry*; Part Two became "Spirits in the Night—New Orleans and Baton Rouge," emphasizing the jazz, blues, and rhythm and blues nightlife of the key cities in Southeastern Louisiana; and Part Three became "Music in the Air—Southwestern Louisiana," highlighting Étienne Viator's observation that, for people like him, growing up in that region, music was an integral part of daily life. As to the film's overall title, *Rhythm 'N' Bayous: A Road Map to Louisiana Music*, this simply acknowledged the project's underlying road trip, and encouraged audiences to visit these diverse musical hotspots, whether in person or through the film.

Starting on February 16, 2001, the film ran for a week at the Screening Room in New York City where, on opening night, I regaled audiences with my sense that Louisiana had either given birth to, or helped to develop, most key forms of traditional American music, not counting assorted forms of Indigenous or Spanish-language music. By this, I meant blues, jazz, rhythm and blues, gospel, country, rockabilly, rock and roll, Cajun, Creole, zydeco, swamp pop, brass bands, Mardi Gras Indian, and so on. The initial run, along with continuing festival screenings, also led to more incredible press, including an awe-inspiring, opening-day rave from Stephen Holden in the New York Times, for which I shall ever be grateful. The first and last paragraph of his review read as follows:

> To describe the recent films of the documentarian Robert Mugge as cultural reference books doesn't mean to imply that these explorations of the musical byways of Southern rural America are lacking in pungent musical sap. It's the careful balance between music and scholarship that lends Mr. Mugge's films a foundation of academic seriousness that flirts with dryness without becoming mired in trivia. Documents of a flourishing below-the-radar culture, often involving older musicians who won't be around much longer, they are archival records as well as entertainments . . . *Rhythm 'N' Bayous*, is finally not about being polished. It's about the organic process by which a culture expresses itself through music and the hybrids that evolve naturally when these cultures begin to mingle. That after all is how rock 'n' roll was born.

***

In late August of 2005, I was living in Jackson, Mississippi with my older son Rob, just having resigned my position as Filmmaker in Residence at Mississippi Public Broadcasting and its foundation and expecting, after Labor Day, to start a new position teaching music filmmaking as part of the Delta Music Institute at Delta State University in Cleveland, Mississippi, then overseen by veteran musician and record producer Norbert Putnam. But on August 29 of that year, Hurricane Katrina struck New Orleans, causing the levees to breach, and also doing enough damage in Mississippi to leave my own area without power for a week and without gas for considerably longer. Regardless, once power returned, my first goal was to learn how my Louisiana-based musician friends were faring, as well as where they were now living.

Closer to home, Katrina had flattened casinos on Mississippi's Gulf Coast, leading to an immediate drop in the money provided to state schools from the taxing of such operations. As a result, the president of Delta State declared that all new hires were canceled, thereby lending further fuel to my idea that perhaps I should try and make a film about what Katrina had done to the New Orleans music community. Just before the storm hit, I had made a new friend in Diana Zelman, the previously mentioned Philadelphia-based financial adviser and sometimes filmmaker, and Diana expressed interest in helping me produce it. Then, I decided to contact my Starz Entertainment Group friends, Stephan Shelanski and Brett Marottoli, who had funded my 2003 film *Last of the Mississippi Jukes* and acquired my 2005 film *Blues Divas* from Mississippi Public Broadcasting (both films are addressed in Chapter Nine). To my delight, they, too, expressed tentative interest in this new idea.

Stephan and Brett brought in their new associate, Michael Ruggierro, formerly with the Independent Film Channel, to serve as the possible film's executive producer, and I urged the three of them to move as quickly as possible so that we could document the devastation in New Orleans while nothing much had been done about it, and to interview top New Orleans musicians while they were scattered around the South and still in shock. They understood what I was saying because, at that point, few yet knew exactly how bad things were in New Orleans, and how long it would be before the people who had fled would be able to return to their damaged or even demolished homes and businesses. However, their hands were tied, because they had no immediately available budget from which to draw production funding. So, the consensus for the moment was that I should figure out who was available to film, and what events were taking place in New Orleans or elsewhere that we could capture. Armed with such information, they would see what they could do about money.

Through calls, emails, and Internet searches, I slowly figured out that, of the New Orleans artists with whom I had worked before, The Iguanas were now living in Austin, Texas; Kermit Ruffins was living in Houston, Texas; Irma Thomas was living in Gonzales, Louisiana; Henry Butler was living in Boulder, Colorado; and so forth. Naturally, I would want to try and get to them.

Yet, just as important to the project, I learned that the annual Voodoo Music Experience, that heretofore had taken place in New Orleans every October, would, for once, be split between its home city and Memphis, Tennessee. That is, for one day, concerts would be presented in New Orleans in order to entertain emergency workers and the small number of residents who had thus far managed to return. Then, the festival would move to Memphis for an all-day-and-evening event at AutoZone Park, the home of the minor league Memphis Redbirds baseball team, along with several days of concerts on Beale Street, largely presented in W. C. Handy Park and entirely sponsored by the Southern Comfort Company. In effect, for that latter period, Memphis would play host to many top New Orleans musicians, some of whom had managed to return to their homes in the so-called Big Easy, but most of whom were still living anywhere they could find refuge. I therefore realized that, if we could get permission to film at both Memphis locations, we could safely and easily capture key performances and interviews needed for the film.

Brett and Michael were intrigued as well and began an epic struggle to find funds within Starz in time for Diana and me to be able to shoot these events in late October, while the four of us also fended off a litany of unrealistic requirements from their Business Affairs Department. But at least having definite dates for a start of shooting focused the group's attention. In short order, and against all odds, we accomplished the following: I secured permission to shoot at the Memphis festival, Diana reserved two minivans at the Memphis airport (an amazing feat, considering that emergency workers would fly there, rent all the vehicles, and drive them to Louisiana), I came up with the title *New Orleans Music in Exile* (helping to romanticize the effort for everyone involved), Starz declared it could spare $30,000 for shooting in Memphis (not enough, but a start), Diana secured New Orleans hotel rooms for several days following the Memphis festival (unbelievable since, initially, she was told that the closest available hotel rooms were three hours away in *Jackson*, which was where I lived), some of my usual crew members began to commit for a two-week trip through the South, and Brett and Michael located funds for potential use beyond Memphis, yet contingent upon everything going perfectly from the start.

Final approval was so elusive that Diana actually flew to Jackson from Philadelphia while I was still negotiating with Brett, while Brett and Michael were still negotiating with others at Starz, and while all of us were faxing and emailing documents back and forth, late into the night, just before Diana and I had to leave for Memphis. Eventually, the deal did come together, but with the following provisos: "Okay, here's the money for shooting at the festival. But before we can underwrite your subsequent shoot in New Orleans, we'll have to see how Memphis goes. And then, before we can fund any additional shooting in Lafayette, Houston, and Austin [major cities then hosting many of the exiled musicians], we'll have to see what you get in New Orleans."

It was an understandable response, because none of us knew exactly what we would find in any of these locations. But it also made things incredibly stressful for Diana, for me, and for our crew members, because we had to fly them in without knowing for sure how many days they would be with us, and they had to decide whether or not to turn away thousands of dollars of competing work being offered for the latter part of our potential shooting schedule. Moreover, Diana had to book additional hotel rooms, the Starz travel agent had to book return air tickets, and I had to rent equipment and order tape stock, most or all of which might never be used. At least I had decided to try a new video format called HDV, which used small and inexpensive tapes (a higher grade of the old mini-DV cassettes) to shoot HD images, so our upfront investment in stock was not so huge as it would have been with 16mm film or another HD video format of that time.

Although my usual cameramen, Chris Li and Dave Sperling, were available and signed on to share the director of photography credit, my invaluable audio director Bill Barth had an unfortunate conflict. Having no idea where I could find another audio person who knew both documentary sound recording and down-and-dirty music recording, I turned to Dave and Chris, who recommended the much younger Seth Tallman out of Connecticut. Seth was enthusiastic, though unavailable for our first two days of shooting. So, I then had to find a local recording person in Memphis to help us kick things off, while also flying Seth in as soon as possible.

The one other crew member would be my son Rob, who would serve as a production assistant and still photographer. Rob had been living with me in Jackson since January of 2005 and had weathered Katrina and the local aftereffects, as had I. Now, to my great relief, Jackson's wonderful Education Center School would allow him to take off for more than two weeks of his senior year in return for his documenting our trip as a school project.

On Thursday, October 27, 2005, Diana, Rob, and I drove to Memphis; picked up Chris, Dave, and our rental minivans at the Memphis airport; and checked into our usual hotel, now with a new name, but still next door to the Peabody and across Union Avenue from AutoZone Park, where we would soon do major filming. Afterwards, we met up with Randy Reinke, our temporary audio person, and then rushed to the New Daisy Theatre on Beale Street for a concert by Cowboy Mouth.

The band put on a great show, which we managed to capture well enough with just our two cameras and a feed from the house audio board. Beforehand, we were invited to join Paul Sanchez and Sonia Tetlow of Cowboy Mouth, Mike Mayeux of fellow New Orleans band Beatin Path, and Jeff Stone of Southern Comfort in the Southern Comfort tour bus in which Cowboy Mouth had been living while on an extended concert tour. It was a somber and somewhat bittersweet affair, as Paul told us about the loss of his New Orleans home to the recent flood waters, waxing philosophic over his and his wife's current situation, and then as Mike Mayeux told us about the loss of his own home, and about the dark humor he found in being told by phone that there was a boat in his backyard and another on his roof.

Robert Mugge (center) and director of photography David Sperling (right) prepare to film a Memphis recording session featuring Louisiana (by way of Sweden) singer/songwriter/ multi-instrumentalist Theresa Andersson. (photographed by Christopher Li, 2005)

The next morning, we met New Orleans singer and multi-instrumentalist Theresa Andersson at Sounds Unreel Studios where my audio engineer friend Dawn Hopkins recorded successive takes of her singing a haunting solo version of Neil Young's classic song "Like A Hurricane," then performing solo violin along with her pre-recorded vocals. Ever since Katrina struck New Orleans and the levees breached, flooding eighty percent of the city, I had envisioned a beautiful angel watching over those flooded streets—much as in the 1987 Wim Wenders film *Wings of Desire*, actors Bruno Ganz and Otto Sander played guardian angels watching over the city of Berlin—and certainly, Swedish-born Theresa looked and sang like we could imagine an angel looking and singing. So, I wanted this performance to open the film, intercut with footage of the actual hurricane battering the city. And thanks also to friend and colleague Jessica Berman-Bogdan, who not only acquired riveting hurricane footage for me but also secured rights to Neil Young's song, I was able to bring it about.

After this session, we rushed to a Southern Comfort party at the historic Hunt-Phelan mansion on Beale Street. There, we conducted interviews and filmed performances which I never managed to use. But it was a nice diversion during our first full day in the city, and our hosts provided free food and drinks. Later that evening, on the main stage at Handy Park, we filmed a set by Beatin Path, featuring witty banter from their two lead singers, Mike Mayeux and Skeet Hanks. Although they played some impressive originals, what I chose to use in the film was a faithful cover of "Band on the Run," the Paul McCartney classic, now almost too ironic to bear.

On Saturday, October 29, we spent the entire day back at Handy Park again. Normally, our priority would have been shooting the Neville Brothers, perhaps the most famous of all New Orleans bands. Yet, over the past week, I had made numerous attempts to contact their management, and none of my calls had been returned. Likewise, we would have loved to film Ivan Neville's Dumpstaphunk, a favorite of Rob's and mine. But Ivan's attorney went on and on about wanting "points" in the production (a Hollywood concept very much out of place here), so we finally dropped the idea. On the other hand, we did film Bonerama, a trombone-centered funk band from New

Orleans. However, they refused to sign releases until seeing edited footage of themselves which, as far as I was concerned, made them more trouble than they were worth.

Fortunately, other artists understood our chief goal, which was shining a light on the post-Katrina plight of New Orleans musicians, and those were the artists with whom we wanted to work. In fact, before each new act took the stage, Diana would skirt past security and approach band members with blank releases, a checkbook, and considerable charm, quickly determining which of them would allow us to film.

Because we could not afford a communication system, our shooting strategies were more basic on this trip. Often, I would stand with Chris at the rear of the audience, watch what Dave was shooting down front, and suggest something complementary for Chris to shoot. Meanwhile, once Seth Tallman flew in, replacing our two-day substitute (who had done fine), he would take a feed from the PA mix, while also doing separate recording of his own.

In the afternoon, we filmed a set by Malcolm "Papa Mali" Welbourne, a Shreveport native, Austin resident, and multidimensional guitarist who was given his nickname during a stint with Jamaican reggae artist Burning Spear. Although present in Memphis to perform with Cyril Neville's band, he also assembled a talented group of his own. Regrettably, I had no room in the film for any of that second performance, but I did feature plenty of Malcolm backing up Cyril, as well as giving us a backstage interview.

Later that evening, we filmed Theresa Andersson again, this time performing with two backup musicians (Carlo Nuccio and Jon Sanchez) as a trio of fiddle, drums, and guitar. The song of hers I chose to use, in large part because of its relevance to the situation in New Orleans, was the crushingly beautiful "It's Gonna Be Okay," written by her former partner and fellow Swedish musician Anders Osborne, along with Joshua Ragsdale. In the film, I intercut that performance with her own terrifying description of fleeing New Orleans by car at the start of the storm, and illustrated it with shots of aid groups in her devastated city.

Although we never received permission to film Art, Charles, Aaron, and Cyril Neville together as a group, the youngest of those famous brothers, the passionate and politically active Cyril, was fine with us filming Tribe 13, which was his other band of the moment. Fronting a rugged congregation of jazz, rock, reggae, and rhythm and blues musicians, including his lovely and talented wife Gaynielle as backup singer, and the ever-adaptable Papa Mali on squealing electric guitar, Cyril brought an urgency to his performance, addressing, through song, what was happening in New Orleans. Perhaps the most persuasive of these musical screeds was "I Will Survive," which I knew, immediately, would be included in the film.

Our last day in Memphis (October 30) was split between AutoZone Park and the so-called "Voodoo on Beale Street" presentations. Therefore, early in the day, we headed to AutoZone and conducted interviews with Cowboy Mouth frontman Fred LeBlanc, young New Orleans rock band World Leader Pretend, and Voodoo Festival founder Stephen Rehage. Then, at the big stage erected on the edge of the ball field, we filmed sets by both World Leader Pretend and Cowboy Mouth, trying to work around the festival's own cameramen already on the stage. Songs making the film from that day included World Leader Pretend's "A Grammarian Stuck in a Medical Drama" and Cowboy Mouth's clearly more relevant "Voodoo Shoppe" and "Home." The latter song, newly composed by Paul Sanchez with an assist from Fred LeBlanc, expressed their fervent longing for pre-Katrina New Orleans, and in cutting it, I switched back and forth between their New Daisy and AutoZone Park renditions.

Afterwards, we raced to Beale Street and, at a retro burger joint called Dyer's on Beale, filmed a joint interview with Jon Hornyak, senior executive director of the Memphis chapter of the Recording Academy, and Reid Wick, a New Orleans musician hired by Jon to oversee Katrina-related operations for their charitable organization MusiCares. At the time we interviewed them, they had already assisted 1,600 New Orleans musicians with places to stay, new instruments, living expenses, and more.

From there, we ran back across Beale again to film a full set by Mac "Dr. John" Rebennack, one of the greatest musicians ever produced by the Crescent City. Only because my Memphis-based friend Joe Mulherin was helping us on the project, and happened to be old friends with Dr. John's road manager, were we allowed to film the set, even though we agreed that no releases would be signed or interviews recorded until we had worked things out with Dr. John's primary manager, Peter Himberger. But whatever they asked of us was fine because, according to Mike Ruggiero, Starz considered the involvement of Dr. John to be essential. So, primarily thanks to Joe, we were able to film and record two Dr. John classics, "Right Place, Wrong Time" and "I Walk On Guilded Splinters," as well as the highly applicable song "Sweet Home New Orleans" (recently rewritten by Mac and his wife), and the deal with Peter could be worked out later. As always in documentary filmmaking, anything not captured in the moment it happens is literally gone forever.

Monday morning, we packed our two minivans and drove the six hours from Memphis to New Orleans. Fortunately, our recent reports had convinced Starz execs that it was worth proceeding to Stage Two, which meant exploring whatever was left of New Orleans after the hurricane and breached levees. On the other hand, people who had recently been through the city warned us of what to expect, beginning with murky, sometimes unbreathable air filled with particles of unknown origin, much as cleanup workers had faced on and after 9/11 at the site of the leveled World Trade Center. Therefore, the night before leaving Memphis, we found a twenty-four-hour pharmacy where we loaded up on bottled water, surgical and N95 face masks, Purell hand sanitizer, and antiseptic wipes (all of which became sadly essential again in March of 2020 when Covid-19 invaded the world).

Upon reaching New Orleans at last, we headed straight to the Bywater home of Jon Cleary, formerly a transplanted British guitarist, and now a world-class New Orleans keyboard player. Coincidentally, Jon himself had only just returned home after months on the road with Bonnie Raitt and was still evaluating moderate damage to his house there. In fact, earlier in the day, National Guardsmen had helped with what he called "a New Orleans rite of passage": hauling his refrigerator from his upper floor living quarters to the sidewalk below. To their great frustration, partway down the stairs, the freezer compartment had opened, sending spoiled meat tumbling onto the landing and Jon and the National Guardsmen vomiting into the street.

In a sense, Jon's house was easy to find, because it was the only one in his neighborhood that currently had power. In fact, as we would soon learn, in the two months since Katrina, many parts of the city were still entirely dark. And if that had been the case here, we would not have been able to film. Yet, Jon's surprisingly good fortune was ours as well, and despite all that he, his wife, and his city had weathered, they nonetheless greeted us with the warm cordiality for which New Orleans is known.

Once we had set up lights around Jon's piano, he told us about listening to his uncle's New Orleans records while growing up in the UK, about moving to the Carrollton neighborhood of Uptown New Orleans at the age of seventeen, about offering to paint the Maple Leaf Bar so he could listen to nightly performances there, and about teaching himself the full range of New Orleans piano, which he now performs around the world. Asked to demonstrate, he played a lovely composition of his own titled "Moonburn," and then, like Henry Butler did for us six years before, an overview of New Orleans piano styles. Although I was able to fit "Moonburn" into the film, sadly, we had to settle for using the longer overview as a home video bonus feature.

From there, we raced to the much-loved Maple Leaf Bar, which owner Hank Staples somehow managed to open and operate soon after the waters abated, even though, ironically, the club itself was still without running water (as the lavatories brutally attested). For whatever reason, Hank did not wish to give us an interview. But he did permit us to film that night's show by John Gros and Papa Grows Funk. Because it was Halloween, music would start late and go even later, and that worked well for us. It provided time for Dave, Chris, and Seth to set up lights, tripods, and recording equipment while Diana, Rob, and I walked blocks in the dark to find the neighborhood's one newly reopened sandwich shop. Only hours after arriving in New Orleans, we could see that simply staying fed and hydrated would be our biggest challenge.

Papa Grows Funk put on a wild show, for which the increasingly costumed and intoxicated crowd showed notable appreciation, whether by applauding, singing along, or dancing without restraint. In fact, considering the high spirits on display, it was difficult to believe this was a city under siege, without even a rest room where drinkers could pee in private.

Meanwhile, I had a problem of my own, which was choosing only one of John's prime-grade funk numbers for inclusion in the film. Eventually, though, I selected the edgy and propulsive song "Rat a Tang Tang," paired with his tale of returning to the city, heading straight for the Maple Leaf, and then performing solo with only a generator to power his keyboard.

After packing up again, we found our way to the Parc St. Charles Hotel at St. Charles and Poydras where, remarkably, Diana had scored rooms for our crew. With hundreds of hotels severely damaged and indefinitely shut down, or serving as temporary living quarters for emergency workers and their own staffs, it seemed a miracle that Decatur Hotels group had rushed several hotels into service again. Of course, even here, we found ourselves living side-by-side with Red Cross workers, FEMA staff, and Blackwater mercenaries wearing black boots, slacks, T-shirts, and berets, and with automatic weapons hanging at their sides. And even though an hour or so after we checked in, my son Rob had to be moved to another room, because initially unnoticed black mold on the walls was causing his asthma to erupt, at least we had a place to stay.

On our way into the city (which, yes, was like entering a war zone), Diana had spent ninety minutes on her phone trying to buy me a new laptop (so I could view some of our footage, shortly after we shot it), yet constantly lost her signal. At that point, we were not even sure where to have it safely delivered. Yet, somehow, we managed to reach my good friend Irma Thomas, who was staying at her daughter's home in Gonzalez, Louisiana. Irma graciously agreed to let the package be sent to her overnight, and then to bring it the following day when she met us at her damaged New Orleans home and music club. To our continuing frustration, cell service would not improve throughout our stay, which is why we mostly resorted to texting. Wi-fi, too, was virtually nonexistent, though with occasional exceptions; gas was in short supply here as it was throughout the region; and again, finding eating establishments open and stocked with food was an ongoing struggle. Yes, our hotel contained a small eatery, but it, too, was closed until further notice. So what proved literally lifesaving for us was the fact that an old favorite, Mother's Restaurant, was less than three blocks up Poydras, and they were open for breakfast. Every morning, without fail, we trudged on over, never sure what they would be able to offer us. But whether it was po' boys, étouffée, or eggs and toast, we were always grateful.

It was now Tuesday, November 1, and kicking off our first full work day in the city, we raced to the Lion's Den, the legendary music club owned by Irma's husband Emile, and the same place my crew and I had filmed her in concert a dozen years before. I knew it would not be possible to film her giving another performance, so I planned simply to reuse "Smoke Filled Room" from my Rounder Records portrait. Still, I asked Irma to meet us at the club so we could tag along as she investigated the damage there for the first time. Doing so meant following the black, six-foot-high water line around the building's exterior, interpreting the rescuer hieroglyphics painted beside the front door, examining the club's former sign lying face up in nearby rubble, and once inside, surveying a dark and musty mess. As Irma herself pointed out, the Christmas lights we had hung behind the stage all those years before were still in place, but portions of the ceiling had caved in, and the air was unbreathable. Indeed, coupled with this bitter new reality, those "Smoke Filled Room" lyrics took on entirely new meaning.

From there, we followed Irma to her visibly damaged home in an upscale New Orleans development, her ruined furnishings heaped into piles out front, taped-up refrigerators lining the sidewalk, her interior wallboard fully stripped away (the universal treatment for black mold infestation), and the circular swimming pool at the rear of her house now totally black. Inside, Irma pointed to a three-dimensional image of herself, now appearing to have a tear falling from one eye, and then to remaining black mold clinging to the ceiling (the reason she suggested my son stay outside).

Walking out front again, we found armed National Guardsmen patrolling the neighborhood, making sure it was free of looters and people in distress. Naturally, Irma being the generous soul she is, she greeted them, asked them where they were from, asked if their own homes or families had been affected by Hurricanes Katrina or Rita, and offered each of them a grateful hug. Before taking leave of one of our favorite humans, we also shot additional views of the abandoned refrigerators, as well as of nearby houses with holes cut in their roofs so the inhabitants could be rescued.

Perusing the city in sunlight for the first time, we saw stacks of abandoned automobiles in open fields and below overpasses; signs on stores announcing generators for sale or warning that looters would be shot; and emptied-out homes and buildings standing open with shutters, drapes, or doors flapping eerily in the wind. After our afternoon tour, we made our way to the Bywater area again, where nearly all power remained off. Diana had found an online notice that voodoo priestess Sallie Ann Glassman would be leading an All Saints Day parade from her Island of Salvation Botanica headquarters on Piety Street, in an effort to bring the dead city back to life. Intrigued, Diana had phoned Sallie Ann, asking if she would mind our filming her parade, and both she and an assistant said it would be fine. However, when we arrived there at dusk, despite the oncoming darkness, the parade had not yet begun.

Assuming pre-parade rituals were taking place inside the small, candlelit headquarters, Diana entered alone, making sure that aggressive male filmmakers with lights and cameras would not be a distraction. Once again, she was told it was okay. The alley leading to Sallie Ann's building included a long fence painted with mystical images, and after seeing Diana's signal, we tried to be as discreet as possible in shooting along the way. But once we entered, switched on camera lights, and began filming in dimly lit rooms filled with colorful, voodoo artifacts, many of those present were not happy. So, we hung back as much as we could while documenting dancing and other activities taking place inside, and then the ceremony overseen by Sallie Ann herself, including use of colored powders to create images and words on the floor. To our amazement, right as she reached the climax of her ceremony, the electrical lights switched on in her building, as well as throughout the Bywater neighborhood. Although

I would not have believed it myself, the documentary evidence is in our film.

The next day, we arranged to meet with Mark Samuels, the owner of Basin Street Records, a New Orleans jazz and rhythm and blues label featuring such top local artists as Kermit Ruffins, Theresa Andersson, and Jon Cleary. As previously agreed, we first showed up at Mark's offices, a freestanding building where he and a female assistant were organizing boxes of product, while also cleaning up from water damage. After showing us around and telling us the basics of his independent label, Mark led us to his home in the Lakeview section of the city, not far from the I-wall breach of the 17th Street Canal. There, he showed us around his large, modern home, pointing out the high water line on his interior walls, the empty sections where dry wall had been removed, the musical instruments now calcified from the flooding, and so forth. Then, he took us to a point in the canal where the protective wall had given way and spoke about flaws in the original construction.

As we discussed all of this, looking out over the damaged houses below the useless levee, a man named Stephen Assaf walked up to greet us. He soon made clear that his was the house directly in front of us that had been washed off its foundation, had landed flush against the house next door to it, had lost at least one of its walls, and now seemed almost ready to collapse. As anxious to show us around as we were to come and film, Stephen took us briefly inside where we examined the black mold on walls and ceilings and the piles of waterlogged possessions. He next drew our attention to a nonfunctioning metronome in one of those piles, then to a half-buried keyboard outside, at which point we knew we had stumbled upon another New Orleans musician.

Stephen next took us to see his mother's larger but similarly ransacked house, showed us the car that had wound up in her backyard swimming pool ("We call it the carpool."), and sat on her back balcony singing a highly appropriate classic song while accompanying himself on guitar: "All of me . . . why not take all of me. Can't you see . . . I'm no good without you . . . You took the best, so why not take the rest. Baby, take all of me." It was not clear whether he intended the irony or whether it was simply instinctive. However, we would eventually be joined by his mother, who was equally friendly, but whose brightly colored clothing and makeup, and whose dramatic manner, made her resemble a character in a Fellini film.

Somehow, Diana learned that a top-rated French eatery, Herbsaint Bar and Restaurant, had reopened for business a few weeks before. So, at our urging, she called for a reservation, and we approached it like starving cartoon characters, tongues dragging in the sand as they near an oasis in the desert. And even if the Herbsaint menu was limited under current conditions, this was anything but a mirage. Our meals were beautifully prepared and blessedly complemented by bottles of French wine. And for that short time, life seemed almost normal again, for which we were immeasurably grateful.

Feeling transformed, we returned to the hotel for a prearranged meeting with Keith Spera, the longtime music critic of the Times-Picayune newspaper, and a close friend of Michael Tisserand. Keith gave us a journalistic view of what it was like returning to New Orleans directly after Katrina and broken levees did their worst. But he also spoke of what he and his wife had endured personally and expressed their sincere hopes for the city's renewal.

By now, whatever was in the air was beginning to have a negative effect on Diana's skin, and an equally bad effect on our group's breathing. However, we had another full day of filming to accomplish before heading to Lafayette, and then to Houston and Austin. Still, our load was made lighter knowing our reports back to Brett and Michael had been well-received, that additional funding had been approved, and that a new tentative agreement had been faxed to the hotel, ready to be signed and sent back again. In short, Starz had given us the go-ahead to complete our mission, and we were happy to get on with it.

Director Robert Mugge, director of photography David Sperling, audio director Seth Tallman, and director of photography Christopher Li prepare to film an interview with Colonel Lewis Setliff III, regional head of the Army Corps of Engineers, while producer Diana Zelman gets releases signed by James H. Taylor, the Corps public relations person. (photographed by Rob Marvin Mugge, 2005)

On Thursday, we started off our day by interviewing Colonel Lewis Setliff III, the regional head of the Army Corps of Engineers, who had been sent there to fix this mess, and James H. Taylor, who handled public relations. They were then reeling from charges that incomplete or shoddy work by the Corps had led the levees to breach, and therefore were relieved that Diana and I wanted only to understand the situation on the ground and how the music community, in particular, had been affected. As a result, in addition to giving us great interviews, they offered us a helicopter ride the following day so that we could document damage across the city, especially in the hard-hit Ninth Ward, which was inaccessible by car to anyone but emergency workers. We happily accepted, then rushed to our second shoot of the day.

Our next stop was the office of *OffBeat*, the magazine of New Orleans music and culture. There, we were warmly greeted by managing editor Joseph Irrera, who took us to the second-floor office of publisher and editor-in-chief Jan Ramsey. Seated at a reassuringly cluttered desk, and occasionally glancing out of her impressively large window onto Frenchmen Street below, she spoke about the rough conditions facing New Orleans musicians and of the need to repair the city sufficiently so that everyone could return from exile and reestablish their lives. Long the most stalwart defender of the New Orleans music community, Jan was grateful to cities that had welcomed Louisiana artists, yet disdainful of efforts to keep them beyond the current crisis. It should also be noted that, due to Katrina, *OffBeat* had lost its staff and its printer, yet Jan and Joseph soldiered on alone, making theirs the first locally-based magazine to return to publishing.

From *OffBeat*, we drove to Tipitina's in the Uptown section of the city. This most famous of New Orleans music clubs was named after "Tipitina," a song by the great Professor Longhair (Henry Roeland Byrd), who played there frequently until his death in 1980 and resides there still in the form of a bronze bust that greets arriving customers. On this occasion, we had come to interview Bill Taylor and Adam Shipley about efforts of the Tipitina's Foundation to provide instruments for marching bands and school music programs and, more recently, to give aid to musicians negatively impacted by the storm and its aftermath. We conducted their joint interview in the covered backyard of the Tchoup House next door, then being run by Adam, while also discussing their own struggles since Katrina.

Joining us as well was David Freedman, the general manager of New Orleans public radio station WWOZ, the city's principal broadcaster of traditional Louisiana music ever since its early days when based in an apartment over Tipitina's and a microphone would be lowered through the floor in order to broadcast concerts from the stage below. Sadly, according to David, their more recent headquarters had sustained damage, and only the station's dedicated staff and volunteers, working largely out of Baton Rouge and supported by dozens of community radio stations around the country, had kept them on the air.

Finally, Bill offered to phone Big Chief Monk Boudreaux, who also joined us at the Tchoup House, bringing along a black suitcase containing his elaborate Mardi Gras Indian crown (elsewhere known as an Indian headdress) and a tambourine. To our delight, as we filmed, Monk placed the crown over his head and played the tambourine while singing two classic New Orleans songs, "Meet the Boys on the Battlefront" and "Lightning and Thunder." We loved both, of course, but I used the latter of the two in the film because of its obvious relevance.

Following that intimate performance, we were finished for the day, though not before learning that our invitation for a helicopter ride had been canceled due to orders that they take the Prince of Wales for a tour instead. Our embarrassed hosts did offer us a rain check, but it was difficult to know when we could collect on that, since we were leaving for Lafayette the following afternoon and had no immediate plans to return.

Friday morning, November 4, we checked out of our hotel and drove to the Check Your Bucket Café at 2107 Banks Street on the edge of Mid-City New Orleans. What made it unique was that it was owned by Eddie Bo, the well-known New Orleans singer, songwriter, musician, and producer who had purchased a run-down medical building and, using his own construction skills, built it into his personal "stress free zone," which he operated with Veronica Randolph, his close friend and so-called "sister." Now, due to recent damage, the café was closed, yet still offered quite a story. Eddie had been performing in Paris when Katrina hit, and in the storm's aftermath, with all flights to New Orleans canceled, he had only made it as far as Philadelphia. Since then, he had resided in Church Point, near Lafayette, with his friend and booking agent Karen Hamilton. And now, Eddie, Veronica, and Karen had agreed to meet us at Check Your Bucket so we could shoot what they found inside.

Noting the dark flood water lines on the exterior walls of musician Eddie Bo's Check Your Bucket coffeehouse, producer Diana Zelman, audio director Seth Tallman, and director of photography David Sperling interview Bo about the building's future while, inside, Robert Mugge and director of photography Christopher Li record the reasons why that future is bleak. (photographed by Rob Marvin Mugge, 2005)

Before we entered, wearing facial masks because of the fumes, Eddie pointed out the black high-water mark on the outside of the building. Then, once inside, we saw that tables and chairs had floated around the room, cases of soft drinks had exploded, refrigerators had fallen on their sides, and the keys on Eddie's electric piano had frozen in place. Eddie and the two women all appeared to share a financial interest in the café, but he spoke for the three of them when declaring that restoring the building to its former condition would require too much money and effort, and that they should simply sell it, letting future owners worry about repairs.

From there, we drove a couple of hours to our usual Lafayette hotel. Because we had now been on the road for more than a week, Diana arranged to have our laundry picked up and given to a woman outside the hotel who would take it to a laundromat, clean it, dry it, fold it, and return it to us within twenty-four hours. Then, that evening, our six-person crew responded to an earlier invitation from

Karen Hamilton, driving the short distance to her lovely home in Church Point, Louisiana and dining there with her, Eddie, and Veronica.

After dinner, we were taken to the home of a neighbor who generously offered us use of her upright piano to shoot Eddie performing. Eddie was a bit feisty that night, but he performed a glorious version of "My Dearest Darling," a song he had co-written and released on Chess Records in 1957, then reworked in 1960 for singer Etta James. After that, we returned to our Lafayette hotel, and all slept especially well.

Saturday, November 5 was our one full day in Lafayette, and we made good use of it. To begin with, we drove to the offices of public radio station KRVS on the University of Louisiana at Lafayette campus where we met up with my friend David Spizale, still general manager of the station. Then, after setting up cameras, tripods, a reflector, and an audio boom on the edge of a small bayou in the middle of campus, we filmed David telling the story of how, on August 31, he and his grown son, Matthew, had joined a flotilla of flat-bottomed boat owners who drove to New Orleans and assisted with rescue operations in the flooded city streets. Afterwards, David gave me a CD of photos he and his son had taken during their adventure, and I later created an eighteen-minute bonus feature for use with home video releases of the film. Originally, I had planned to include David's story and photos as part of the film itself, but that was while I still dreamed of making it three or four hours long.

With one shoot out of the way, we treated ourselves to a meal at our number one Lafayette restaurant, Prejean's. Then, at dusk, we found our way to Grant Street Dance Hall, a revered music venue for touring musicians, including house favorite (and personal favorite of ours) Austin-based Marcia Ball. As we set up to shoot the first of Marcia's sets that night, we also filmed an interview with current owner Don Kight, and then another with Marcia herself.

Midway through Marcia's interview, Eddie Bo arrived, and we were able to film the touching moment as she gave him a brand-new electric piano. It was intended to replace the one destroyed in Check

Your Bucket and, according to Marcia, was paid for by a group of his Austin fans, and not by her alone.

The show that night by Marcia and her five-piece band was dependably rip-roaring, and we did our best to capture it with just two cameras and an audio feed from the house PA system. Although Marcia offered us many great choices, I wound up using her powerful tribute to New Orleans nightlife, "That's Enough of That Stuff," and her soul-stirring cover of Randy Newman's "Louisiana 1927," which creates a first-person response to how the floods of that year threatened "to wash us away." Few songs could have offered greater resonance for contemporary New Orleans musicians, whether already back in their flooded city or forced to reside elsewhere.

The following day, we drove three and a half hours west on I-10 and, typically for this post-Katrina period, found more and more expensive gas along the way. Arriving in Houston, we checked into our latest hotel and, like Kermit Ruffins before us, headed straight to the Red Cat Jazz Café. The Red Cat was basically a single-room saloon comprised of a bar, an eating area, and a stage along the right wall. There, both Kermit and Red Cat manager Christopher Hayes relayed how Kermit had flown to Houston as a potential safe haven, arrived at the local airport, and then asked his taxi driver to take him to "the city's best jazz club," which turned out to be the Red Cat. According to Hayes, Kermit later asked if he could sit in during the club's Tuesday night open jam, and once he did, they realized who this was and began booking him with his band. Kermit added that the people of Houston had shown them incredible hospitality, even helping his band members to acquire new instruments to replace ones left behind and destroyed. During his performance that evening, Kermit played his usual range of material. But for the film, I decided his current take on "When the Saints Go Marching In"—sometimes upbeat and sometimes subdued—was a perfect reflection of his present exile. (As it happened, Dr. John had performed an equally mournful version of the song during his show in Memphis, aptly demonstrating the common emotions now being experienced by New Orleans musicians, wherever they had landed in Katrina's wake.)

We only stayed in Houston a single night, but would not leave the area until the following afternoon. As Diana had arranged, after checking out of our hotel on Monday morning, we drove to a nearby park where we met up with Philip Frazier, leader of the Rebirth Brass Band, along with a hastily assembled version of his group. As we knew, Rebirth had been founded in 1983 in the Tremé neighborhood of New Orleans by tuba and sousaphone player Philip Frazier, bass drum player (and Philip's brother) Keith Frazier, and trumpet player Kermit Ruffins. Despite Kermit leaving the group in 1993 in order to front his own jazz ensemble, the Frazier brothers carried on. Now, however, band members had taken refuge in various cities, so the version of Rebirth shown performing "Lord, Lord, Lord" that day was made up of whomever Philip could gather on short notice, which was fine. The more important point was that, even if staging such a performance here in Houston (rather than in their home city of New Orleans) implied severe cultural dislocation, *all* of these musicians, both individually and together, were carrying on.

Prior to Starz approving, and backing, our full shooting schedule, Dave Sperling had committed to another production that was starting before ours could finish. So, bidding Philip and the others goodbye, and very much wishing them well, we stopped for a bite to eat, then dropped off Dave at George Bush Intercontinental Airport for his flight back to Newark. Afterwards, we headed west on I-10 again, arriving in Austin some three and a half hours later. Once there, we checked into still another hotel, ate again, and conversed with Dieter Kaupp, a local cameraman who would briefly fill in for Dave.

On Tuesday morning, we drove to the Continental Club where our first order of business was interviewing its owner, Stephen Wertheimer. Stephen had been instrumental in attracting New Orleans musicians to Austin, where he helped them to find new housing, arrange bookings, and get their kids enrolled in local schools. Among those he had helped were my old friends The Iguanas, and they agreed to meet us at the club and perform several numbers (though, due to the short notice and time of day, doing so without an audience). Four members of the band—Joe Cabral, René Coman,

Doug Garrison, and Rod Hodges—had made the move with their families, but second saxophone player Derek Huston had elected not to relocate, preferring to set off on his own. For the moment, Derek's place had been taken by trumpet player Eric Lucero, whereas later, they would revert to a foursome.

We first interviewed the group inside the club, during which Joe Cabral opened his laptop and showed us recently shot video of the interior of his home back in New Orleans. The footage revealed how several feet of water had sent his possessions floating and seemingly ruined all of his musical instruments. Then we went out behind the club where the five musicians leaned against the rear wall, looking understandably glum. In the course of this second discussion, Joe mentioned how some of them were also performing in a side band called the Texiles, which was made up of Texas musicians and New Orleans exiles. But perhaps René summed up their situation best when he said, "Austin's a beautiful town, and there's really nothing not to like about it. New Orleans, at the moment, is not itself. We really long for a city that doesn't exist right now, you know? And it's really crushing to even contemplate the idea that you wouldn't be able to go back; that it wouldn't be as it once was, at least to some degree."

In the film, I used two songs from their performance inside the club. One was "Un Avion (A Plane)," which was a typically upbeat songwriting collaboration between Rod Hodges and Joe Cabral, featuring Spanish lyrics and a saxophone solo by Joe. The other was their cover of a strikingly applicable Nick Cave composition, "Right Now I'm A Roamin'," a slow, melancholy song in which Rod expressed a longing to be home again with his family, yet also a fatalistic view that, for now, he had no choice but to continue roaming. At this point, I should also mention that Starz had agreed to pay a token fee of $1,000 to the writers of every song used in the film. But when our clearance person, Barry Ennis, told Australian musician and songwriter Nick Cave that the project was supporting exiled New Orleans musicians, Nick refused to accept any payment.

From the Continental Club, we moved to Threadgill's, an even better known venue where we would film an outdoor concert by

Tribe 13, once again featuring Cyril and Gaynielle Neville (newly relocated to Austin) and their fellow Louisiana musician Papa Mali (an Austin resident for nearly two decades, though he would eventually return to New Orleans). Although Cyril liked to describe collaborations between Louisiana and Texas musicians as "the gumbo has spilled into the chili," the special meals Gaynielle and her daughter prepared for shows at Threadgill's featured exclusively Louisiana food, made especially for those who were very much missing it.

As expected, Tribe 13 performed an entire set that night, but I could only fit two more of Cyril's songs into the film. One was his cover of the Meters classic, "Hey Pocky Way," and the other was "Blues for New Orleans," which Cyril simply improvised about his beleaguered home city. In an interview that same night, he described how, as soon as he and Gaynielle had decided to move to Austin, Marcia Ball, currently on the road herself, phoned him to say that a few of her friends would shortly be in touch. Then, he said, the very next call was from Eddie Wilson, owner of Threadgill's, inviting him to perform Louisiana music at his club every Tuesday night, with Cyril's wife Gaynielle preparing Louisiana food. According to Cyril, this weekly event became known as "Louisiana Cookin' and Jookin'," and our crew was fortunate to be there on exactly such a night. Eddie echoed some of this same information while introducing the band on stage, adding that, when Marcia phoned him from the road about Cyril and Gaynielle's arrival, she instructed him to look after them, or else his "ass" would be "grass."

On Wednesday morning, November 9, Chris Li took the wheel of one of the minivans, and I took the wheel of the other, as we prepared to follow I-10 from Austin all the way back to New Orleans again. Even without stops, it normally would have taken seven and a half hours for Chris, Diana, Rob, and me to make that trip. But we also made a stop for lunch somewhere near Houston, then dropped off Seth Tallman at George Bush Intercontinental Airport, so he could fly home to Connecticut. Naturally, it then took the rest of the day for us to make it to New Orleans and eventually check back into the Parc St. Charles Hotel, where Diana had somehow secured rooms for us again. In fact, the only reason we returned to New Orleans that night was because she also had been in touch with the Army Corps of Engineers, and they had assured her that, on Thursday, we would be able to take our delayed helicopter ride over the city, which I considered to be essential for the story we were telling.

The following day, after checking out for the final time, we made our way back to the Corps offices. There, we were introduced to our pilot, who pointed out that his helicopter had four seats, which meant that Chris and his camera could be seated up front with the pilot, and Diana and I could sit behind them. Sadly, Rob would have to wait with Corps staff until we returned. But to my great relief, he was fine with that.

Once the four of us had our seat belts fastened and our headphones on, the helicopter lifted straight up, then flew quickly across the skyline. Highlights of our trip, all of which Chris recorded, included circling around the Superdome, a center of so much anguish during flooding of the city; sites of key levee breaches; points where assorted boats and cargo ships had washed onto shore; Lower Ninth neighborhoods where houses appeared to have been smacked down or moved out of place; and the Ninth Ward home of musician Fats Domino, who was wrongly rumored to have died, and on whose roof someone had prematurely spray-painted the words, "R.I.P. Fats. You will be missed."

Director of photography Christopher Li and producer Diana Zelman pose in murky air while exploring reconstruction efforts at a New Orleans levee. (photographed by Robert Mugge, 2005)

At one point, the pilot asked if we would like to touch down where a levee was being repaired, walk around among the workers, and grab a few shots. So, we made the stop, did some shooting, posed for photos in the mud, then headed back to the Army Corps of Engineers headquarters where Rob was waiting for us. Afterwards, we thanked our hosts for permitting Chris to shoot helicopter footage every bit as valuable for the opening of *New Orleans Music in Exile* as his helicopter footage in Memphis had been for the opening of *Deep Blues*.

With that accomplished, we drove to Louis Armstrong New Orleans International Airport, as it had been named since July of 2001, when the greatest of New Orleans musicians turned 100. There, we said goodbye to Chris, who flew home to Washington, DC; Diana got behind the wheel of the minivan Chris had been driving; and she, Rob, and I prepared to drive the three hours back to Jackson, Mississippi. However, on our way out of the city, we were stunned to find a fully functioning Popeye's restaurant, which we took as one more sign of the city coming to life again. And since this Popeye's offered both shrimp *and* oyster po' boys, which those elsewhere in the country did not, we were sent happily on our way.

Later that evening, upon arriving home in Jackson, we washed and dried clothes again, then, as I had on so many past projects, generally collapsed. But not for long, because the Starz Business Affairs Department suddenly wanted updated budgets, copies of all collected releases, a list of every person we had interviewed on camera, a list of every person who had performed on camera, and a *separate* list of those who had both performed *and* been interviewed on camera. Naturally, they wanted these reports immediately, or else we could forget about coming payments necessary for remaining stages of the project. Not long thereafter, they also demanded that we secure written releases for every building or piece of sculpture that happened to appear in any shot of the film, and for every newspaper or periodical in which we had filmed a mere headline, until, in complete exasperation, I sent other Starz executives published articles regarding the concept of "fair use" in film and television production and was finally able to shut down these ludicrous, time-consuming requirements.

The following day (Friday, November 11), Diana and I drove our two rented minivans the three hours back to Memphis, turned them in at the airport, picked up my own minivan we had left there, ate dinner, and drove back to Jackson again. Then, over the weekend, Diana flew home to Philadelphia, at which point I immediately started missing her.

Over the next few months, I raced to organize and edit a huge amount of footage and to prepare for final postproduction, because Starz wanted the completed film in hand by late February, just three and a half months after we had finished shooting under sometimes brutal conditions. However, late in the year, I was approached by Roger Naber and Judy Alexander of the Legendary Rhythm & Blues Cruise, inviting me to sail on their late January cruise to the Caribbean, so that I could observe their operations and discuss the possibility of filming the same cruise a year later. I told them that, despite my current workload, I probably could manage it, but only if I could bring along Rob and Diana, and only if they understood that I would also have to bring a laptop, a hard drive, and speakers, and spend eight hours a day continuing to edit *New Orleans Music in Exile* while at sea with them. It was a bit crazy, but I did not see how else I could both sail on the cruise—which featured performances by hundreds of blues and soul musicians, and typically made three or four stops at Caribbean islands or countries in Latin America—and still finish the New Orleans film by the time Starz wanted it. To our delight, they did agree, and we made it work.

Also, not long before that, I was invited to present a brief retrospective at the Santa Fe Film Festival in early December, and Diana and Rob were free to join me, which included our lodging in a remarkable Tibetan-themed guest house. Other highlights included several well-attended screenings; Steve Terrell's generous piece in the *Santa Fe New Mexican* (the first to chronicle any of our post-Katrina filming stories or Rob's superb accompanying photographs); and my receipt of the festival's Lifetime Achievement Award via the great Lee Eliot Berk, longtime former president of Boston's Berklee College of Music.

Finally, there was the matter of Dr. John. Immediately after filming his performance at the Voodoo Experience in Memphis, he and his musicians had rushed away without signing releases or sitting for interviews. So, when we learned that Mac would be performing at the Keswick Theatre in Glenside, Pennsylvania, a suburb of Philadelphia, I reached out to his manager, Peter Himberger, who graciously arranged for me to interview the good doctor in his dressing room before his performance. The show was scheduled for February 4, 2006, and that afternoon, I arrived at the Keswick with Diana, cameraman Dave Sperling, and audio person Bill Barth, all of whom lived within driving distance of the venue. After we located Dr. John's still-empty dressing room, I asked Dave and Bill to set up lights, camera, recorder, and microphone in the tiny space, while I left briefly to pay homage to someone else on the night's bill, which was Bobby "Blue" Bland, the great rhythm and blues singer whom Diana and I had seen perform just a week or two before on the Blues Cruise, and who had his own dressing room on a different floor.

When Dr. John made his appearance, I presented him with a bag of silly souvenirs from a Doctor John's Lingerie Boutique, a store that we had encountered somewhere on our travels, and that we visited so I could buy him a joke gift in a bag that bore his name. However, once we started the interview, he was as serious and articulate as ever in telling us what was special about New Orleans and why he was so angry about what had happened there. At my request, he went on to recite lyrics to his song "Sweet Home New Orleans," which, again, he and his wife had recently rewritten in response to the Katrina debacle, and his performance of which would end the film. The song included the following lines:

Sweet home New Orleans,
I can sure enough hear you callin'.
But since the levees come fallin',
I say, "Where ya at, my little darlin's?"
Lootin' and shootin'; poor people ain't got a dime.
And poor people been livin' like this for too long a time.
I pray to the spirit world for help from dreams,
In Katrina's wake, to heal my New Orleans.

That same night, across the city of Philadelphia, Diana's latest, beautiful granddaughter, Anabella Grace Hoback, was born. So, once again, our project combined the joyful, the tragic, and the simply bittersweet.

Throughout production, Brett Marottoli had served as our primary contact at Starz, and more often than not, as our own guardian angel. But throughout editing and postproduction, I reported more to executive producer Michael Ruggiero, and he and I also got along great. We did have a few minor disagreements, of course, and in those, he was largely passing along the company line. For instance, thinking like a filmmaker, I wanted to open with Theresa Andersson performing "Like A Hurricane" over shots of Katrina striking New Orleans, then go to actual information about what had resulted. But Michael, thinking like a cable executive, wanted me to start with a quick tease of artists describing what had happened to them. So, I added the tease and generally liked the way it worked, while still missing the more abstract opening I had envisaged from the beginning.

Otherwise, we had gathered so much wonderful footage that I proposed making a four-hour film, half of which would offer the perspective of musicians and others who had returned to New Orleans, and the other half of which would offer perspectives of artists still in exile. But Michael said Starz felt I needed to limit the film to two hours, as originally pitched, which is why I was forced to leave out David Spizale's New Orleans rescue, Jon Cleary's history of New Orleans piano, and more compelling scenes.

Ironically, Spike Lee, who did not start shooting *When the Levees Broke*, his own Katrina doc for HBO, until months after we shot ours, and who did not premiere his finished product until five months after we premiered ours, nonetheless announced his intention to make a four-hour film, exactly as I had proposed to Starz. He also had a budget of $2,000,000 (ten times our budget of $200,000), plus the full-on HBO publicity machine behind his release. But frankly, having received rough treatment from HBO in the past, I was happier working with more modest Starz resources, since the people providing those resources showed genuine commitment to the project, as well as to the ideals behind it. Without Brett, Michael, and Stephan fighting countless corporate battles on our behalf, there is no way we could have made the film that we did, much less on the schedule that we did.

Eventually, Diana and I oversaw postproduction at a facility she had discovered in Philadelphia which, at the time, was called Shooters Post & Transfer, and where our work was lovingly supervised by project manager Andy Williams. Then, from there, *New Orleans Music in Exile* moved quickly into release.

First came the film's March 23, 2006 world premiere as an opening night offering of the Memphis International Film Festival, the response to which included glowing press by film critic John Beifuss in *The Commercial Appeal* (the longtime Memphis daily), by Chris Davis in the weekly *Memphis Flyer*, and by former AFI Theater programmer Eddie Cockrell in *Daily and Weekly Variety*. After that, it played a couple more spring festivals before receiving a spectacular Starz launch in New Orleans on May 13, 2006. The Starz event began with two well-received screenings at Landmark's Canal Place Theatre—a free one for the public, then a private one for invited guests. After the first, two women sought out Diana to say they had seen much coverage of their city's physical devastation, but that our film was the first to show how they and other residents actually *felt*. Then, after the second screening, the Rebirth Brass Band led everyone in a "second line strut" to Tipitina's French Quarter, a second venue operated for a time by owners of the original Tipitina's.

Once at the venue, Rebirth continued to play for a private reception in the upstairs area. Then, in the larger downstairs area, an "invitation-only benefit concert" took place with performances by Irma Thomas, Theresa Andersson, Kermit Ruffins, and World Leader Pretend. But for Diana and me, the most gratifying part of the event came when Starz president Robert Clasen presented two literally gigantic (roughly two feet by five feet) checks for $50,000 each, one to the Tipitina's Foundation's Instruments A Comin' program, and the other to the MusiCares Artist Relief Fund (also known at the time as Hurricane Relief). Although working with corporate funders can be a challenge for independent filmmakers, in the end, not only did we get the film made—bringing wide attention to the post-Katrina struggles of the New Orleans music community, and spotlighting some of the groups who were trying to help—but our efforts also led a corporate television company to provide direct support for traditional American musicians.

On Friday, May 19, just six days after the New Orleans theatrical premiere and party, Starz premiered the film nationwide over its Starz in Black channel (the third name thus far for the Starz channel aimed at African American viewers), and a day after that, on the original mainstream Starz channel. Finally, in the June 2006 issue of *Jazz Times* magazine, my friend Lee Mergner published an excellent feature story by Bill Milkowski, and on Tuesday, April 24, 2007, Diana Zelman and I were presented with a *Gambit Weekly* "Big Easy Music Award" for being "Special Friend[s] of New Orleans Music."

Chapter Nine
Delta Diaspora

Last of the Mississippi Jukes (2003)

Blues Divas (2005)

New Orleans Music in Exile was not the first film I made in collaboration with Starz. In the years after making *Deep Blues*, my trips back to the Mississippi Delta left me feeling that the rural blues scenes we had captured in that film—insisting, in the process, that they were still alive and well—seemed to me finally to be fading. In fact, nearly everyone in *Deep Blues* itself started dying off. For that reason, I began seeking funding for a film I wanted to call *Last of the Mississippi Jukes*. My intention was to document the last vestiges of an important but dying culture, and to create a more wistful follow-up to *Deep Blues*. I even envisioned visiting the same sorts of jukes and other venues we had portrayed in the earlier film, but this time presenting any we could find as the final gasp of regional, down-home blues culture. In reality, this pessimistic view was as much an exaggeration as our earlier optimistic one. Yet, even if commercial and governmental packaging of blues traditions in the state had increased, as I looked around, I did not find the extremes of either talent or vitality we had found before, and most of the artists being touted by friends in the Delta seemed to be weaker versions of those who had preceded them.

At any rate, I could not find the money this new project would require, so I turned my attention elsewhere. Then, three unexpected developments turned everything around. First, early in 2001, a guy named David Hughes called to see if I would like to attend the Crossroads Film Festival in Jackson, Mississippi and show three films relevant to the region: *Deep Blues*, *Hellhounds on My Trail*, and *Gospel According to Al Green*. David lived in nearby Vicksburg, made his living as a collector of music-related memorabilia, and played guitar in local blues clubs. On this occasion, he had been asked to organize some special events for the Jackson festival, and so decided to invite Chicago Tribune movie critic Michael Wilmington (who had written the rave about *Deep Blues* while at the Los Angeles Times), David's friend and fellow collector Terry Stewart of the Rock Hall (who had collaborated with me on *Hellhounds* and *Rhythm 'N' Bayous*), and, at Terry's suggestion, me as well.

The festival took place in early April of that year, and much of Saturday was devoted to screenings of my three films, as well as to a panel discussion moderated by David and featuring Michael, Terry, and me. Naturally, one of the subjects of that discussion was the documentation of Mississippi blues culture, and at that point, I casually mentioned my intention to create a kind of sequel for *Deep Blues* that would be called *Last of the Mississippi Jukes*. Then, when David asked for input from the audience, Hattiesburg-based musician, bandleader, and record producer Vasti Jackson stood up and said that, if my project went forward, he hoped I would concentrate on authentic venues, and not on the sort of slick blues clubs that were taking their place, including as part of recently opened Mississippi casinos. I told him that, as with *Deep Blues*, I intended to do exactly that. Then, as the event was ending, I sought him out, and we exchanged contact information. However, it would not be until weeks later that I realized Vasti was the same incredible young Mississippi-based guitar wizard I had seen performing six years before at Buddy Guy's Legends Club in Chicago, where many of us were gathered to celebrate Bruce Iglauer's recent wedding to Jo Kolanda. As so often seemed to be the case, persons meant to connect inevitably did, and the point was simply to stay alert so as not to miss what was somehow intended.

Speaking of which, later that night, David arranged for Terry, Michael, and me to visit the Subway Lounge, a legendary Jackson juke—

or urban lounge, as some might call it—which featured blues performances every Friday and Saturday night from midnight until nearly
dawn. Decades before, in 1966, the Subway had been founded by local
musician and entrepreneur Jimmy King to offer jazz performances in
the basement of Jackson's Summers Hotel, one of the city's first two
hotels catering to African American travelers. However, years after
the hotel itself closed, Jimmy and his wife Helen were still operating their (literally) underground venue. It also should be noted that,
right from the start, Jimmy called his nightspot the Subway, because
descending the narrow brick exterior stairway into the basement reminded him of entering a subway station in New York City. And even
though, for the first few years, he did stick with jazz, changing tastes
in the community later caused him to switch to blues.

By the time the three of us visited Jimmy's venue in April of 2001,
he had settled into a pair of alternating house bands—the appropriately named House Rockers and the King Edward Blues Band—each
of which would perform both nights, every other weekend, and each
of which was as effortlessly integrated as the crowds for which they
played (something which, at the time, was still somewhat unique in
the city of Jackson). The role of either house band was to kick off the
night's festivities with a set of its own, and then to back a series of
local singers, many of whom would stop by to perform a short set
after their own gigs elsewhere had ended.

As for Terry, Michael, and me, we were greeted warmly at the
door by Helen King, Jimmy's wife, who requested a small cover
fee and, in return, gave us tickets to exchange for metal buckets of
canned beer, which Jimmy doled out at the bar. Then, we took our
seats in the dark, smoky, ramshackle room, and buckled our metaphorical seat belts for what was to come.

Most of the music alternated between hard blues and what people in the South dubbed soul blues: basically soul music featuring a
blues edge, forceful electric guitar, and down-home lyrical content.
It was no surprise that music of this sort would be dominant at
the Subway, because Malaco Records, which was based in Jackson,
produced and released more of it than any other label. Speaking for
myself, however, these lushly soulful sounds, the joy conveyed by

everyone around us, and the welcoming smiles of Jimmy and Helen made me feel as if, in terms both musical and spiritual, I had found my way home.

Before flying out again on Sunday, I thanked David for the gift he had given the three of us. Moreover, I told him I was now determined to include the Subway in a future film, and we each agreed to be alert for potential funders. Then, as I settled back into my usual work routine, I received some recordings Vasti had produced, both in his own name and in that of a female Mississippi vocalist named Patrice Moncell. After only a single listen, I resolved that, regardless of how long it took, I truly needed to produce *Last of the Mississippi Jukes*, and the people I had met in Jackson needed to be involved.

The second development came a month later, in May of 2001, when Mississippi-based movie star Morgan Freeman, Clarksdale and Memphis attorney Bill Luckett, and Blues Foundation executive director Howard Stovall opened Ground Zero Blues Club, their newly minted Clarksdale, Mississippi blues venue, which was intentionally designed to resemble a traditional juke joint. Although essentially a bar, restaurant, and music club taking over the long vacant home of the wholesale Delta Grocery and Cotton Co., Ground Zero was freshly filled with pool tables, mismatched tables and chairs, Christmas tree lights, flags, posters, Delta-related signs, blues iconography, musical instruments, and ever-expanding graffiti, in order to give it the ambience of what Morgan referred to as an old-fashioned "bucket of blood." Even before having the chance to visit there myself, I already knew that, this, too, could play a part in the film I was planning.

The third and final development followed late in the year when I learned from WinStar, my distributor at the time, that Starz had purchased rights to my films *Deep Blues* and *Hellhounds on My Trail* for screenings on their African American cable channel Black Starz (later renamed Starz in Black, to make it easier to find in television directories). Hearing this, I responded exactly as I had two decades before when learning that Andy Park of Britain's Channel 4 Television had purchased rights to my Sun Ra film. That is, I thought to myself, if people at Starz had acquired my work, these were people worth knowing.

Upon learning that Stephan Shelanski and Brett Marottoli were the executives in question, I wrote to them, thanked them for the acquisitions, and asked if they would like to fund a similar film I was then preparing. Titled *Last of the Mississippi Jukes*, I said, it would be much like the aforementioned *Deep Blues*, but with a focus on Mississippi blues as vanishing American culture. Although attracted to the idea, they declared their bosses would never underwrite shooting throughout the state, which is what I had in mind. So, regrouping, I asked, "What if I were to place my primary focus on the Subway Lounge in Jackson, Mississippi, which would permit nearly all the film's performances to be filmed in a single night?" Then I added, "What if I spent a second night filming the hands-on owners of Ground Zero Blues Club in Clarksdale, Mississippi—Morgan Freeman and Bill Luckett—explaining how they had patterned their club after a traditional juke, which, in turn, would establish what the word meant?"

At that point, I felt as if I were watching the scene in Alfred Hitchcock's 1929 film *Blackmail*, wherein one woman mentions a scandalous murder committed with a knife, and a second woman, listening intently, hears only the word "knife," repeated over and over. In the same way, when I laid out my alternative plan for making *Last of the Mississippi Jukes*, Stephan and Brett heard one thing only, which was the name *Morgan Freeman*. To be fair, at the time, the vast majority of Starz programming was Hollywood movies, so the involvement of a top-rated star would be extremely appealing. And when I also told them what I had learned from Bill Luckett, which is that, so long as their heavily subsidized club were implicitly promoted, there would be no need to pay Morgan for his onscreen involvement, I could feel my fish tugging on the line.

With interest from Starz growing, I reconnected with David Hughes and told him that, if he would help organize a multi-artist concert to be staged at the Subway Lounge—much like the one I had seen there back in April—I would be willing to credit him as the film's second producer. In response, David reached out to Subway owner Jimmy King, as well as to key musicians, both Black and white, who had played the Subway over the years and put together an impressive roster of potential performers. I also asked him to include Vasti, which made good sense because, when the somewhat larger-than-life Patrice Moncell was not making explosive appearances at the Subway, she could be found touring casinos with Vasti, in shows that he produced for the two of them, not unlike the way Ike Turner had done for his wife Tina and himself. In addition, we wisely invited Bobby Rush, the funniest, raciest, most talented, and most famous blues artist living in Jackson, as well as Chris Thomas King, the successful progeny of Baton Rouge bluesman Tabby Thomas, and now increasingly well-known for playing blues forebear Tommy (not Robert) Johnson in the Coen brothers film *O Brother Where Art Thou*, much of which had been shot in central Mississippi.

Attorney and Ground Zero co-owner Bill Luckett kept me informed as to when Morgan would likely be home in Mississippi again, and that information helped to determine the successive days on which we could shoot at the Subway in Jackson and at Ground Zero in Clarksdale. I also reached out to Memphis-based bluesman Alvin Youngblood Hart, who had been so good in *Hellhounds on My Trail*, and asked him to perform for us in Clarksdale, perhaps using Delta artists Sam Carr on drums and Anthony Sherrod on bass.

Then, just as all was nearly set for back-to-back shoots at the Subway and Ground Zero, we heard from Jimmy King that a movement had arisen to try and save the Summers Hotel building, which was otherwise due to be condemned and torn down. By 2002, the city of Jackson finally had a Black mayor and a number of African American city and state officials reflective of its population, and they all wanted to preserve the hotel due to its political and historical legacy. Some of that significance came from the fact that, until the early 1940s, when the Summers Hotel opened, Black musicians, theater troupes, church groups, soldiers, tourists, and others passing through the area had to stay with friends or with members of Black churches, because white hotels would not admit them. Additional significance came from the facts that, number one, among those who stayed at the hotel in the early 1960s were freedom riders who were risking their lives in support of voter registration; and number two, the house next door, owned by African American attorney Jack Young, became a meeting place for local and visiting civil rights activists, including Jackson-based NAACP state field secretary Medgar Evers, who was assassinated at his home in June of 1963. In later years, Jimmy would lease the vacant house to sell his "blues dogs" (high-quality hot dogs with assorted fixings) to Subway customers during his late-night Friday and Saturday shows.

Once we heard that a groundbreaking ceremony would take place beside the Summers Hotel on Sunday, April 7, with the hope of pushing along preservation efforts, I also learned from Bill Luckett that Morgan would be in Clarksdale the same weekend. So, we quickly arranged to shoot interviews in Jackson the prior Thursday; shoot a multi-act concert at Jackson's Subway Lounge on Friday night; shoot additional interviews and performances at Clarksdale's Ground Zero on Saturday; and, after a quick return to Jackson Saturday night, shoot the Summers Hotel groundbreaking on Sunday.

To assist me with this densely concentrated effort, I booked many of my regular crew people: directors of photography Chris Li and David Sperling, audio director Bill Barth plus assistant, second unit cinematographer and camera assistant Craig Smith, head grip Quincy McKay, and multitrack music recording and mixing person Greg Hartman of Big Mo, who brought along two assistants of his own. In addition, my longtime friend Dick Waterman—the legendary blues-related author, photographer, and artist manager—offered to shoot production stills, as did Craig Smith. And since my son Rob and David Hughes's brother James were with us anyway, I hired them both as part-time production assistants. Without doubt, this several-day period would be stress-inducing, so I tried to surround myself with easygoing collaborators, if only to compensate for whatever else awaited, and it was good that I did.

I flew into Jackson on Wednesday, April 3 and headed for the Edison Walthall Hotel, an ancient edifice where most of my team would be staying. Some considered it elegant, and it did have a certain musty charm. Regardless, I then touched base with David Hughes and Jimmy King in person, and with Bill Luckett by phone, and everything seemed to be on track.

On Thursday, the rest of my crew either flew in or drove in, and after all were checked into the hotel, we got straight to work. Jimmy

King's wife Helen was now away from home, being treated for a terminal illness. Nevertheless, Jimmy met us at the Subway and allowed us to set up for a series of interviews.

Mississippi blues artist Vasti Jackson visits with Jimmy King (left), the longtime owner of Jackson, Mississippi's legendary Subway Lounge in the basement of the historic Summers Hotel. (photographed by Dick Waterman, 2002)

Over the course of that day, we filmed Jimmy with three artists, each of whom chatted with him, then sang a song, accompanied by guitar or harmonica: Bobby Rush performed a solo version of his classic number "Garbage Man," Eddie Cotton Jr. performed his song "All Night Long," and Chris Thomas King performed "John Law Burned Down the Liquor Sto,'" his original composition he had performed in *O Brother Where Art Thou*. In addition, Bobby told a funny story about tricking a white hotel owner into giving him a room under Jim Crow segregation, while Chris discussed his father's legendary Baton Rouge blues club, the Black retail and entertainment community of which it was a part, and the ironic loss of community cohesion and financial control that came with integration. Afterwards, I took our group to eat at the Mayflower Café on Capitol

Street, "the oldest operating restaurant in the capital city." Fair or not, everywhere we went that day, I felt as if we were cinematic rescue workers, searching through the rubble for signs of life. And with our next stop, that feeling only deepened.

After dinner, Jimmy took us to the home of Mrs. Elma Summers, the elderly and somewhat fragile widow of W. J. Summers, the African American businessman who had opened and operated the Summers Hotel. It was the first wife of Mr. Summers who had helped him to run the hotel, primarily in the forties and fifties. Elma Summers, his second wife, started helping out in the sixties, and since she now controlled what was left of the hotel, we had long been hoping to interview her. In fact, Jimmy, who looked after many of her needs (bringing her meals and her medicine on a regular basis), had tried for weeks to convince her to speak with us about the hotel's colorful history, and about the interactions between W. J. Summers and various civil rights activists, from the freedom riders to Medgar Evers. At last, she did agree to be interviewed in the parlor of her dimly lit home, but only if said interview were conducted by the owner of the liquor store where she occasionally shopped, suddenly presenting himself as her "business adviser."

Once we agreed to his initial terms and proceeded with the interview, it quickly became clear that Elma had not been present for the most eventful years at the hotel. Then again, she did possess worthwhile information, which I would readily have used in the film. But as we finished our chat, her so-called "advisor" said she would not sign a release until he could "negotiate with Starz" on her behalf. This was disturbing because, reportedly, the man had a questionable reputation in the Black community. But Jimmy told us not to worry, reminding us that he, too, had Elma's ear, and he would do his best to straighten things out.

The following morning, in a large hotel room at the Edison Walthall, we filmed blues photographer, author, and artist manager Dick Waterman showing David Hughes some of the color photos he had shot of jukes across the state, as well as large, black and white images of his late friends and clients, among them Son House, Skip James, Mississippi John Hurt, and other legendary masters of the country blues. To be honest, the reason I asked David to conduct project interviews, beginning with Dick, was because I found his intensity distracting, and I therefore figured, if I could keep him busy in front of the camera, he would have fewer opportunities to bother me behind it. Nevertheless, the arrangement worked well in other respects, in that David's hip musicality, his brown leather jacket, his unshaven whiskers, and his raspy, accented voice brought the film a measure of Mississippi cool, as did Vasti, Jimmy, Bobby Rush, and others.

After we finished the work at our hotel, we headed back to the Subway, met up with Jimmy King, and began setting up lights for that evening. This was not easy, of course, because the ostensible "stage" was merely a small space at the front of the room, and the ceiling was so low that musicians could reach up and touch it, precluding our ability to light from above. Instead, Dave and Chris found a way to light the musicians from the side, from the back of the room, and from just below, which gave everything an eerie sort of look, like the Egyptian columns we had filmed that way for the Sun Ra film. In the earlier case, the columns had been designed to be lit from above by the sun, but Larry McConkey had lit them from below, creating an intriguing sort of disorientation. Similarly, what the guys did here, placing Chris's fluorescent lights at the feet of the performers, resulted in almost a horror film look, which was a step beyond our usual "film noir concert."

We also established camera positions, and Chris set up the table holding my communication system and video monitors (only two of the latter this time, since that's how many cameramen I could afford). At some point, of course, we also were joined by Greg Hartman, who pulled his multitrack recording truck up to the exterior door nearest the performance area and had his assistants run cable and set up microphones. The Subway being a dark, dank, dilapidated room with a building above it in seeming danger of imminent collapse, our high-tech equipment once again seemed out of place, as on so many of our projects. But my goal was to treat traditional artists and out-of-the-way venues with the same respect that more commercial ones enjoyed.

Despite these lofty intentions, I also knew that we could never duplicate a typical night at the Subway Lounge. For one thing, the music would begin playing, and we would begin shooting, hours before the usual twelve o'clock starting time; for another, rather than use just one of the alternating house bands, we had hired them both; and for still another, we had invited more singers and musicians than ever had performed here on a single night. Still, imposing order over all this would be up to David, who would now have the chance to earn his secondary title as music director, and who already had arranged which of the musicians would back up which of the singers. I had confidence David could handle this on his own, though, like Maggie Lewis Warwick in Shreveport, he did seem to invite virtually every musician he knew, which portended a very late night.

As the sun prepared to set that day, still another joker entered the deck I was dealt. Apparently, Starz was still nervous about funding such a project, by which I mean, one taking place thousands of miles from its Colorado headquarters, in a region with a radically different history and culture. For this reason, I was informed that a junior executive of note would arrive sometime prior to the Subway event. And suddenly, even as more and more bohemian musicians were joining our ranks, here, too, was that very junior exec, looking clean-cut, corporate, and ready to interfere.

By the rudest of cosmic jokes, right about then, we also were joined by Mrs. Summers's businessman friend who said that, unless Starz was prepared to write Mrs. Summers a check for one million dollars, not only could we not use any of her interview, but we could not film in the Subway that night. In other words, if we did not cut him a massive check, right that minute—one literally five times the size of our entire project budget—we all had to clear the hell out. Having met plenty of con men in my time, I simply looked to Jimmy King, asking him again if he had full legal control of this space, whatever the case with the rest of the building. Invariably calm and collected, Jimmy told me again that, of course he did. "Great," I said. "Then we're fine."

And yet, we were not. Suddenly, like a military recruit eying armed, approaching troops for the first time, the junior exec flipped out on me. According to him, by his authority as a representative of Starz, we were hereby ordered to pack up our equipment and depart the building. "Absolutely not," I replied. I then went on to explain how much time, effort, money, and good will would be lost if we did not proceed. I also told him that the guy to whom he was deferring was not an attorney, that he was simply a local con artist trying to bluff us into actions not in our own best interests, that Jimmy King had far more credibility in the community than this guy had, and that, if Jimmy said we were fine, then we truly were fine.

To the great frustration of everyone present, the junior exec was unmoved. He declared, again, that he was in charge, and that he was ordering all of us to cease and desist. But that was not going to happen. Instead, I moved directly into his face, pointing out that there was one of him versus many of us, and that, if he, himself, did not cease and desist, my crew and I would gaffer tape his hands and feet and throw him into one of our minivans until our work there was finished. Fortunately, he realized this was an argument he could not win, at least for now. So, he backed off, while still warning that further repercussions would follow. Ironically, he also went on to enjoy the show. (Note: Gaffer tape is like a higher quality version of duct tape that is used on film, television, and theatrical productions, especially for hanging lights.)

At Jackson, Mississippi's Subway Lounge, J. T. Watkins (second from left) and Levon Lindsey (third from left) perform a duet, backed by the King Edward Blues Band. King Edward is at left. (photographed by Dick Waterman, 2002)

Overall, it was a long but incredible night. As expected, far more songs were performed than I could ever have used, but I at least want to mention what made the film: Greg "Fingers" Taylor (with Casey Phillips and the Hounds) performing "Subway Swing"; Dennis Fountain and Pat Brown (with Casey Phillips and the Hounds plus Jesse Robinson) performing the Little Milton classic, "The Blues Is Alright"; Patrice Moncell (with the House Rockers) performing the "T-Bone" Walker classic, "Stormy Monday"; Vasti Jackson (with the King Edward Blues Band) performing his own "Casino in the Cottonfield"; Patrice Moncell and Vasti Jackson (with the House Rockers) performing Clarence Carter's risqué "Strokin'"; Levon Lindsey and J. T. Watkins (with the King Edward Blues Band) performing McKinley Mitchell's "You Know I've Tried"; the King Edward Blues Band performing the Mel Waiters classic "Hole in the Wall"; David Hughes (with Virgil Brawley) performing his own newly composed "Last of the Mississippi Jukes"; songwriter George Jackson (with the King Edward Blues Band) performing his co-composition, "Still Called the Blues"; Levon Lindsey and J. T. Watkins (with the King Edwards Blues Band) performing McKinley Mitchell's "End of the Rainbow"; Lucille and her band (with Greg "Fingers" Taylor) performing her song, "What Goes Around, Comes Around"; and Abdul Rasheed (with the House Rockers) performing Larry Duane Addison's classic, "Members Only," which perfectly described a venue like the Subway where, in the midst of longtime Southern segregation—implicit, if not always explicit—people of various races and backgrounds were able to come together around a shared love of largely African American music.

Although the clock slowly meandered towards morning, we did not quit work until every artist present had performed, had been filmed and recorded, had been paid, and had signed a release. Then, shortly before dawn, we returned to the hotel and caught a few hours of sleep before driving nearly three hours to Ground Zero Blues Club in Clarksdale. There, we interviewed Bill Luckett and Morgan Freeman about their intention to recreate the look and spirit of a traditional juke joint, and Morgan reminisced about experiencing such places himself while growing up in the Delta. After that, my camera crew set up lights, and Greg and his team set up microphones, in order to film and record Memphis-based musician Alvin Youngblood Hart offering a solo rendition of "Pony Blues" (a classic song by pioneering Delta bluesman Charlie Patton), and then, as planned, a group performance of his own composition "Joe Friday," backed by veteran Jelly Roll Kings drummer Sam Carr, and by young Delta guitarist Anthony Sherrod on bass. Finally, rounding out the evening, Anthony rejoined his own band, Clarksdale-based The Deep Cuts, for a performance of singer Josh "Razorblade" Stewart's "Every Goodbye Don't Mean I'm Gone." Unfortunately, I could not fit the latter song into the film, but I did include it on the film's original soundtrack CD.

Sunday, April 7, as Greg Hartman's Big Mo recording truck returned to Washington, DC, the rest of us set about filming assorted preservationists as they donned hard hats for a group groundbreaking outside of the seriously deteriorating Summers Hotel. After the ceremony, we interviewed the mayor, state and local politicians, community activists, and Jackson Clarion-Ledger reporter Arnold Lindsay about hopes that the Summers Hotel building could, indeed, be saved, even as the reality looked bleak. Next, as light began to fade, I asked Vasti Jackson to discuss the future of blues in Mississippi, and asked four members of the House Rockers band what decades of playing the lounge had meant to them. To quote House Rockers bandleader and drummer, Dudley Tardo: "The Subway has been a real blessing to our band and to this community. It's the one place where [Black singer J. T. Watkins] and I can come and have a common bond, and that bond is the blues."

Even then, of course, our long weekend was not yet over. After once again setting up lights and cameras inside the Subway Lounge, we interviewed Jimmy about his future plans, especially considering his wife's terminal illness and increasing threats to the building that housed his concerts. Finally, we filmed Steve Cheseborough, author of *Blues Traveling: The Holy Sites of Delta Blues*, affirming to Jimmy that his Subway was one of the last functioning juke joints in the state, reminding him that Mississippi blues great Bo Carter had lived only a short distance away, and using his own shiny National guitar to perform Carter's classic number, "Cigarette Blues."

The following day (Monday, April 8), the rest of us headed our separate ways, and I looked forward to editing all of our amazing concert footage. Of course, location filming this troubled was bound to lead to an equally troubled postproduction period, and that was what happened. The Starz Business Affairs Department took an inordinate amount of time to decide if the film I was completing could even be released, which, in practical terms, meant their dragging out the process for several additional months, yet refusing to pay me for my additional time spent on the project. Ultimately, they did rule that I could finish the film, but stipulated that I could not use any of the interview we had shot with Mrs. Summers. That, in turn, meant my having to cut the heart out of the civil rights portion of the film, all because of interference from a local con man who had achieved nothing at all for Mrs. Summers or himself, but who, instead, did limit my ability to tell the inspiring story of her late husband.

Regardless of my ongoing battle with Business Affairs at Starz, I went on to make a second trip to Mississippi in June. My greatest regret during our previous stay had been that Jimmy King's wife Helen was away receiving treatment and, therefore, was not available for me to film her taking tickets in the Subway doorway. Moreover, during later calls with Jimmy King, I learned that Helen was continuing to decline. As a result, I arranged with Craig Smith to rent a film camera in Nashville, then to meet me in Jackson on Tuesday, June 25.

Shortly after our arrival, Craig and I filmed Helen at the Subway, looking every bit as lovely as when she had first greeted Terry Stewart, Michael Wilmington, and me for our initial experience there. We also filmed Jimmy King using a bulldozer to pull down a rear section of the Summers Hotel that was dangerously close to giving way. Then, over the next couple of days, we returned to Clarksdale to shoot additional images at Ground Zero Blues Club and at Hopson Plantation's Shack Up Inn (former sharecropper shacks grouped together and made available for overnight stays by tourists). Finally, Craig and I drove to Tunica and (somewhat surreptitiously) gathered images of casinos I could use to illustrate Vasti Jackson's song "Casino in the Cottonfield."

I have mentioned before that Craig Smith is a very funny fellow. So, for me to spend a couple of days shooting alone with him on this occasion was a treat. In a sense, Craig represented a lot of what Northerners do not understand about the modern South. Because he grew up in rural Tennessee, he presented himself as a big, friendly, attractive, grinning white guy with a heavy Southern accent. However, Craig grew up with a well-educated father who owned multiple small-town banks, and once you got to know him, you realized that he was a smart, progressive, educated, caring, and self-effacing person, as well as a sensitive still photographer and camera operator. He also was a born comedian with a seemingly endless supply of so-called "redneck jokes." For instance, question: "What are a redneck's last words?" Answer: "Hell, that ain't nothin'. Watch this!" And when we teamed cameraman and camera assistant Craig Smith with Memphis-raised, African American head grip and driver Quincy McKay—a man who had had a stroke relatively young, and so developed a stammer, which he surmounted with quick one-liners, a hearty laugh, and comically disapproving facial expressions, and who took time from his job at a Memphis television station in order to work with us—we created a sweet, hilarious comedy team that got us through a great many stressful days, but that also gave us hope for race relations, not only in the South, but across our still struggling country.

Eventually, my friend Ron Henderson, the cofounder and long-time director of what, at the time, was called the Starz Denver International Film Festival, negotiated a truce between Starz executives and myself, making it possible for us to come together for a mid-October festival world premiere. Often, when showing one of my films, Ron would hire one of its featured acts to perform after the screening. However, in 2002, with Starz and the festival working together, they managed to bring in Chris Thomas King, Vasti Jackson, Patrice Moncell, Lucille, David Hughes, and some local Denver backup musicians. It was a fun affair, which included Starz publicity people interviewing us for their coming television premiere.

Jimmy King was invited to the Denver premiere as well, but was forced to decline, due to the worsening of Helen's condition. A few weeks later, I learned that she had died and flew to Jackson for the funeral. Sadly, I arrived a few hours too late, but simply making the trip felt like paying proper respects. So, too, did making a last-minute addition of the following title at the end of the film: "Dedicated to the memory of Mrs. Helen Johnson King, 1949-2002." In my own mind, as in Jimmy's, I feel sure, it was impossible to separate his gradual loss of Helen from his simultaneous loss of the Subway. In both cases, something very beautiful was slipping away, and the two losses were inextricably linked.

At 8:00 p.m. on Saturday, February 16, 2003, *Last of the Mississippi Jukes* was premiered over the Black Starz channel. Then, on March 18, 2003, the film was released on DVD, and the same day, the soundtrack CD I had produced also was released, though with David Hughes unexpectedly listed as a second CD producer (a reminder from Business Affairs that they were still in charge). However, I was far more interested in what was happening on April 11, almost exactly a year from when we had shot at the Subway.

For the past two decades, the American Film Institute had been showing my films at the AFI Theater at the Kennedy Center in Washington, DC, as well as at the AFI Fest in Los Angeles. This was thanks to programmers Ken Wlaschin in L. A. and Eddie Cockrell, Michael Jeck, and Ray Barry in DC. But now, the AFI was departing its theater at the Kennedy Center and opening a new, state-of-the-art cinema in my hometown of Silver Spring, Maryland, a suburb just northwest of the city. Called the AFI Silver, because it was taking over the former home of the Silver Theater (which my friends and I had attended while growing up), the new cinema would include two smaller screens in spaces to the left of the original movie palace area, and during the opening week of Friday, April 11 through Thursday April 17, each of these three would offer a separate program.

Thanks to Michael Jeck, who had been a longtime programmer for the AFI Theater at the Kennedy Center and who now would serve that role at the AFI Silver, the newer theater would host the world theatrical premiere of *Last of the Mississippi Jukes* on April 11, then, for the next week, would alternate screenings of that film with screenings of my two earlier Mississippi blues films, *Deep Blues* and *Hellhounds on my Trail*. All of this would take place on the medium-sized screen in AFI Silver II, and the evening of April 11, I would be present to introduce the film, accompanied by Vasti Jackson and Patrice Moncell, who would perform afterwards.

At least, that was the plan, and that was what had been publicized by the American Film Institute, which was hugely proud of its flashy new East Coast theater. But just before opening night, the same troublesome attorney in the Starz Business Affairs Department who had meddled repeatedly during production and postproduction of the film now decided I did not have permission to organize this theatrical premiere on my own. He therefore issued instructions that I was to cancel the opening, but I refused. Further incensed, he then contacted the theater itself and ordered them to cease and desist. However, to my great delight, Ms. Jean Picker Firstenberg, the director and CEO of the American Film Institute, had flown in from the West Coast to oversee the long-awaited opening of this jewel in the AFI crown, and she was not about to have it ruined by some self-important corporate lawyer in Denver, Colorado. Without a second thought, she tossed him aside like a bug caught in her car's windshield wipers.

For most of the year after we filmed at the Subway, Jimmy had struggled to vacuum up water that continued to collect in his performance space, and would open for business only when he felt it was safe and sanitary to do so. However, in May of 2003, he decided to close the lounge and try tearing away the middle of the hotel building, because that section was in the greatest disrepair. Unfortunately, doing so also weakened the front part of the structure, which was overtop of the Subway. Therefore, Jimmy then brought in engineers to evaluate the situation, and they concluded that the remainder of the building could be saved, but only for a prohibitive amount of money.

Almost two years later, during the period in which I was living in Jackson with my son Rob and working for Mississippi Public Broadcasting, Jimmy phoned to tell me he would shortly tear down the rest of the building. Therefore, on February 3, 2005, I grabbed an MPB cameraman and sound man and met Jimmy at the old Summers Hotel and Subway Lounge site. After our arrival, Jimmy signaled a man behind the controls of a large steam shovel that he could begin his work and, as the man slowly flattened what was left of the building, I filmed an interview with Jimmy in which he explained what had led him to this fateful decision. Then, from the footage shot that day, I created an update to the original film, which I featured on my website and on a subsequent DVD released by MVD Visual, into which I also folded my original soundtrack album.

In the years since I completed *Last of the Mississippi Jukes*, some reviewers have misunderstood the title. It perhaps is a subtle point, but if I had wanted to say that the Subway had been the final juke joint functioning in Mississippi, and that an entire era in blues culture was fully over, I would have called the film *(The) Last of the Mississippi Jukes*. Instead, I left off "The," because I wanted to suggest only that this was a fading tradition, and that, sadly, we would soon see the end of this particular venue, which had provided so much joy, and a tenuous form of racial integration, in the capital of a former Confederate state. I also wanted it known that, even if the building was falling apart, the people who had performed there, and who had partied there, would carry the spirit of the place for the rest of their lives. As Greg "Fingers" Taylor suggested in the opening of his song, "Subway Swing," Jimmy, Helen, and the rest of the gang would always be with us: "Now, there's a little place down a dead end street. It's called the Subway Lounge; it's really a-reet [jazz slang for "all right"]. It ain't much to look at; just a hole in the wall. But every Saturday night, we have ourselves a natural ball."

***

In the summer of 2003, I became filmmaker in residence for Mississippi Public Broadcasting in Jackson, and eventually for its foundation as well. In addition, just before being hired, I collaborated with MPB in shooting B. B. King's annual late spring show in Indianola, Mississippi, bringing together several of my longtime crew members (Dave Sperling, Chris Li, Bill Barth, Tim Healey, etc.) with MPB's production staff and remote HD video truck, as well as new associate Mark Williams using Greg Hartman's Big Mo music recording truck to record and mix multitrack audio. That year, the concert took place on Friday night, June 6, though our work went well into the early hours of June 7. Under my direction, and the technical supervision of MPB's Darryl Moses, we captured video and audio for B. B. King's forty-five-minute midnight show at Club Ebony, Indianola's legendary stop on the so-called Chitlin' Circuit (the loosely connected group of Black-owned music clubs and theaters which provided places for African American musicians to perform during the era of segregation), as well as assorted other Mississippi blues artists earlier in the evening, including David Lee Durham, Bobby Whalen, Bill Abel, Levan Lortkipanidze, Mickey Rogers, Barbara Pope Looney, Lil' Dave Thompson, Lee Shot Williams, Vasti Jackson, and Patrice Moncell.

Then, after moving to Jackson in early July and going on the MPB payroll, I got straight to work gathering pertinent interviews and archival images to flesh out Club Ebony's colorful history, and edited those together with some of the aforementioned performance excerpts. Unfortunately, although I did complete a feature-length documentary titled *A Night at Club Ebony*, as well as a separate forty-eight-minute B. B. King concert film titled *The Road Home: B. B. King in Indianola*, MPB's management never cleared rights for the B. B. King concert footage used in both films, so neither film was ever released (though I currently make my original rough-cuts of both films available on my website).

During those same early months in Mississippi, I also brought in Steve Cheseborough, author of *Blues Traveling: The Holy Sites of Delta Blues*, to serve as onscreen guide for *Blues Breaks*, the thirteen sixty-second films I had decided to produce, direct, write, and edit as introductions to Mississippi blues culture. The subjects of nine of these minimovies were blues streets, blues highways, blues venues, blues plantations, blues graves, blues foods, Delta crossroads, W. C. Handy, and the Stovall Plantation shack in which Muddy Waters once lived, and the rest were built around new performances by Willie King, Vasti Jackson, and James "Super Chikan" Johnson (the nephew of Big Jack Johnson, who had starred in my film *Deep Blues*). These at least made it onto the air in Mississippi and a few other places, coinciding with the fall 1993 premiere of Martin Scorsese's *The Blues*, a series of seven feature-length programs on PBS (directed by Scorsese and six other feature film directors, most of whom had little experience with either documentary filmmaking or the blues). In fact, I had made *Blues Breaks* in the hope of complementing that series, as well as, where necessary, counteracting what I assumed would be a lot of misinformation. However, the producers of the series ultimately decided to show it without breaks, which greatly limited the number of stations able to utilize my thirteen sixty-second blues films. So, just as with my portrait of Club Ebony, I once again felt I was putting a lot of work into productions that were receiving little or no distribution, and therefore, I was seeking a change.

Approximately eight months into my time at Mississippi Public Broadcasting, I moved to the Foundation for Public Broadcasting in Mississippi, whose job it was to keep MPB funded. Still regarded as filmmaker in residence for the overall institution, I was asked to originate projects that would appeal to residents of the state, but also have potential for national and international distribution. So, right off the bat, I proposed a project called *Blues Divas*, which would involve staging concerts by seven female artists (later expanded to eight) working in various musical genres, but all related in some way to blues traditions. My idea was, first, to focus on extraordinary women in a field that tends to be male-dominated, and second, to illustrate a kind of blues diaspora with origins in the Mississippi Delta. If all went as planned, the concerts would be filmed at Ground Zero Blues Club in Clarksdale, with co-owner Morgan Freeman serving as emcee, and also conducting interviews at nearby Madidi, a French restaurant owned by Morgan and his Ground Zero partner Bill Luckett.

At Clarksdale, Mississippi's French restaurant, Madidi, owned by Morgan Freeman and his partner Bill Luckett, Robert Mugge prepares to film Morgan's interview with "soul queen of New Orleans" Irma Thomas. (photographed by Dick Waterman, 2004)

Not surprisingly, some of those I contacted were unavailable. For instance, Shemekia Copeland, Marcia Ball, and Cassandra Wilson all had prior commitments. However, I quickly booked seven outstanding female performers, among them New Orleans soul queen Irma Thomas, soul and gospel star Mavis Staples (of the beloved Staples Singers), folk and blues legend Odetta, recently reemerging soul singer Bettye LaVette, racy soul blues singer Denise LaSalle, Hi Records veteran Ann Peebles, and contemporary blues singer and guitarist Deborah Coleman. Then, Minnesota-based music manager Miki Mulvehill contacted me about a slightly more jazz-oriented artist named Reneé Austin, smartly offering terms that would not bust my budget. And so, suddenly, there would be eight headliners, rather than seven.

My plan was now to stage eight separate concerts at Ground Zero over the course of a weekend—two on Friday, three on Saturday, and three on Sunday—and again, to shoot interviews with all eight headliners at Madidi between sets. So long as Morgan would be available, the perfect weekend would be three days following the annual Thursday night Blues Awards ceremony held by the Blues Foundation in Memphis, because blues fans who had flown in for the awards show could then drive a mere hour and a quarter to Clarksdale to watch our subsequent eight concerts. One factor making this such a smart endeavor was that, after only three long days of shooting, I figured I could edit an eight-hour public television series, eight feature-length portraits for home video release, and a two-hour film sampler with an introduction by Morgan. But then I thought of something likely to make the project even more cost-effective, which is always important when focusing on artists who are outside the commercial mainstream.

My new idea was to work out a deal with the Blues Foundation wherein we would shoot and record their several-hour W. C. Handy Blues Awards celebration (as it was then known), and edit highlights into a two-hour special for broadcast and home video release. From our end, this made sense for several reasons: first, because it would give us an additional program to broadcast and market; second, because any outside technicians and equipment brought in for shooting would cost us little more, if any, for four days of work than for three; third, because the Blues Foundation was already absorbing the costs of bringing in talent and staging the show, which meant we could simply piggyback on their efforts; and fourth, because MPB had enough technicians of its own that it could assign one group to spend several days setting up for the three days of shooting at Ground Zero, another group to handle last-minute preparations for the Blues Foundation shoot, and then a single group of camera and audio people to converge briefly on Memphis before settling into Clarksdale for the subsequent three days and nights. Happily, the Blues Foundation was enthusiastic, so we expanded our plans accordingly.

Still, with regard to the major setup and shooting at Ground Zero, in spite of our having MPB's talented Darryl Moses to serve as production coordinator, I knew we would need additional help from outside. For that reason, I recruited all of the following: my Memphis-based friend Joe Mulherin to construct a stage, set up a PA system, secure a grand piano for Odetta's accompanist, and produce all eight of the project concerts; (at Joe's suggestion) my future friend Dawn Hopkins to serve as stage manager; (at Bill Luckett's suggestion) my friend Roger Stolle (owner of Cat Head Delta Blues & Folk Art) to serve as artist liaison; my friend Tim Healey to fly in from Los Angeles and serve as line producer; my new friend Mark Williams to use Greg Hartman's Big Mo Recording truck in overseeing multitrack music recording; and my friend Greg Hartman himself to mix the recorded music. With an army like this, I had little concern about our prospects for success.

On Thursday, April 29, our shooting and recording of the Handy Awards show at the Memphis Cook Convention Center was a breeze, in that we had five MPB cameramen and Greg's multitrack recording truck to capture a lot of great music and the periodic giving of awards. In fact, over the course of the evening, we successfully captured performances by Pinetop Perkins, Charlie Musselwhite, Kim Wilson, Bobby Rush with Alvin Youngblood Hart, Henry Butler with Vasti Jackson, Michael Burks, Maria Muldaur, Eddie Shaw, Rory Block, Otis Taylor, Bettye LaVette, Willie Kent, E. C. Scott, Eric Bibb, Fruteland Jackson, E. G. Kite, and Ellis Hooks with Deborah Coleman, as well as conducting interviews with "Little Milton" Campbell Jr., Bobby Rush, and many others.

However, at the time, none of us realized that my boss at MPB's foundation would never be able to raise the money he had promised to pay all the performing artists. So, even though I would later edit all of this material into a two-hour film titled *Memphis Blues Again: The 25th Anniversary W. C. Handy Blues Awards*—also supervising music mixing, audio mixing, online editing, and the rest—MPB would never have the means to release the film. Naturally, this infuriated the head of the Blues Foundation and left me disappointed as well, even if pleased at having been able to document fine performances by some truly great musicians.

Nevertheless, after finishing work at the Blues Awards, we all drove to Clarksdale and checked into rooms at the local Comfort Inn. Then, on Friday morning, April 30, we got right to work again, finishing preparations for three more days of concerts. Our two shows that first night featured Reneé Austin and band at 7:00 p.m., and Deborah Coleman and band at 10:00 p.m.

These two acts could not have been more different, but both surpassed expectations. Reneé played a jazz-influenced form of blues, including a breathtaking composition of her own titled "Fool Moon," which she dedicated to jazz singer Ella Fitzgerald. By contrast, Deborah, a skillful electric guitarist, performed a long, sultry version of Koko Taylor's "I'm A Woman," including an endlessly inventive guitar solo.

The next day, we had three sets scheduled—Bette LaVette at 3:00 p.m., Irma Thomas at 6:00 p.m., and Mavis Staples at 9:00 p.m.—all supported by their respective bands, and with Yvonne Staples providing backup vocals for her sister Mavis. Bettye was still at the point in her comeback where she was performing emotionally draining soul numbers, among them "Let Me Down Easy," "Your Turn To Cry (Your Time To Cry)," and "Serves Him Right." For her part, Irma Thomas performed soulful hits of her own including "Chains of Love," "I Needed Somebody," and her cover of Otis Redding's "I've Been Loving You Too Long." By contrast, Mavis Staples performed in a variety of soul-and-blues-related styles, including two songs with overt spiritual content: "Will the Circle Be Unbroken" and "God Is Not Sleeping."

Legendary folk blues singer Odetta performs at Clarksdale's Ground Zero Blues Club. (photographed by Dick Waterman, 2004)

Finally, on Sunday, May 2, we filmed and recorded Odetta with virtuoso New York piano accompanist Seth Farber at noon, Ann Peebles with a Memphis-based band at 3:00 p.m., and Denise LaSalle with her Jackson, Tennessee-based band at 6:00 p.m. To begin the day, Odetta sang such folk and urban blues classics as Lead Belly's "Careless Love" and "Bourgeous Blues" and W. C. Handy's "St. Louis Blues," all presented with the sort of dignity and elegance she had honed in years of performing traditional material in upscale concert halls. Odetta was followed by Willie Mitchell's sole female star at Hi Records, Ann Peebles, who, in a program of her better known songs, included both "Full Time Lover" and the major hit she co-authored, "I Can't Stand the Rain." Then, closing out the show at 6:00 p.m. (on a Sunday, no less!) was sexy soul blues queen Denise LaSalle, belting out her richly suggestive "Don't Mess With My Man," "Your Husband Is Cheating On Us," and "Still the Queen," all of which she wrote or co-wrote.

One of the more fascinating lessons of focusing a series (and a two-hour compilation film) entirely on female headliners is that they cared no less than men about the quality of their performances, yet clearly cared a good deal more about their respective appearances. So, even though our eight divas showed as much diversity in their dress as in their music, each of them provided a striking visual impact, not unlike that of both male and female artists I had filmed in Hawai'i. And yet, to quote a classic song by bluesman Johnny Taylor, no matter how much you dress it up, "It's still called the blues."

I undertook these productions during a several-month period when my younger son Rich was living with me and attending the private Education Center School near our Jackson home. The two of us were on our own at the time, so I had no choice but to bring him with me to Memphis and Clarksdale during our four days of shooting in those cities. And of course, I thought he might actually be impressed by the hundreds of world-class singers and musicians sharing their talents, or by the dozens of technical people racing around at each venue, in the hope of keeping things running smoothly. But no, he was nearly fifteen, and he did not wish to be there.

Since Rich showed no interest in taking part, during the Ground Zero shows, I had him sit beside me as I studied the five video monitors in front of us, and used my headset to issue instructions to five nearby cameramen, as well as to the TV truck and music recording truck parked outside the building. Incredibly, hour after hour, with remarkable dedication, he would ignore everything going on around him and focus instead on his handheld video game. However, every so often, line producer Tim Healey, whom Rich knew well, or one of the MPB bosses would say something to him, and he would begrudgingly respond. But mostly, he ignored us all.

Nevertheless, one person refused to be ignored, and that was someone with an equally strong will. Noting Rich's sullen expression, Morgan Freeman would periodically walk by our table and impishly toss a wad of crumpled paper at him, or sneak up behind him and, using fingers from both hands, pull Rich's frown into an involuntary smile. All of us nearby would be gently amused, but not Rich. Sadly, even the attention of an internationally acclaimed movie star was not enough to pull him out of his self-imposed, adolescent funk.

Later that summer, clearly missing his friends in suburban Philadelphia, Rich returned to live with his mother there, at which point his older brother Rob offered to move down in his place. Rob was now sixteen, hated his four-thousand-student high school, loved the idea of attending a small private school in Jackson with a much later starting time, and had gotten deeply enough into music that he liked the thought of living three hours from Memphis, three hours from New Orleans, and a couple hours from the Mississippi Delta.

On August 14, 2004, while Rob was visiting and we were making plans for his eventual move, he and I met Morgan and an MPB cameraman and sound man at Ground Zero Blues Club to shoot an introduction for the two-hour *Blues Divas* film, which I was then completing. As we stood in the sun in front of Ground Zero, I was stunned by how quickly Morgan committed my words to memory, then delivered them with typically resonant inflection. I also took a couple of photos which, along with Dick Waterman's great photos of the original Ground Zero concerts and Madidi interviews, were used to promote the film. Of course, Morgan being Morgan, he also engaged in a bit of

sweet ribbing of my long-haired, elder son, which was taken a bit better by Rob than it had been by his younger brother Rich.

*In front of Clarksdale, Mississippi's Ground Zero Blues Club, actor and club co-owner
Morgan Freeman delivers an introduction for the two-hour film version of Blues Divas.
(photographed by Robert Mugge, 2004)*

By that fall, when Rob was finally given permission to move, I
had completed offline edits of all eight long-form *Divas* programs,
Greg Hartman had mixed the music for all eight, and MPB staff had
carried out audio mixes and HD online edits for them all. So, not
long before Rob joined me, I arranged with my friends Zoe Elton
and Mark Fishkin at the Mill Valley Film Festival to present the
long-form Bettye LaVette and Odetta portraits on October 13 and 14
(accompanied by my MPB boss), and with my friend Ron Henderson
at the Starz Denver International Film Festival to present the long-
form portraits of Deborah Coleman, Irma Thomas, and Mavis Staples
in two programs on October 23. What made the Denver premieres
special was my being accompanied there not only by my foundation
boss but, more importantly, by Deborah Coleman, who performed
a concert with her band, and by Morgan Freeman, who appeared at
our three screenings and then was feted in a special program of his

own. That latter program featured clips from his key films, an on-stage interview with a local film critic, and his receipt of the "Mayor's Lifetime Achievement Award."

The only sour note in Denver came when, just prior to her concert, Deborah announced that she and her band would not perform unless paid up front in cash. Clearly, this was not easy to arrange on a Saturday evening in late October. But somehow, with his usual ingenuity and grace, Ron pulled it off, and the evening went forward without further ado.

Meanwhile, my friend Michael Jeck, programmer at the AFI Silver in Silver Spring, Maryland, arranged the world premiere of the two-hour film version of *Blues Divas* for Saturday, January 22 and Sunday, January 23, 2005. Odetta, who lived in New York City, committed to appearing at the Saturday screening; Bettye LaVette, who lived in North Jersey, committed to appearing at the one on Sunday; and Deborah Coleman, who lived in Norfolk, Virginia, informally promised to come on Sunday as well. Unfortunately, snow warnings caused Bettye LaVette to cancel, and Deborah Coleman simply failed to show. However, during the actual snowstorm, Odetta, remarkable trouper that she was, boarded a plane to DC and thrilled our Silver Spring audience with her charming presence.

After those auspicious premieres, the project grew increasingly troubled. For instance, my efforts to secure an international home video deal were stymied by the potential cost of music rights for precisely one hundred songs, which was the cumulative number of those used in the eight long-form portraits. And after initially agreeing to release a *Blues Divas* soundtrack CD on its in-house label, Starbucks bowed out when Mavis Staples refused to participate, claiming that her voice had not been at its best during our Clarkdale concerts (and thereby painfully evoking my initial experience with Alison Krauss in Owensboro, Kentucky). At least, Mississippi Public Broadcasting did premiere my eight-hour TV series within the state, and later made it available to other public stations throughout the US, but this brought MPB no additional income. So, I contacted my friend Brett Marottoli at Starz, asking if she would purchase cable rights for the two-hour film version for $100,000.

Happily, in the couple of years since I had collaborated with Starz executives on the making of *Last of the Mississippi Jukes*, most of our past issues had been forgotten. Moreover, for a company heavily invested in movie channels, Morgan Freeman was still a major draw. So, after some internal discussion, Brett was able to offer us $50,000 for three years of rights, which at least gave MPB sufficient funds to pay off remaining project debt. Most other costs had been borne by Entergy Mississippi, marking the only time in my career I had been funded by a public utility.

Throughout the spring and summer of 2005, I worked out plans for a series I had titled *Native Sons* (after the 1940 Richard Wright novel), which was to be a companion piece for *Blues Divas*, this time highlighting major bluesmen with connections to the state. But in early August, two weeks before we were scheduled to shoot again at Ground Zero Blues Club, I resigned from the foundation due to excessive meddling from my boss, who had promised me complete creative autonomy. MPB went forward with the shoots I had scheduled, though under a new project name (since, incredibly, they thought my title suggested something to do with Native Americans), and with none of the thematic underpinnings I always brought to such projects. Truth be told, I was pleased to hear that Morgan Freeman elected not to participate, and that it took a dozen years for MPB to figure out how to edit what they had shot. Apparently, it was not so easy, after all.

As I mentioned earlier, come September, I expected to design a new "music filmmaking" curriculum for Delta State University in Cleveland, Mississippi. But the arrival of Hurricane Katrina on August 29, 2005 changed everything, killing the funding that would have underwritten my position, and leading instead to my working with Starz again, plus my new partner Diana Zelman, on production of *New Orleans Music in Exile*. Looking back, I can only assume that the angel watching over New Orleans was also watching over me, even as, together, Diana and I sought to watch over the city's exiled music community.

Chapter Ten
Water Music

Deep Sea Blues (2007)

All Jams On Deck (2011)

n August of 2006, with *New Orleans Music in Exile* having been premiered over Starz in May, and eighteen-year-old Rob having graduated from the Education Center School in Jackson the same month, he and I moved north again to the ironically named Media, Pennsylvania, a suburb of Philadelphia, and rented a roomy, if overly expensive, house with Diana Zelman. There, Rob enrolled at Delaware County Community College, Diana continued doing financial work for The Hartford, and I began making plans to shoot the Legendary Rhythm & Blues Cruise to the Caribbean in late January. Viewing this cruise as a kind of modern-day equivalent of the so-called Chitlin' Circuit, the loosely connected grouping of Black-owned music clubs and theaters, among which African American musicians had toured for decades, I also saw filming such a cruise as my ultimate musical road movie. In this case, a Holland America ship called the MS Westerdam would depart from Fort Lauderdale, Florida on January 13, 2007, carrying hundreds of performing musicians and well over a thousand blues fan "cruisers" for seven days of music on the high seas. Along the way, there would also be music-filled stops at the islands of Turks & Caicos, St. Thomas and St. John, and St. Barts, before the ship's weary and musically satiated passengers returned to Fort Lauderdale, arriving early on January 20.

On the island of St. Barts, overlooking Holland America's MS Westerdam, Robert Mugge interviews Legendary Rhythm & Blues Cruise president Roger Naber and attorney Judy Alexander. (photographed by Christopher Li, 2007)

According to Roger Naber, the Kansas City, Missouri-based music promoter who operated the twice-yearly Blues Cruise—and Judy Alexander, the LRBC attorney, and one of Roger's several partners in the venture—they wanted me to film all aspects of their coming cruise as a means of publicizing it. Yet, they also were happy to make the production a partnership between us and to have me produce what I saw as a serious film about another group supporting traditional American musicians. This time around, of course, the artists we filmed would be removed from this or that milieu out of which their music had arisen. On the other hand, I knew from the previous year's cruise that the weeklong bonding of musicians and fans created an environment of respect that was well worth chronicling.

Diana, having accompanied me on the cruise the year before, faced a challenge getting off work for the second January in a row. So, even though she continued to assist me behind the scenes, my buddy Tim Healey agreed to fly in from California again and serve as line producer. I also brought together other favorite crew members, including Bill Barth as audio director (the last time we would work together before, tragically, he succumbed to a rare lung disease), Dave Sperling and Chris Li as directors of photography, Craig Smith as our third concert cameraman, and Peter Ruhl, a young protégé of Bill's, as both our fourth concert cameraman and our chief audio assistant. My son Rob would also serve as an audio assistant, and he and a friend from Philly would work as production assistants.

Greg Hartman of Big Mo, along with his associate Mark Williams, would once again oversee multitrack music recording for us, which would be complicated on this ship. Performances would take place in as many as five different locations, and we could only afford to have equipment in two of them. So, Mark oversaw multitrack recording in the Vista Lounge, a large opera house type theater at the front of the ship, and Greg oversaw it at the specially constructed stage on the rear Pool Deck. Smaller-scale performances would take place in the more intimate Queen's Lounge, the Piano Bar, and the Crow's Nest (an upper-level lounge), and any of those we chose to cover would be handled by Bill using a stereo recorder, microphones, and a small mixer. As for the cameramen and me, we would retain established positions at the two ends of the ship, but as circumstances required, would be ready to run to any of the three performance spaces elsewhere onboard. And of course, we had a secret weapon in this effort, which was Roger's extremely competent staff—Scott, Tracy, LeAnne, Mardi, and Shar—who were always ready to assist.

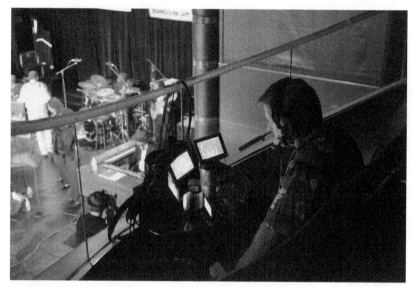

In the right balcony area of the MS Westerdam's Vista Lounge (basically a floating opera house), Robert Mugge watches a concert by Otis Clay and his band via video feeds from four cameras and offers guidance to the camera operators as they document Otis's performance. (photographed by Joseph A. Rosen, 2007)

Most days, music on the ship started in the early afternoon and ran until late night. In accordance with Roger's established plan, every act booked was scheduled to perform at least three times throughout the week, and since performances on different stages conflicted or overlapped, I would have to schedule carefully when to film each act so that no one important was entirely missed. In addition, acoustic performances in the Piano Lounge could carry on until dawn; jams by so-called "semi-pro" musicians could take place in the Crow's Nest at any time; and every night at 1:00 a.m. on the Pool Deck stage, a preselected band would perform a brief set and then gradually work in more and more professional musicians for a so-called "Pro Jam," going until as late as 5:00 a.m.

That left only mornings free, which is when many fans of late-night listening would sleep. However, on days when the ship was at sea rather than stopped at an island or Central American port, Roger would schedule late morning and early afternoon panels and workshops in various lounges. For instance, on this cruise, that would include a musician workshop featuring female guitarists, a photography workshop taught by my friend Joseph A. "Joe" Rosen, a songwriters workshop, a Delta bluesman panel, a harmonica workshop, and a blues-related industry panel. And of course, various other events were scheduled for later in the day, including musician autograph parties, a charitable silent auction, a Caribbean culinary demo, and themed costume dinners and parades, not to mention conventional cruise offerings such as bars, cafés, a spa, an exercise room, and gambling in the onboard casino. However, since my own primary interest, and therefore that of my crew, was to capture as many musical performances and supporting interviews as possible, we did only the most cursory filming of informational sessions and special interest activities.

On Saturday, January 13, most of my invited crew gathered at our home in Media, then flew together to Fort Lauderdale. There, on Sunday afternoon, we rushed to the docks and were given priority assistance in hauling our gear and personal items onto the MS Westerdam. The next several hours were spent getting our bearings on the ship, constructing Big Mo's recording fortresses adjacent to the Vista Lounge and Pool Deck stages, and also beginning to shoot routine activities such as the mandatory lifeboat drill and the erecting of the Pool Deck stage. Then, at around dusk, Roger Naber welcomed everyone with brief speeches and a champagne toast from the outdoor stage, food and other drinks were made available nearby, Tab Benoit performed a set of Cajun blues, and the ship slowly began to pull away from its dock, cruised along the coastline, and finally headed out to sea.

Among the other artists we filmed over the course of the week were the following: Taj Mahal (who allowed us to use his Caribbean culinary demo in the film but, strangely, not his performance), the Fabulous Thunderbirds (with Kim Wilson), Bobby Rush, Tommy Castro, Deanna Bogart, Michael Burks, Lil' Ed and the Blues Imperials, Otis Clay, Ruthie Foster, Buckwheat Zydeco, Mel Waiters, Watermelon Slim, Mitch Woods, the Phantom Blues Band featuring Tasha Taylor, Joey Gilmore, Earl Thomas, Leon Blue, George "Commander Cody" Frayne, and the newly constituted Legendary Rhythm

& Blues Revue which, on this initial occasion, featured Tommy Castro and his band, Deanna Bogart, Ronnie Baker Brooks, and Magic Dick of the J. Geils Band. Most of these artists were filmed performing their standard shows, but we also shot and recorded groupings of musicians in unique situations, including the following: a racy duet performance of "Ride in My Automobile" by Bobby Rush and Deanna Bogart during the Monday morning Returnee Party; Joey Gilmore and his band performing William Bell's "Bit Off More Than I Could Chew" in an open-air beach club bar on St. John; Watermelon Slim and band performing the Katrina-related "Black Water" on the Pool Deck stage with the St. Barts harbor looming in the background; Lil' Ed and the Blues Imperials performing the humorous "Icycles in My Meatloaf" beside an outdoor pool at a resort on Turks and Caicos; and blues photographer and author Dick Waterman marrying his beautiful fiancée Cinda Tidmore on a Turks and Caicos beach (although recently married for real, they went through the motions again for friends and fellow cruisers). This special ceremony included Taj Mahal escorting the bride to the beach as trumpet player Darrel Leonard of the Phantom Blues Band played Mendelssohn's Wedding March at water's edge; Bobby Rush conducting the tongue-in-cheek, sexually suggestive ceremony before a large group of delighted musician and cruiser onlookers; Otis Clay serenading the happy couple with the lovely soul ballad, "I Am"; Kim Wilson adding a few celebratory notes of his own; Dick struggling to find an opening in which he could pay heartfelt tribute to his new wife; and Bobby Rush asking if anyone else in the crowd wanted to get married, "or even divorced!"

On the beach at Turks and Caicos, with the MS Westerdam docked nearby, the wedding of blues community royalty Dick and Cinda Waterman is restaged for cruisers, with musician Bobby Rush presiding and musician Otis Clay serenading the couple. (photographed by Joseph A. Rosen, 2007)

Still, many of the performances we captured in routine circumstances on the Pool Deck or in the Vista Lounge could be just as extraordinary. Among those were Chicago-based soul and gospel singer Otis Clay, backed by the late Tyrone Davis's crackerjack band, performing an extended version of O. V. Wright's classic "A Nickel and a Nail"; Michael Burks strolling around the Pool Deck in bright sunlight playing a masterful, and seemingly endless, guitar solo for blues standard "As the Years Go Passing By"; Ruthie Foster, barefoot on the Vista Lounge stage, belting out the mesmerizing "Traveling Shoes"; Tommy Castro singing a soulful and winking "Nasty Habits" on the Pool Deck at night; Commander Cody reviving his countercultural classic, "Seeds and Stems Again," for appreciative former hippies; and soul blues giant Mel Waiters wrapping up the week in a metaphorical bow with a sweetly still-water version of the Isley Brothers classic "Smooth Sailing Tonight."

I could never explain the sheer joy of hearing, with or without the influence of free-flowing alcohol, the deeply felt and skillfully performed blues, soul, funk, and gospel music playing around the clock as the Caribbean sun shines down warmly in late January, and sea breezes blow their own cooling counterpoint. But for musicians and fans alike, this is a unique and satisfying experience. As the musicians themselves point out, at mainland music festivals, they rarely have time to relax together, to reminisce, and to jam into the night, as once happened in juke joints, urban lounges, and other stops on the Chitlin' Circuit. At a festival, you show up, you play your set, and you leave again; while, on the cruise, you spend a stress-free week together, while getting to know your most passionate fans and engaging with admiring younger musicians. So, as one set of musical traditions fades away, another rises to take its place, thanks in large measure to caring professionals like Roger Naber and his partners, who saw the continuation of culture as the ultimate reward of their business. That, in short, was the message of a film I could not help calling *Deep Sea Blues*.

The film's twin world premieres took place in November 2007 at the Starz Denver International Film Festival and, appropriately enough, at the Fort Lauderdale International Film Festival. I attended both, with Roger and Diana accompanying me to Denver.

***

In August of 2009, I moved to Muncie, Indiana, where I was given a five-year appointment as an endowed chair professor at Ball State University, and a few months later, was joined by Diana. My primary role at Ball State was to train film and video students in the art, craft, and business of independent filmmaking, especially regarding documentary production, and my favorite way of doing that was, once each year, to transport a small group of graduate and undergraduate students somewhere in the world, where they would serve as crew for my latest feature-length documentary. One of those projects involved shooting and editing a second Blues Cruise documentary, this time as part of the October 2010 cruise, which sailed from San Diego, California to the Mexican Riviera on the MS Zaandam.

In the time since Diana and I had finished work on *Deep Sea Blues*, Roger Naber had become one of our closest friends, and we enjoyed sailing with him on additional cruises, meeting him at music festivals, or watching him race one of his horses (which was Roger's *other* passion in life). And somewhere along the way, he admitted that, as much as he loved *Deep Sea Blues*, his one regret was that my crew's brutal schedule during the January 2007 cruise had precluded our having time to document most of the late-night Pro Jams. Again, those were the minimally structured performance sessions held every night on the Pool Deck stage, usually from 1:00 a.m. until the musicians tired of jamming or the seemingly tireless audiences stumbled to their cabins. In fact, Roger eventually proposed that we center a *second* film on those very jams, which he considered to be the heart and soul of his cruises.

My response was that I found Roger's idea intriguing, so long as my primary focus could be on blues jamming itself. With *Saxophone Colossus* and *Sun Ra: A Joyful Noise*, I had delved into group and solo improvisation in jazz, and I thought I would enjoy exploring similar skills, both social and musical, as they were utilized in blues. Roger was fine with my spin, and certainly, both of us knew that we, too, were jamming our way to an understanding—each of us offering his respective variations on a theme which, together, created a larger possibility than either one of us might have created alone.

Roger's only concern was that he could not afford to fund a second film at the generous level he had managed for our first collaboration. But I assured him that, because he and I could each adjust our approaches, because Diana and I could bring along four of my more talented students to serve as crew, and because I was currently receiving a solid salary from Ball State University, our overall financial needs would be decidedly less. He then added that an audio engineer would be onboard to handle PA miking and recording for a key Blues Cruise artist, and this engineer could likely do basic multitrack recording of the late-night jams and of any other key performances I planned to shoot. So, relatively quickly, we worked out a cost-effective strategy that, while somewhat risky in its bare-bones approaches, at least would make a second film possible without prior need for endless fundraising.

As it happened, Roger's coming cruise was scheduled for October 17 to 24, 2010, and my supportive department chair, Dr. Joe Misiewicz, was perfectly amenable to Diana and me dragging four production students along on a cruise to Mexico, so long as my classes were covered for that week and the students kept up with their official studies. As he and I agreed, the four students would not be paid, and neither would they receive any course credit. But all their expenses would be covered by Roger, and it was the consensus in our department that this could be an incredible learning experience. In fact, when first hired at Ball State, I had been asked to include as many students as possible on my professional productions.

In my experience, the two BSU graduate students then most proficient at camerawork and lighting were Joe Vella and Andrew Bissonnette, so they were the two I asked to be camera operators on the cruise. Others interested included two undergraduate students, Derek Cox and Darik Hall, who were well-qualified to alternate between recording audio and acting as our third camera person. Happily, all four of these students also owned equipment we could rent, in addition to whatever we secured from a rental company in San Diego and picked up prior to the cruise. So, with just the four students, Diana, and me going aboard, plus minimal equipment, ours would be a smaller and scrappier crew than before. But with so much youthful energy, we were sure to accomplish a lot.

This time around, the ship would be at sea for the first two days; would stop in Cabo San Lucas on the third day, in Puerto Vallarta on the fourth, and in Mazatlán on the fifth; and then would spend two more days at sea before arriving back in San Diego very early on the eighth. And of course, during our week onboard, our primary goal was to cover every late-night Pro Jam, no matter how late it went. Roger liked to have the first night's jam controlled by a veteran of the form, because it required skill to figure which interested musicians to bring onstage and when, what sort of chemistry was likely to result, and how many participants were too many. If you handled such decisions with intelligence, creativity, and diplomacy, the results could be remarkable. But if you handled them poorly, you could wind up with anarchy, as well as with a surplus of bad feelings.

This is why Tommy Castro, someone popular with musicians and fans alike, was appointed Roger's "showrunner," if you will, for opening night, and he deftly set the tone for all late-night jams to come. Tommy and his band started off playing, on their own, songs that were favorites on blues radio, including "A Good Fool Is Hard to Find" and "I Feel That Old Feeling Coming On," both of which I later used in the film. As the set continued, however, Castro added (and sometimes switched out) musicians until the stage was increasingly full.

Monday night, Lowrider Band, mostly founding members of the disbanded group War, performed many of that group's funky, audience-pleasing hits, gradually allowing more and more musicians onstage. In the end, I wound up using a long chunk of an extended jam, much of it dominated by original War harp player Lee Oskar, and not recognizable as one of War's costly (in licensing terms) hits. Highlights included a blistering guitar solo from Midwestern bluesman Larry McCray, and West Coast singer Sista Monica Parker inserting a subversive rendition of James Brown's "Licking Stick."

Next, on Tuesday night, another experienced jam leader, Marcia Ball, took charge, performing one spirited Texas-Louisiana style blues number after another and slowly opening up both the play list and the number of musicians joining in. By the time she initiated an extended jam of "I Woke Up Screaming," a hit for the late Bobby

"Blue" Bland, she was ecstatic over her huge horn section and powerful guitar and organ soloists. As she said at the time, and again as we later joined her and her friend Margie Pouisson for guacamole and margaritas in an open-air, dockside tourist spot in Puerto Vallarta, "This is how I hear it in my dreams!"

Two nights later, Kim Wilson's jam included memorable contributions from California blues guitarists Elvin Bishop and Coco Montoya, as well as a cover of Houston Stackhouse's "Take A Little Walk With Me," featuring successive blasts from harp greats John Nemeth and Rick Estrin, backed up by their peers, Lee Oskar and Wilson himself. Then, on Friday, Coco hosted the final Pro Jam in the Vista Lounge, playing some typically fine guitar during his song "Last Dirty Deal" before watching Mississippi's Vasti Jackson tear into his own song ("Hurricane Season"), leave the stage, and slash and burn his way through the visibly approving crowd below.

Throughout the week, we also filmed groups of musicians demonstrating blues jamming techniques peculiar to their instruments. For instance, Vasti traded guitar licks and advice with fellow guitar master Laith Al-Saadi; Commander Cody and Rev. Billy C. Wirtz traded piano philosophy and techniques, as well as quite a few jokes; and Kim Wilson and Lee Oskar ruminated on everything harp-related, while also trading licks of their own. In addition, guitarists Coco Montoya, Jimmy Thackery, and Larry McCray described some notable jamming experiences, and bandleaders Tommy Castro and Elvin Bishop reminisced about memorable jams they had run themselves, including one early in Elvin's career in which he had to fend off countless musicians who wanted to climb onstage with Jimi Hendrix. And finally, SiriusXM Bluesville program director Bill Wax, and blues and jazz record producer and historian Bob Porter, provided their own observations about how blues jamming originated and evolved.

Speaking of Elvin Bishop, the great Oklahoma-to-Chicago-to-California musician brought along a star-studded company of top West Coast sidemen who performed as Elvin Bishop's Raisin' Hell Revue. My young crew and I filmed one of their full sets, and in the film, I used a version of Bishop's biggest hit, "Fooled Around and Fell In

Love," with John Nemeth ably handling the lead vocals. We also interviewed Elvin about his career and each of the musicians in his revue, and then I cut clips of that together with related performances to create a separate Elvin Bishop film. Unfortunately, Elvin and I could not agree on the structure for that one, since I wanted to stick to the order in which his songs had been performed, and he wanted me to change the order so that songs he sang himself came first, and those sung by others came later. I could not accommodate his wishes, because doing so would have played havoc with screen logic, leading to certain players appearing on one song, disappearing for a few more, showing up again after that, and so forth, yet with no sign of them entering or exiting. At any rate, because of this minor disagreement, instead of formally releasing a separate *Elvin Bishop's Raisin' Hell Revue* film, as Roger and I had intended, I simply posted my version on my website.

The guys and I also filmed a raucous, all-keyboard jam in the Vista Lounge featuring, in order of their first solos, Leon Blue, Kelley Hunt, Commander Cody, Steve Willis, and Eden Brent, with Marcia Ball and Rev. Billy C. Wirtz eventually sitting in as well. Finally, we filmed keyboard and saxophone player Edgar Winter sitting in with his guitarist brother Johnny Winter for the first time in years, and guitarist Elvin Bishop duetting with Johnny as well.

On the October 2010 West Coast Blues Cruise to the Mexican Riviera, guitarist Elvin Bishop (right) jams with guitarist Johnny Winter. (frame from film, 2010)

Wanting to give the students a chance for more than just work, after having lunch with Marcia Ball in Puerto Vallarta, Diana and I flagged down a private car being driven by a professional tour guide and worked out a deal. He then drove all of us by the older part of the city and the impressive sand sculptures lining the road near the beach. After that, he took us onto a high hill for a view of both city and ocean, and then to an open-air market with thatch-covered huts deep in the rainforest. There, we could sample—and were encouraged to purchase—bottles of tequila in every imaginable flavor, from mango to chocolate, as well as some with high alcohol content. Diana and I did purchase a few bottles in assorted flavors, one of which never made it home with us because, as we were going through security again in San Diego, it fell from my hands, breaking into hundreds of pieces and briefly delaying the line of groggy returning cruisers.

Aside from that last-minute, early-morning faux pas, we thought the production had gone splendidly. However, it turned out that, relying on someone to do *free* multitrack recordings of numerous large-scale concerts for us could lead to problems, if only because the number of musicians and types of instruments onstage was constantly changing, which, in turn, meant that miking and recording inputs were changing as well. It turned out that, with recordings of a few of the late-night jams, certain instruments did not make it into our digital audio files, which was concerning, as were some distorted vocals in one case. But to my very great relief, we were able to turn to Northern California audio technician Steve Savage, who managed to reclaim, rebuild, or even newly record vital missing tracks for us, and thereby save the day. Thanks to Steve, performances in the film all sound wonderful, with no indication at all of the problems we encountered.

The 2011 release of *All Jams On Deck*, as I came to call the film, gave the Legendary Rhythm & Blues Cruise a second film they could use to promote the many positive attributes of their January and October cruises, gave me the chance to document still more aspects of traditional American music making, and gave four of my students their first professional credits. Roger Naber initially gave away DVDs of the film to people sailing on his subsequent cruises, to blues fans met at festivals, to the press, and more. Then, later, when Ed Seaman's home video company MVD Visual acquired rights to do new releases of a couple dozen of my films, paying for me to remaster many of them in 2K or 4K quality, Roger and I agreed to a Blu-ray release for *Deep Sea Blues* that would also include *All Jams On Deck* as a bonus.

As expected, during the week that Diana, my students, and I spent on the October 2010 West Coast Blues Cruise, we acquired a great deal of information about blues jamming, as well as performance footage illustrating every possible variation in the interactions among improvising musicians. Yet, if there was one quote that summed up our findings better than any other, it would have to be what Elvin Bishop said to Tommy Castro toward the end of their joint interview: "It's just a matter of takin' turns. When it's your time, go ahead and shine as hard as you can. And before and after that time, you try and back up the other guy as tastefully as you can. You just use those old three musician's commandments, you know: C sharp, B natural, and when in doubt, lay out." Laughter followed.

Chapter Eleven
Spirit Guides (Respect, Regret, Renewal)

Big Shoes: Walking and Talking the Blues (2010)

Giving Up the Ghosts: Closing Time at Doc's Music Hall (2014)

For someone who cares about traditional American music, Central Indiana is not the place to live. The rural Midwest is largely flat, conservative, and sorry to say, bereft of much culture of its own. Sure, Chicago is three and a half hours away, and it has much to offer in the way of blues, jazz, theatre, comedy, art, film, and more. But beyond that, Nashville is a five-hour drive, Memphis is an eight-hour drive, and New Orleans is six hours past Memphis, with the Delta in between. So, if one tends to focus on such places, and on the musical traditions each one embodies, living in a city like Muncie, Indiana offers a true sense of dislocation. And yet, in every region of America, no matter how seemingly devoid of musical nourishment, one still can find islands of history and performance, and a handful of people with similar interests, and that has been true even here.

Of the five feature-length documentaries I produced out of Muncie while teaching at Ball State, two of them did not center directly on music. One, a two-hour film titled *Souvenirs of Bucovina: A Romanian Survival Guide*, was a documentary Diana and I produced, aided by four of my students during a three-and-a-half week stay in Northern Romania, with a side trip to southern Ukraine. While the film included exotic performances of traditional Romanian songs, Roma (historically termed "gypsies," which Roma find offensive) brass band music, singer-songwriter numbers, klezmer, and even regional heavy metal—many of them introduced to us by our trusted guides, the wonderful Kisczuk family of Radauti, Romania—music was incidental to the film's primary themes, which centered on the treatment of Jews and Roma before, during, and after World War II. The other of these nonmusical films was *Steve Bell Storyteller: A Newsman Living History*, a two-hour portrait of former ABC news correspondent and anchor Steve Bell, with emphasis on many of the biggest national and international stories he covered, from three political assassinations to the Vietnam War. Even though *Storyteller* featured a fine original score composed and performed by Dr. John Peterson, in no other sense could it be termed a "music film." Again, aside from *All Jams On Deck*, just two other films I made with student crews dealt directly with music, and those are the subjects of this final chapter.

A few months after I arrived in Indiana, I heard from my friend Ted Drozdowski (a respected blues musician and music journalist based in Nashville with his wife, artist Laurie Hoffma) that he was scheduling a brief Midwestern tour for the original version of his two-person band Scissormen. Since I already planned to teach a course in music filmmaking during my second semester at Ball State, accompanying Ted and his original Scissormen drummer on a tour of Indiana and Ohio seemed a perfect form of extracurricular activity. In addition, ever since my *Deep Blues* collaboration with music writer and part-time musician Robert Palmer, I had thought about comparing the analytical approaches of the music journalist with the performance approaches of the professional musician, especially as sometimes embodied within the same person. And finally, Ted and I liked the idea of investigating historic performance venues and music-related sites in this unlikeliest region of the country. So, we appeared to have the basis for a fun new project, and one that could be made with little more than money from my annual endowed chair fund, which was a perk of my academic employment.

In practical terms, I knew we needed to film and record the bulk of Scissormen's performance sequences at a single location not far from Muncie so that we could marshal university students and equipment, as well as draft my TCOM (Telecommunications Department) colleague Stan Sollars to record and mix the music without the need for costly travel. Ted had the perfect answer, which was to get his band booked for a performance at the Key Palace Theatre, a hidden gem in the town of Red Key, Indiana about a half-hour away. There, a local man named Charlie Noble, who had spent an extended period in Chicago during which time he fell in love with the blues, returned home, purchased an abandoned movie theater, and turned it into a rural blues palace. Now, twenty years later, Charlie and his theater were both increasingly run-down, but he continued to host weekend concerts for much of the year; sold burgers, beer, popcorn, and candy in rooms just outside of the concert area; and housed visiting musicians in cottages he had built out back to resemble Mississippi sharecropper shacks, which also were available to rent.

This remarkable man, who now was fighting cancer and living out of the theater's former projection booth, was more than happy to book Ted's band and to have us film there. So, in addition to asking Stan Sollars to record audio along with student assistants, I asked one of my sharper students, Andrew Bissonnette, to serve as director of photography. He had impressed me the previous semester as I oversaw a large group of students in creating an archive of footage of potential shooting locations around Indiana for use by the state film commissioner. I also drafted production student Joe Vella to operate Steadicam for the concert. (The following fall, when Joe and Andrew became grad students, they were half of the student crew Diana and I took on the October Blues Cruise.)

The project kicked into gear on Monday, February 22, 2010 as guitarist Ted Drozdowski and drummer R. L. "Rob" Hulsman drove from Nashville to Indianapolis in preparation for a Scissormen appearance the following day. Hal Yeagy Jr., owner with his wife Carol of the Slippery Noodle Inn, Indy's premier venue for live blues, had invited the two for a Tuesday night performance at his club, preceded by a slide guitar clinic presented by Ted. In other words, in the early evening, Drozdowski would don his music journalist and scholar hat as he demonstrated traditional slide guitar techniques, as well as more modern applications of them. Then, a short time later, he and Hulsman would present a full-blown Scissormen concert.

Already planning to film the band performing in Red Key on Wednesday, we elected to skip the show at the Slippery Noodle. However, Diana and I drove down with a few students on Tuesday afternoon, set up some lights in the front bar area, and filmed a discussion between Hal on one side of the bar and Ted and R. L. on the other. During their discussion, Drozdowski described how he founded Scissormen as a vehicle for performing not only classic Delta and hill country blues classics, but also his own modern updates of inherited forms and techniques. In turn, Yeagy related the history of the Slippery Noodle Inn (the oldest bar in Indiana, having been established in 1850 as the Tremont House) and how he and his wife Carol were committed to presenting live blues. Hal went on to talk about hosting artists such as John Mayall, Albert Collins, and Bobby Rush; about how their building had once been a stop on the Underground Railroad, sheltering escaped slaves in its basement on their way to Canada; and how the John Dillinger gang and others would drink in the back room and also use it for target practice.

Finally, we filmed Ted in his guitar clinic discussing what he termed "North Mississippi hill country open-tune slide," and a good bit more. In his own words, "There are three principal tunings that a lot of the folks in the hill country and the Delta use. There's open D, open E, and open G." Then, with R. L.'s help, he demonstrated how a single guitarist, using these particular slide techniques and backed by a drummer, could create more than enough sound to please any Mississippi blues audience, whether past or present.

The following morning, a large group of us headed north to Red Key, parked outside of the Key Palace Theater, carried in our equipment, and set up additional lights on the stage there, as well as cameras and recording equipment on the sloping movie theater floor. Then, in the afternoon, a few of us walked through snow behind the theater in order to film Ted, R. L., and Charlie Noble chatting on the front porch of one of Charlie's cabins. In their conversation, they discussed how, living in Chicago in the late fifties and early sixties, Noble had seen Elmore James, Hound Dog Taylor, and Jimmy Rogers. Then, as mentioned previously, he had moved to Red Key, bought and restored the theater himself, and seeing the sharecropper shacks at Hopson Plantation's Shack Up Inn near Clarksdale, had built his own facsimiles to house the bands performing for him. "You know, these are singles here," he said, "and then the other two over there are doubles. So, that takes care of ten people." As they talked, it quickly became clear that both Ted and Charlie, each in his own way, were working to keep blues traditions alive, even in a small rural town in Indiana, surrounded by cornfields rather than cotton.

The show itself was electric, unpredictable, and loud, and the sparse but exuberant crowd responded warmly on the chilliest of nights. Drozdowski is 6' 3", and his long arms fanned across the stage, flailing at his vibrating guitar strings, his metal slide caressing them up and down, in partial recognition of Hulsman's pounding, tapping, or brushing behind him. At the start, however, Ted's guitar was simply a slight, pulsing melody in the distance until, suddenly, he entered from the rear of the house, already playing through the speakers onstage, and followed by R. L., who was tapping one beat per measure on a tambourine. From there, they strolled slowly down the aisle to the front, ascended the stairs to the stage, and took their places: Hulsman seated at his center-stage drum kit, and Drozdowski standing expectantly between R. L.'s drums and the lip of the stage.

At the Key Palace Theatre in Red Key, Indiana, blues artist Ted Drozdowski plays a slide guitar solo with his guitar straddling the lap of a surprised audience member. (photographed by Chris Bergin for the Star Press in Muncie, Indiana, 2010)

Once the two were in place, the intensity of Ted's performance would rise and fall until, suddenly, he would race into the crowd again, thunder in his wake, as if he were wielding Thor's hammer instead of a faded yellow and white guitar. On some such occasions, Ted might approach a seated audience member, rest his guitar across her lap, and play it like a lap steel; on others, he might play while lying horizontally along an empty row of seats; and on still others, he might saunter through a door to the bar area, serenading men who were standing there drinking, mostly out of sight of the seated audience. Of course, toward the end of each song, Drozdowski would return to the stage again, play the final few chords, and introduce another song, often with a personal anecdote. Beyond that, not even Ted knew what to expect.

Interspersed among the songs Drozdowski and Hulsman performed by, or about, hill country giants R. L. Burnside, Jessie Mae Hemphill, and Mississippi Fred McDowell were Ted's darker, more impressionistic, or even psychedelic numbers such as "The Devil Is

Laughing," "Tupelo," "Delta Train," and "Whiskey and Maryjane." They also played Ted's latest song called "Big Shoes," which he wrote in recognition of my planned title for the film (Big Shoes: Walking and Talking the Blues). With that title, both of us were acknowledging that Ted's North Mississippi and Delta blues idols offered big shoes to fill. And yet, Ted's deepest ambitions were both to "walk" in their shoes (emulating them through performing and touring) and "talk" up their work (analyzing and promoting progenitors in his role as music journalist).

The following day, we had two stops to make. The first was in Richmond, Indiana, an hour southeast of Muncie. There, we visited Bob Jacobsen, board member of the Starr-Gennett Foundation, the job of which is to preserve, promote, and honor the heritage of Gennett Records and the Starr Piano Company which had created it. Aided by historical signs and murals, Bob explained to us that Richmond's Starr Piano Company was founded in 1892, eventually building a factory in the gorge of the Whitewater River, which was one of the largest in the world for producing pianos. Yet, in 1916, as phonographs began to replace pianos as the primary source of home entertainment, Starr also began manufacturing those, and a year later, recording and distributing records to be played on them. Afraid that other phonograph companies would not want to sell records in their stores under the name of a rival company, Starr created a label called Gennett Records, named after Starr's own president, Henry Gennett, rather than after the piano and phonograph company itself.

Jacobsen pointed out further how Gennett was one of the first independent American record labels, paving the way for modern independents such as the previously mentioned Alligator, Rounder, Arhoolie, Delmark, Milestone, Basin Street, Stax, Hi, Fania, Fat Possum, Swallow, Jin, Maison de Soul, and Malaco Records. In addition, to the company's credit, it sought to record a wide range of American music, because it wanted to reach as many different audiences as it could. As a result, Gennett made early recordings for such major jazz artists as Louis Armstrong, King Oliver, Sidney Bechet, Bix Beiderbecke, Jelly Roll Morton, Earl Hines, Duke Ellington, Fats Waller, Fletcher Henderson, Red Nichols, Artie Shaw, Coleman Hawkins, and Armstrong's musician wife, Lil Hardin Armstrong; major blues and gospel artists such as Charlie Patton, Blind Lemon Jefferson, Lonnie Johnson, Alberta Hunter, Roosevelt Sykes, Big Bill Broonzy, Scrapper Blackwell, and Georgia Tom Dorsey (a.k.a. Thomas A. Dorsey); and other artists as diverse as Gene Autry, Dave Macon, Mitch Miller, Lawrence Welk, Guy Lombardo, and Jimmy Durante. But the label is perhaps best known for its 1927 recording of Indiana songwriter Hoagie Carmichael performing his worldwide smash, "Stardust," even as its guilty secret was recording such mid-1920s Klan classics as "Klansman Keep the Cross Burning" and "Daddy Swiped Our Last Clean Sheet and Joined the KKK."

As part of his tour, Bob also took us by the old piano factory where, later on, phonographs were manufactured and music recorded; large outdoor murals of top artists who recorded there; the historic Pennsylvania Railroad Station where musicians would disembark after traveling to Richmond (in the case of Black artists, often arriving at night, so as to avoid the aforementioned Klan, as much a force in Indiana as throughout the South); the foundation's more recent Starr Gennett Gallery, complete with gift shop; and a newly produced Lonnie Johnson marker, soon to be added to the Gennett Walk of Fame, the latter prompting Ted and R. L. to perform an impromptu version of gospel standard "Jesus on the Mainline." Afterwards, Bob took us to the outdoor Walk of Fame itself, close by the old piano factory and protected from the Whitewater River by a tall flood wall.

The ground already was obscured by several inches of snow, and more was falling as we approached. But despite the snowfall and the extreme cold, Ted and R. L. were determined to see some of the key markers. So, out of Drozdowski's minivan came the only available tools, which were a travel-sized plastic snow shovel and snow brush. Thus armed, the two of them set about locating and revealing the widely spaced sidewalk markers and expressed their joy over each new discovery. First came the incomparable jazz composer and bandleader Duke Ellington, followed by songwriter Hoagie Carmichael, and then pioneering bluesman Charlie Patton. Thrilled over that latest revelation, Ted stopped to discuss what a marvelous showman Patton had been, even throwing his guitar into the air and catching it in mid-song, which clearly inspired some of Ted's recent antics. And as Ted, R. L., Bob, the small student crew, and I (but not Diana, who, understandably, was too frozen to exit the car) continued uncovering more and more musical greats of the past, it was easy to feel these were vital connections between our Midwestern landscape and the history of American music—something all too easily lost in inclement weather, but also in the changing priorities (and unchanging prejudice) of the American heartland.

Involving as that was, it was only our first shoot of the day. The second required a return to Muncie, where TCOM audio czar Stan Sollars would meet us in his David Letterman Building audio studios, fitted out with glorious recording and mixing equipment almost a century newer than the equipment first used by Gennett Records. Once we arrived, Stan placed R. L. behind a drum set in an isolation booth, set up Ted and his guitar in the central room, then watched over them both from his own glass-enclosed booth, preparing to use twenty-first century tools to record timeless American blues.

The following day, while I taught film classes and ran assorted errands, Drozdowski and Hulsman drove an hour up I-69 to Fort Wayne for a performance at the Brass Rail, a regular stop on what some termed the "Deep Blues Circuit," open to performers like Ted and R. L. who tried to duplicate or extend the hill country blues legacy. Then, the day after that, we all made the five-hour drive to Cleveland, Ohio where my friend Terry Stewart, president of the Rock and Roll Hall of Fame, agreed to meet us on a Saturday. After we checked out the Rock Hall's blues-related exhibits, Terry sat down with Ted and R. L. to trade stories of their shared blues idols, from Jessie Mae Hemphill to Howlin' Wolf. Finally, Ted showed Terry a guitar signed by some of his own favorite guitarists, and then a tiny splinter of wood from the sharecropper's shack in which blues giant Muddy Waters had once lived. As Drozdowski made clear, he carried this artifact in his guitar case like a "relic of the true cross."

Leaving the Rock Hall, we still had one more event to film, which was a performance at a hip Cleveland club known as the Beachland Ballroom & Tavern. There, co-owner Cindy Barber welcomed Ted and R. L. (especially R. L., who had performed there before with another band), and explained how she had purchased this building in 2000 and turned it into a venue where diverse touring musicians could play. Then, as the two visiting musicians performed in the tavern, Drozdowski walked atop the bar, playing with the same wild abandon as "honker" saxophone players of generations past. Ted also dropped his guitar onto a young woman's outstretched arms and momentarily played it there, only to have her male companion, either jealous or intoxicated, pour beer on the bridge of Ted's guitar. In addition, at the break, R. L. stood outside the club, lightly falling snowflakes swirling around him like fireflies, and spoke about the pleasure of accompanying Ted from a stationary drum set as his friend wandered the room.

(Note: Not until 2022 did I learn of the untimely death of my Cleveland-based friend Nick Amster, who always greeted me warmly when I attended the Cleveland International Film Festival, and who, at the Rock Hall in 1998, convinced an irascible Robert Lockwood Jr. to give me an interview for my Robert Johnson film. From Nick's obituaries, originally published in April 2020, I also learned that Nick had been Cindy Barber's silent partner in the opening and operation of the Beachland Ballroom & Tavern, which sounded entirely in keeping with his singular legacy as a patron of the arts. At the same time, I was reminded again how the threads of my own musical and cinematic adventures were inextricably linked to those of countless others with similar interests and ideals.)

In completing the film, I cut from the final scenes in Cleveland to Drozdowski and Hulsman driving past snow-covered fields as they reflected, still again, upon their continuing musical commitment. Then, after that, I cut back to the Key Palace stage as Ted introduced his song "Big Shoes" in the following way:

We wrote a new song the other day, and we're going to try it out for you. It's called "Big Shoes," and I've got size twelves, for the record . . . "Big Shoes": it's about kind of finding your own place in the blues tradition, and trying to make sure that tradition lives on to the future, which is one of the important things that this band tries to do. It's kind of our mission in life, as we drive around the country in our minivan . . . All you need is a minivan, a couple of guitars, a drum kit . . . and we're on a mission!

And with that, the two of them launched into long-enduring notes and rhythms, but with their own contemporary, high-volume spin.

Knowing that Charlie Noble's cancer was wending its way through his body, I raced to edit the film as quickly as I could, despite university obligations, Diana's suddenly scheduled spinal surgery, and preparations for another upcoming film. At the same time, Stan Sollars worked just as hard to get the music and audio mixed so that, by summer, we were able to arrange a private screening for Charlie in the Letterman Building where Stan and I both taught. When the time came, ignoring his illness, Charlie managed to drive his dilapidated car onto campus, which I then took to the appropriate lot and parked for him, because simply walking into our building from the street was almost more than he could endure. Nonetheless, he was pleased with the film and also with the part that he and his Key Palace Theatre had played, and we were equally pleased to be able to share it with him.

On Saturday, October 16, 2010, still recovering from her spring surgery, Diana joined the student crew and me in flying to San Diego where we prepared to shoot *All Jams On Deck* on the West Coast Blues Cruise. While onboard, we also presented *Big Shoes: Walking and Talking the Blues*, which received as warm a response as Ted, R. L., Charlie, and the rest deserved. Sadly, though, on November 1, a week after we returned home, Charlie succumbed to his cancer at the age of 72. And even though I had come to this place barely a year before, I felt as if a part of its soul was dying with him.

Five days later, on November 6, I introduced the film's official world premiere at the Starz Denver International Film Festival. Then, during the first half of 2011, Ted and I arranged screenings at the Clarksdale Film Festival in Mississippi; the Gasparilla International Film Festival in Tampa; and the Museum of Fine Arts in Boston, all accompanied by live Scissormen performances. Yet, for everyone involved, including Charlie's own family, the most special of our screenings was the one we arranged on April 2, 2011 at the Key Palace Theatre, followed by still another live concert. This screening, like our original shoot the year before, received generous coverage from popular Muncie Starr Press journalist John Carlson, who attended both the initial concert and the later screening with his wife, Dr. Nancy Carlson, who had helped to bring me to Ball State in the first place. The latter showing was also promoted by my department as a whole, with university tech people setting up a topnotch video projector and screen in the theater, and many other thoughtful colleagues joining us for the event. As smaller American cities like Jackson, Mississippi and Muncie, Indiana had shown me again and again, what they lacked in the way of major cultural diversions was more than balanced by a close-knit and supportive community.

Finally, on March 20, 2012, Ted and the VizzTone label released a special edition, two-disc set featuring a DVD of the film and a live CD of Scissormen's remastered concert at the Key Palace Theatre. As I wrote in the set's liner notes, "My primary goal with this film was to demonstrate how Ted simultaneously honors the past masters of blues while also seeking to extend their important legacy." Like all great critics and musicians, he provides a link to both the past and the future.

***

Although the *Big Shoes* project had revealed several musical oases in the Midwest, Diana and I still felt like strangers in a bland, essentially culture-free land. Of course, part of that alienation was our own lack of familiarity with the modest, yet still genuine, local music scene. That changed in early April 2012 when the two of us received a letter, hand-written on lined yellow paper, which read as follows:

Professors Mugge & Zelman: I have appreciated your support for blues & jazz—especially your interest in Charlie Noble & the Key Palace in Red Key. I knew Charlie for @ 25 yrs. and helped him with the stage & sound system—when he 1st opened up the Key—while playing in a band called Borrowed Time & opening for Delbert McClinton when he played at the Key during its 1st year. At about that time, I purchased an old building in downtown Muncie—which later became Doc's Music Hall. On many occasions Charlie and I commiserated—comparing notes on how to survive financially—in our support of live music performance.—Dr. John Peterson.

Attached was a paperback copy of his autobiography titled *The True-Life Adventures of Captain Wa Wah—Fifty Years of Music, Meditation and Politics.*

Although I was then extremely busy with teaching, increasing problems resulting from Diana's 2010 spinal surgery, the planning of our November 2012 wedding and Blues Cruise pre-honeymoon, and the editing of footage we had shot in Romania, I nevertheless planned to follow up with Dr. Peterson. Meanwhile, some of my Ball State colleagues heard of our note from John and confirmed that Doc (as the whole city knew him) was an outstanding doctor (who incorporated the ancient Ayurveda system of natural healing into his family medical practice), and that his wife Vicki taught Transcendental Meditation. They also noted that he was an accomplished keyboard player who had enjoyed early success as a recorded musician while growing up in northern Iowa, who continued to write music and play with regional bands after relocating to Indiana, and who, twenty years earlier, had capped all of this by purchasing an unused building in Muncie's increasingly abandoned downtown. With the help of his wife Vicki and a parade of mostly volunteers, John had then turned that building into a small urban Mecca where visual artists could work and exhibit, where musicians (and later comics) could practice and perform, and where locals could eat healthy food in an equally healthy environment.

To be frank, I was less interested in John's medical practice or in Vicki's meditation classes than I was in the idea of John's downtown building. Over the years, it had been known by many names, among them, the Creative Opportunity Center, the Dead Pigeon Café (so-called because of the dead pigeons found when they moved into the building), the Full Circle Arts Co-op, and again, simply Doc's. Eventually, though, it had evolved into a kind of countercultural night-club called Doc's Music Hall which was managed for John by younger local musician Mike Martin.

In this final iteration, the upstairs area remained available for unrestricted creativity, while street level rooms were now centered around a commercial bar and performance spaces where both area and touring musicians could perform. And yet, in spite of this latest attempt to broaden the venue's appeal and make it financially self-sustaining (rather than being subsidized by John's medical practice), it still retained much of the original spirit with which John and his followers (especially jack-of-all-trades Paul Troxell, who had rebuilt it after a bad fire) had infused it from the beginning. In fact, John himself still performed with small ensembles on Thursday and Friday evenings in the smaller of the two performance spaces (jazz on Thursday and rhythm and blues on Friday). Devoted fans of John's would stop by to drink together and listen to him play in the early evening. Then, later, a cover was sometimes charged for younger, louder, and more current bands performing on the large stage in the adjoining room.

Diana decided to begin seeing Dr. Peterson as her primary physician and returned from her first appointment on October 2, 2012 with news that, after two decades of operating his downtown venue, he was preparing to shut it down. Even in its current form, the club and art space was failing to make money, and John could no longer afford to subsidize it alone. Therefore, at long last, he had announced its closing at the end of that week, with the building passing to another owner the week after that.

Not one to stand by while important transitions were in the works, I immediately told my students that an opportunity for extra credit was at hand, reserved some department equipment for late in the week, and stopped by John's final Thursday night performance to have a word with him. Introducing myself between sets, I asked if he would mind a crew of students under my supervision capturing the final gasp of his noble experiment in downtown creativity and urban revitalization. John happily agreed, but noted that his friend Nick Melander, unable to make the last-ever performance on Saturday, would be doing multitrack recording of his Friday night show. Recognizing the value of having professionally recorded and mixed audio recordings to synchronize with our video, I readily switched from a Saturday shoot to a Friday night one, even though doing so left only hours in which to entice students who were subject to full-time academic commitments, employment, social lives, and, in some cases, long-distance commuting time to join me for an ambitious shoot the *following night*. Somehow, though, we made it work.

The next afternoon (Friday, October 5), Diana and I returned to Doc's Music Hall with a full crew of students, led by Turner Fair, a charming, dreadlocked student who always made me laugh. Turner's constant enthusiasm could sometimes be at odds with a tendency to be a bit scattered, but I decided to risk having him serve as director of photography, if only because of the energy he brought to any endeavor. In fact, this was a great bunch of students overall—both talented and likable—and once again, some even owned their own cameras. Nick Melander, too, turned out to be a positive force in every respect, and brought skillful collaborators who provided flawless audio to accompany our video.

As always, John and his band set up with their backs to the nearly floor-to-ceiling windows along the front wall of the club and facing the bar, with just enough space in between for two rows of chairs, and even a little room left for potential dancing. Just behind them was downtown Walnut Street, where anyone not yet taking his or her place inside Doc's was smoking and chatting before entering. The band was positioned with John at the far left, seated amid his keyboards, Phil Dunn standing a few feet to the right of him with trumpet and saxophone at the ready, Doug Hunt standing a few feet past Phil with an electric guitar strapped to his body, and Kyle Ivey seated diagonally at his drum kit a few feet more to the right.

From left, musicians Dr. John Peterson, Phil Dunn, Doug Hunt, and Kyle Ivey give a farewell performance at Doc's Music Hall in Muncie, Indiana as the venue prepares to cease operation after a twenty-year run. (frame from film, 2012)

John kicked off the concert with a composition of his own titled "Tribute to Monk," a lively tribute to legendary jazz pianist and composer Thelonious Monk that included multiple opportunities for soloing. This instrumental was just one of three Peterson compositions making it into the film, the others being a sweet ballad titled "In A Special Way (My Baby's Eyes)," which he had written for a girlfriend when very young, and "Still Talking About The Doors," a psychedelic song that John paired with the early Doors classic, "Light My Fire," and which recounted the time when he and his first professional band opened for that not-yet-famous California group and considered them to be likely one-hit-wonders. John sang lead on both of those originals, as he did on covers of such classic rock and pop hits as "We've Gotta Get Out of This Place" and "You Can Call Me Al," while Phil sang more soulful numbers such as "It's Your Thing," "All Night Long," and "The Roof Is on Fire," as well as performing old movie themes such as "Somewhere Over the Rainbow" and "Whatever Will Be, Will Be."

Whether consciously or unconsciously, a number of those songs had to have been selected because their lyrics offered unique relevance for those in attendance—whether young or old, Black or white—who had long considered this building to be a second home, and who were devastated over losing it. (With this in mind, perhaps a better selection by the Doors would have been "The End" or "When the Music's Over.") Yet, one song, "My Girl," which Smokey Robinson and his Miracles bandmate Ronald White wrote in 1964 for fellow Motown artists, the Temptations, was performed simply because it was so beautiful, especially as sung with the ethereal voice of drummer Kyle Ivey, who was not even born until decades after the song's release. On this particular night, it was a song that could hold everyone in its grip, briefly suppressing knowledge that this noisy, laughter-filled celebration was really a wake.

Filming with five cameras in such a small space was fun, even though I knew that, in the editing, I would have to compensate for slightly different looks from one type of HD camera to another. Generally speaking, we had no real problems and were able to send home our talented young crew with a sense of satisfaction. Nonetheless, Turner, one other young cameraman, and I returned to the building the following night, waited outside until John's final performance at Doc's had ended, then filmed as he climbed a ladder and, to the cheers and tears of all his slightly intoxicated followers, removed the giant D, O, C, and S, one at a time from the outside wall over the front entrance. Yet, as powerful as this ritual proved to be, it was not the one offering final resolution.

During the two decades that Doc's had been a day-and-night gathering place for creative local residents, there had been many reported sightings of ghosts, especially late at night and on the dark and creaky upper level where young people practiced their arts and crafts and sometimes stayed the night. Over the years, speculation had varied as to who or what these spectral visions could be, with some seeing it relevant that Muncie had once been a small but booming city made prosperous from manufacturing automobile parts for the car companies in Detroit, a few hours away. Such prosperity had led to an equally active nightlife, the nickname "Little Chicago," the frequent presence of big-time gangsters including John Dillinger, and the operation of several legitimate theaters. Consequently, some residents believed that these were the spirits of a more thriving and affluent Muncie, Indiana, and especially of actors who had walked the boards of majestic downtown theaters, most of which had long since disappeared for lack of a paying audience.

Now, with even Doc's Music Hall shutting down, John and Vicki Peterson, their friend Paul Troxell, and others worried that these ghosts would continue to be captive in a building dating to Muncie's heyday. Therefore, they decided to hire Sherita Campbell, a psychic medium and tarot card reader of their acquaintance, to oversee a ceremonial rite of passage meant to release the ghosts from the building, as well as from the downward spiral in which Muncie and other rust belt communities had been trapped for decades. At long last, Muncie, for one, was slowly extricating itself from that spiral through the growth of Ball State University and Ball Memorial Hospital, and the stubborn presence in its semi-abandoned downtown of businesses such as Vera Mae's Bistro, the Heorot Pub and Draught House, and the various versions of Doc's, all of which had stood bravely together as so many other establishments fled, especially in the hours after dark. However, these ghosts were another matter entirely. So, the following Wednesday evening, a small group of Doc's regulars would gather together to free them and provide closure for this decades-long venture.

Late afternoon on October 10, Diana, Turner, and I once again brought a good-sized student crew to John's now-empty building. We arrived early enough to film and record interviews with John Peterson, Vicki Peterson, Paul Troxell, and Mike Martin in order to establish some of the twenty-year history of Doc's, as well as the personal history of the Peterson clan. Then, as assorted others arrived, John and Vicki had them form a wide circle on the floor, gently illuminated by only our film lights and a couple of lit candles in their midst.

Finally, Sherita swept into the room wearing a green and purple wizard's robe, decorated with white stars and crescent moons; a golden, multicolored hat that looked like a cross between a turban and a shower cap; and large silver amulets dangling from her neck. After being welcomed, she was helped into the last remaining chair next to where John was seated on the floor, closed her eyes, and held her tarot cards tightly in both hands as John played a solemn, unaccompanied melody on his melodica. John then gestured to Sherita with his hands in prayer position, and she began to speak, praising what Doc's had done for the city and urging the building's "spirit guides" to take their flight. Throughout the rest of what John labeled a "ceremony of reassurance"—presumably, reassurance for both the people and the spirits who had spent endless hours there—participants lit the candles they had been holding and took turns sharing personal memories of what Doc's had meant to them. Even though I was unable to fit the latter part of this session into the film, the sad expressions on faces said all that was needed.

Eight weeks later, on December 3, 2012, student Turner Fair and I stopped by John's offices to film an additional interview with him, this one concerning his medical practice. During that interview, in which he was framed against a wall full of medical degrees, he happened to engage with one of his patients, and I asked if he would mind demonstrating his method of Ayurvedic pulse diagnosis. This is a fascinating practice, taught to him by top Indian *Vaidyas*, in which an experienced doctor is able to place three fingers on the wrist of a patient and, by properly positioning those fingers and adjusting for relative depth, detect three so-called *dochas*, each of which contains five *subdochas*, and which offer reports on the proper or improper functioning of the body. To someone unfamiliar with Ayurvedic medicine, this can sound like a parlor trick. Yet it is a serious diagnostic tool that can reveal acute physical imbalances, to which Dr. Peterson may then respond with Western medical tests in order to assemble the most complete picture of possible afflictions.

Diagnosis and treatment are key to how Dr. John Peterson functions as a human being. They are the two sides of being a healer, and John is a healer, not just in medical and spiritual terms, but also in musical ones—perhaps most vividly apparent in his recognition that young artists and musicians of his city needed a place to express themselves, and that the city itself needed revitalization of its abandoned downtown, prompting a prescription that helped to cure them both. My own recognition of John's larger role as a healer is why, in the film we made together, I termed him a "Doctor of Music."

Because I was teaching full-time through the summer of 2014 and trying to complete three feature-length films simultaneously, it took me a highly uncharacteristic two years to finish this one. Arguably, though, the wait helped Doc's Music Hall patrons to make their way through the five stages of grief, and then to be ready for the sixth stage—that of the Muncie Civic Theater, from which John and I presented the film on Saturday night, January 10, 2015 (which happened to be his sixty-seventh birthday). On that occasion, John and I each made brief introductory remarks, after which we screened the film in public for the first time. Then, Vicki and other family members came onstage to present John with a cake large enough to serve much of the audience, followed by a musical set from John, Phil, Doug, and Kyle, along with percussionist Garland Simmons, another longtime musical collaborator of John's. It was the perfect tribute to one of Muncie, Indiana's favorite sons, by way of Grand Forks and Mason City, Iowa (where he was born and raised), not to mention ancient India.

Six weeks later, on February 26, 2015, we screened the film again in the David Letterman Building at Ball State University where I had taught video production and cinema studies for the previous five years, thereby turning our farewell to Doc's Music Hall into my own goodbye to Ball State as well. And finally, eight months after that, on October 13, 2015, we released *Giving Up the Ghosts: Closing Time at Doc's Music Hall* on Blu-ray, making it one of twenty-two of my newer films and remastered older ones to be released over a relatively short period by MVD Visual.

In a sense, this film offers the smallest of stories, from one of the most out-of-the-way places, featuring talented musicians who are virtually unknown. And yet, for me, it is one of the most resonant. Certainly, if I have learned anything in more than four decades of filmmaking, it is not to search for meaning in the obvious, the immediate, or the blindingly self-absorbed.

Sometimes, as in this case, the story itself does the searching, and I need only stay attuned, because the spirit guides show me the way.

Postscript

I n newspaper, magazine, radio, and television interviews I gave about my earliest music-related films, as well as in subsequent press, media, and Internet coverage during the next four decades, I have consistently made three primary points about my work. One is that I consider myself to be a *music filmmaker*, which I mentioned in the preface, and which I have always thought to be self-explanatory. In 1986, when a French journalist, Louis Skorecki, said of me in the publication *Libération* that I was "the best music filmmaker on the planet," that was encouraging. Yet, for me, the most significant part of the quote was that, even in a different language, he was concisely acknowledging what it is that I do. A second point I have made for decades involves my belief that the best music documentaries are ones that focus on *more than just music*. In other words, even if films explore American musical styles, genres, performers, composers, and more, they also should examine human personality, racial and ethnic identity, religious belief, political doctrine, social interaction, cultural tradition, regional geography, and community support, all of which can influence the music being made or, in turn, be influenced by it. But perhaps most important is my longtime third point, which is that music is a *metaphor for the human spirit*, and which I mean not simply in religious terms, but also in the more basic sense of what it means to be a human being. That is, music can reveal aspects of our humanity, not only through the lyrics of our songs, but also through their rhythms, melodies, harmonies, textures, instrumental and vocal techniques, and so forth.

More than any other art form, music speaks to us about the lives, the beliefs, and the feelings of its creators, of its interpreters, and of its more attentive listeners, even if it expresses them in the most abstract of terms. And just as music tells us much of what we need to know about its makers, I like to think that, in the same way, my films tell you everything you need to know about me, and about the art, artists, ideas, and human values I believe to be most essential. But for those who have not found my work to be 100% transparent, both about me and about the films themselves, I decided to write this book.

Looking back on my career to date, including the films that were explored in these pages (as well as those that were not, because they focus primarily on subjects other than music), those efforts seem like dreams to me now. Like all memories, they become less and less distinct over time—more memories of earlier memories than of the events themselves—occasionally replenished by new visits with old films, including trotting out long-orphaned out-takes on social media or my website, and rereading my dusty old project calendars, notebooks, and checkbooks. Without such resources, I could not have reconstructed my journeys, nor attempted a coherent book on the subject.

The thing about journeys is that they always end, after which we return to predictable routines. Fortunately, I was able to document these particular journeys, as well as scores of participating artists, many of whom have since died, as we all will over time. Therefore, perhaps the most important aspect of the storytelling craft I practice is in its name—documentary filmmaking—because what I attempt to say with these films matters less than what I do with them, which is to *document*. As I used to tell my students, when you turn on your camera, and that rectangular box appears, you can focus on anything in the world around you. And of course, the choice you make endows that person, object, location, or event with value, over and above everything else around it. Moreover, whether during shooting or editing, as soon as you make your second choice—cutting or panning to something else or simply following your original subject—you begin to express yourself because, out of a succession of images comes meaning. Irrespective of words spoken or written onscreen, with the first images you select, a dialogue begins between you and your subject, and between you and your audience.

In short, as much as I love telling stories, developing themes, establishing visual metaphors, and using all the tools available to me as a nonfiction filmmaker, I suppose what means the most to me is what I have shot, edited, and shared; in other words, what I have managed to *preserve* (or at least grasp onto for as long as humanly possible). And not just surfaces. What I most aim to capture is what is *inside* my subjects: personality, character, and especially *spirit!* My favorite director, the late Polish genius Krzysztof Kieślowski, who created such mysterious and illuminating cinema as the *Three Colors* trilogy, the ten-part *Dekalog*, and *The Double Life of Veronique* (as well as several other features and numerous short documentaries), always claimed that films could not capture a person's inner life. Yet, to my mind, no one has done so more skillfully, more subtly, or to more devastating effect than did Kieślowski. (His work with music—especially the compositions of his frequent collaborator Zbigniew Preisner—was stunning as well.)

According to my own definition, works that merely recycle old film clips, audio clips, and photos, even for the laudable goal of reclaiming history, are not documentary films. What do they document, aside from newly expressed opinions about long past events? For me, true documentary filmmaking involves exactly what the words imply—documentation, out in the world, while history is still being made—and in the best cases, *spirit-catching*, which does not happen in an editing room alone. As much as anything, my films are about the remarkable spirits my crews and I have "captured" in their natural (musical) habitats: Sun Ra and Sonny Rollins, Al Green and Gil Scott-Heron, Rubén Blades and The Iguanas, George Crumb and Bill Morrissey, Irma Thomas and Marcia Ball, Peter Rowan and Raymond Kāne, Junior Kimbrough and R. L. Burnside, Mavis Staples and Tish Hinojosa, Beau Jocque and Boozoo Chavis, Koko Taylor and Katie Webster, Eddie Bo and Dr. John, Odetta and Denise LaSalle, Ralph Stanley and Doc Watson, Kermit Ruffins and Mutabaruka, Theresa Andersson and Vicky Holt Takamine, Cyril Neville and Papa Mali, Bobby Rush and Vasti Jackson, Rita Marley and Judy Mowatt, Ted Drozdowski and Dr. John Peterson, and hundreds more who have brightened my life and enriched my work.

Like you, perhaps, I have often been asked (in one form or another), "If you had to go to a desert island, what would you take with you?" But for me, the better question was always: What would I leave behind? My films are the answer to that question, and my musical journeys a means to that end.

Robert Mugge Filmography

Steve Bell Storyteller: A Newsman Living History (2020)
Ship to Shore: Launching the Legendary Rhythm & Blues Revue (2018)
Zydeco Crossroads: A Tale of Two Cities (2015)
Rosie's in the House Tonight (2015)
Giving Up the Ghosts: Closing Time at Doc's Music Hall (2014)
Souvenirs of Bucovina: A Romanian Survival Guide (2013)
Elvin Bishop's Raisin' Hell Revue (2011)
All Jams On Deck (2011)
Big Shoes: Walking and Talking the Blues (2010)
Deep Sea Blues (2007)
New Orleans Music in Exile (2006)
Memphis Blues Again: The 25th Anniversary W.C. Handy Blues Awards (2005)
Blues Divas (2005)
A Night at Club Ebony (2005)
The Road Home: B. B. King in Indianola (2004)
Blues Breaks (2003)
Last of the Mississippi Jukes (2002)
Rhythm 'N' Bayous: A Road Map to Louisiana Music (2000)
Hellhounds on My Trail: The Afterlife of Robert Johnson (1999)
Iguanas in the House (1996)
True Believers: The Musical Family of Rounder Records (1994)
The Kingdom of Zydeco (1994)
Gather at the River: A Bluegrass Celebration (1994)
Pride and Joy: The Story of Alligator Records (1992)
Deep Blues (1991)
Kumu Hula: Keepers of a Culture (1989)
Entertaining the Troops: American Entertainers in World War II (1988)
Hawaiian Rainbow (1987)
Saxophone Colossus (w/Sonny Rollins) (1986)

The Return of Rubén Blades (1985)
Gospel According to Al Green (1984)
Cool Runnings: The Reggae Movie (1983)
Black Wax (w/Gil Scott-Heron) (1982)
Sun Ra: A Joyful Noise (1980)
Amateur Night at City Hall: The Story of Frank L. Rizzo (1978)
George Crumb: Voice of the Whale (1976)
Frostburg (1973)

ABOUT THE AUTHOR

Since 1976, music filmmaker Robert Mugge has produced three dozen documentaries about various aspects of American culture, with particular emphasis on traditional forms of American music. In *Notes from the Road: A Filmmaker's Journey Through American Music*, he describes the making of what he considers to be his twenty-five key music films, including *Sun Ra: A Joyful Noise*, *Black Wax* with Gil Scott-Heron, *Gospel According to Al Green*, *Saxophone Colossus* with Sonny Rollins, *Kumu Hula: Keepers of a Culture*, *Deep Blues*, *The Kingdom of Zydeco*, *Hellhounds on My Trail: The Afterlife of Robert Johnson*, *Rhythm 'N' Bayous: A Road Map to Louisiana Music*, *Last of the Mississippi Jukes*, *Blues Divas*, *New Orleans Music in Exile*, and many more. His key funders have included Britain's Channel 4 Television, BMG, Starz, CPB, NEA, and the States of Hawaii and Louisiana. He also has served as Filmmaker in Residence for Mississippi Public Broadcasting and as an Endowed Chair Professor at Ball State University.

ABOUT THE PUBLISHER

The Sager Group was founded in 1984. In 2012 it was chartered as a multimedia content brand, with the intent of empowering those who create art—an umbrella beneath which makers can pursue, and profit from, their craft directly, without gatekeepers. TSG publishes books; ministers to artists and provides modest grants; and produces documentary, feature, and commercial films. By harnessing the means of production, The Sager Group helps artists help themselves. For more information, please see TheSagerGroup.net.

MORE BOOKS FROM THE SAGER GROUP

Students Write the Darnedest Things: Gaffes, Goofs, Blunders and Unintended Wisdom from Actual College Papers
by Pamela Hill Nettleton, PhD

Big Noise from LaPorte: A Diary of the Disillusioned
by Holly Schroeder Link

Meeting Mozart: A Novel Drawn from the Secret Diaries of Lorenzo Da Ponte
by Howard Jay Smith

Lavender in Your Lemonade: A Funny and Touching COVID Diary
by Chris Erskine

*Sarabeth and the Five Spirits:
A Novel about Channeling, Consciousness, Healing, and Murder*
by Mike Sager

*The Deadliest Man Alive:
Count Dante, The Mob and the War for American Martial Arts*
by Benji Feldheim

Lifeboat No. 8: Surviving the Titanic
by Elizabeth Kaye

*The Pope of Pot:
And Other True Stories of Marijuana and Related High Jinks*
by Mike Sager

See our entire library at TheSagerGroup.net

Artifex Te Adiuva